ARC 1

TO BE KING

Elemental: Shadow and Fire Series

BY BRANTLEY A. MASON

TABLE OF CONTENTS

ACKNOWLEDGMENTS

Interior Art Design- Brett Upshaw
Beta Reader- Rebecca Strickland
Photographer- Rebecca Strickland
Design Editor- Andrea Hurst

"Do not take revenge, my dear friends, but leave room for God's wrath, for it is written: "It is mine to avenge; I will repay," says the Lord." —Romans 12:19

VERSYRIUM

By GrandMaster Traés

A BRIEF HISTORY OF
THE GREAT WAR

Thank you for humoring an aging man the privilege of giving you, the reader, a bit of understanding of this tragic war that has happened. With how we have handled this event, I would like to make this writing for future scholars to have a better understanding of the events surrounding the end of that war.

After winning the Wraith Wars, a civil war within the Darklands, the Dark Lords turned their hate and desire for power to other places. They were led to this by someone I had once considered a friend, a brother. And he led these zealot warriors to war on the world.

Those of the Druids broke from this war and based themselves on a false claim of neutrality, before then beginning to play both sides in secret to sell their souls, their services, to do the quiet and dark deeds that the good natured would not do, and the dark natured could not accomplish. Thus, the Shadow League was born, increasing the escalation of the war to a height that no one could have predicted.

After the war had lasted nearly a full season rotation, the war had almost stalled. The line cuts through the continent, the Fire Realm and Darklands in the north with the Nature Folk and Lightning Provinces in the south. Effectively cutting the continent in half, North and South. The Fire Realm had joined in three moon cycles into the war on the side of the Dark Lords under the false pretense of stability and duty, to right the world's faults.

I was able to reach the king and, after two moons of secret meetings, was able to convince him that he had joined the wrong side. In doing so, the scales of the war tipped into the Alliance of Nations and they were able to push the Wraiths, and Dark Lords' forces back within the Dark Lands.

This betrayal of the Realm was not without cost, for the Dark Lords had sent a contingent to the Realm for aid against the Water Imperial invasion from the Northern Sea. This army was then turned upon the Realm's Capitol, a night most of the clans and Realm now call, the Purge. It was a horrid deal to witness, and I will not go into detail other than that the royal family was sent to the winds, the Realm's capitol sacked, and the king was lost.

The Lightning Knights arrived too late and could only chase the enemy to the Mist Mountains. They continued their advance on the retreating army as the Alliance front lines broke through and pushed the enemy back from the south. Most of the enemy forces were dead or injured and the rest of them barricaded themselves within Castle Doom, their capital. An infiltration team, commanded by myself, underwent the task of infiltrating and killing the remaining Dark Lords.

Once the castle fell, the war itself was over, but the people still deal with the aftermath. The Realm may never recover, though, attempts are being put forth. The Royal family is still in hiding, for fear of assassins from my brethren.

Hopefully, my Order of Owls will resolve this before any harm comes to the Royal family from my brethren assassins. But for now, the world is attempting to right itself from this tragic war that most fear has not ended, including myself.

I hope these suspicions are wrong. But as I attempt to track down missing Wraiths and rogue assassins of the Shadow League, I fear that we have only postponed this fight to a later date. When that is, I hope is not within my lifetime. But…with how long it takes us Druids to age, my hopes may be outpaced in the end.

May the Shadows guide whoever is reading this. And allow them to understand a bit more of Versyrium, this broken world this war has left us in.

EXILED PRINCE

1

THE FIRE WITHIN

Three seasons after the Great War

The day it all began...

Skipping down the street, the little boy tore off a piece of jerky and chewed it with a big smile on his face. As the sun descended steadily towards the west, the boy wished for a comfortable bed to sleep in until morning. The hard ground hadn't been too pleasant the previous night, and he hoped the men had chosen an inn that would take them on.

He moved through the busy street, munching upon his treat, without drawing attention to himself in his plain clothes. As he had always thought everyone was nice, like back at the castle. Though his mother had always said there were mean people out there in the world, he would need to be nice to them when he met them.

She was correct, he thought, as he waved to a man selling warm bread wearing a funny white hat. Though some people aren't nice, it was always better for you to smile and be kind to them. Even if you felt angry inside. To be a good person. And his father would agree... if he had been there, that is.

Remembering one of the last conversations he had with the imposing man. *"Your mother is right, son. If you treat others how you want to be treated, eventually they will treat you that way."*

The boy understood his father but resented him for not actually doing what he had said to do. The boy munched on his jerky, dispelling the thought as he turned the corner of the market.

When returning from Central City, they typically bought dried meat or bread and cheese, but if they were running low on funds, which was why his mom would consider asking his aunt for help. It had taken nearly eight days to reach the city and seemed all for naught to the boy.

After leaving the same day, they had arrived. He had come to the understanding that his aunt had not been pleasant. His mother had told him to wait with their small escort of guards in the spare room as his mother and aunt spoke.

The boy was unsure what his mother had spoken to his aunt about, but he knew it had to do with his father and the throne. But as the boy skipped across the cobblestone, waving at a smiling lady near a fruit stand, the boy thought it was none of his concern. All he knew was that his aunt had been rude to his mother, and he believed his aunt had tossed them out. Though his mother denied this and said that she needed some space to think.

The boy was getting used to the treatment these days. Even though he was never the one given the criticism, the adults always seemed to be singled out by others and called mean names and told to move along.

In fact, it seemed to be the case as the little boy pulled up to the inn he had last left his mother at. The boy watched them for a moment and saw Nicodemus, the Captain of the Guard, talking with a serious expression. The man wore his red and black dragon armor and had his helm under one arm as he spoke with the innkeeper, who was almost yelling at this point. Beside the Captain stood two Clan Ignus Huntsman in their leather armor and robe like clothing underneath. The boy glanced at the sign and could see the picture of a shouting bird crest of a hissing dragon head, a clan that he was pretty sure didn't like clan Ignus. But it was always too much for the boy to keep straight. He was only just learning from Gran about the clans. Saying his father should have been the one to teach him, but it was now up to her to take that role.

Gran suggested taking the clan dragons to the city, but the boy's mother was uncomfortable around them. The boy always loved flying on them. And the dragons always mesmerized him with their power and strength. Like his father's Regal, Freis the Black. One of the most powerful dragons of this age.

The boy slowed his skip to a walk now as he approached the alley next to the inn. He could see the three guards standing on the porch talking with the innkeeper they were attempting to stay the night in. Words like, "You stoking Ignus aren't welcome here," met with "but her majesty will pay you," were all the snippets the boy heard as he turned to the alley.

Another memory of when he had walked in on his father and mother standing on their balcony smiling and swaying to a song playing in the distant city below. *"Son,"* his father called, *"make sure that you find a woman like your mother here and you treat her respectfully. Not like a man respects a man. But how the sun treats the moon. With a delicate kiss of light and a warm embrace. And you make sure you protect her like a dragon protects its horde. Protect her, your family, and those of yours.* **That** *is your first duty."*

As the boy stepped into the alley, the memory brought back.. other memories. Memories he wished he never had. Memories of the night his father had thrown his life away and left the boy to take up the place as the man of the house. And he would. He would do it better than his father had after throwing himself away when he...

The boy stopped in his tracks. The light of the sun was low here in the depths of the alley, the building too high for light to reach at this time of day. But as the boy's eyes had come into focus, adjusting to the light, he could make out two figures at the end of the alley where it split into an intersection.

Slowly, the boy stepped forward. He could just make out the figures now. His mother stood with her back to the building wall that intersected the alleys. And between her and him, a man in a blue coat and white hair was stepping closer to her. A whisper that the boy couldn't hear passed between the two.

Then his mother's eyes went wide, and she made to speak out, but the man clamped a hand over her mouth. A brief struggle took place then as the man forced the boy's mother to the wall. The muffled screams of his mother, lost to within the alley as the man cupped her mouth with his hand and gripped her shoulder with the other. She thrashed for two breaths, kicking and attempting to punch the man in the blue coat.

The man seemed to not even feel the weak attempt and only clamped his hand tighter around her mouth, pushing her into the wall with his body. The boy had the sudden urge to run to his mother's aid, to hit the man, to strike him down just like his father said. But just as he did, he watched as two things happened within the same breath.

First his eyes met his mother's, and her thrashing seemed to slow a bit as she saw him there in the ally. He watched as her eyes registered him, widened even further and with the man still trying to clamper her mouth shut motioned her head and pointed at a stack of crates and bags of what looked like grain. The boy's thoughts though, were to go back down the alley to where the guards, strong powerful men. Those able to manage this man and bring him to justice...

Second, the shining glint of a small blade...the boy's eyes were drawn to the thing as it seemed to form out of thin air with mist and ice crackling the air as it formed an ice dagger in the assailant's hand. The almost translucent blade appeared in the man's opposite hand as he pulled the blade back and then the man's arm was ramming it into his mother's pinned body.

The boy froze then, unable to move from the spot as he heard a grunt from his mother, and then another as the man rammed the blade into her side again. The boy watched as his mother seemed to grow limp in the man's hold, her eyes drooping and her arm falling. The man stumbled as his mother seemed to collapse then, her legs giving and her weight falling onto him. He began to guide her to the ground and the boy caught a glint of the man's eye, not real features as the shadows hid the man's face, but the blade in the man's right hand as he guided the boy's mother to the ground was enough to put the boy to action.

With a sudden panic the boy dove behind the crate and held his breath. Hoping the man hadn't seen him. With how dark the alley was, the boy was surprised he had made out his mother, the shadows hid her assailant far too much for the boy to make out, other than the strange blue coat.

After two heart beats the boy peered around the corner to see the man now leaning over her slumped form. Whispering something, but the man didn't finish before the boy heard a roar of fury and whirled around.

The old bald captain drew his black steel blade, tossing his helm aside in favor of gripping the long sword with both hands.

Then, faster than the boy could track, the old captain was flying past him and towards his mother and the assailant. The man seemed to have been launch down the alley by something. Like an arrow released from a bow.

The boy could hardly follow as the man came down the alley. But when the boy turned to look at his mother's assailant the man nowhere to be seen. The captain reached the boy's mother and knelt quickly, after the captain said a few words he burst to his feet, turned, and launched down the alleyway, hopefully after her assailant. The sound of the man's roar echoed as he chased after the blue coat man.

The two guards rushed to the boy's mother and bent to peer under her traveling cloak at where her assailant had most certainly stabbed her.

The boy stepped out from behind the crates then and hesitantly stepped forward as the men propped her up against the wall and began asking her questions. "What happened, your majesty?" "Who was he, my lady?" "What did he want?" "Did he say anything?"

But the boy's mother only looked to him, a faint smile upon her lips as she looked him over. As if glad he wasn't hurt, but a pain behind her eyes.

"Come...come here, my little Fire," she called in a whisper. Her voice strained as she spoke.

The boy hurried over, the guards parting to make room. The boy could feel the tears building in his eyes as he reached her and then embraced her.

"I'm sorry, mother!" the boy wept into her shoulder. One of her hands stroked his shaking back, like she had when he had burnt his hands practicing elemancy. "I—I couldn't—"

"Shhhh—shhhh, it's okay. It is not your fault, my Fire." She assured him as he clung to her. "It is *not* your fault."

The guards spoke in low voices before the sounds of boots on cobble stone raced off down the alley while one guard bent down and looked over the injured side as the boy hugged her from the other side, just barely able to make the guard out through his tears.

"I wanted to help..." the boy cried.

"I know." His mother's breathing became labored as she affirmed, "You were so brave in trying... but I'm glad that you listened to me and weren't hurt... It was good that you didn't do it...I would have been so sad if you had been hurt too..."

The boy's body shook as he felt his mother's hand begin to slow.

"Your majesty," the guard checking her side began, "Your majesty, please save your strength. Kimp is going for a healer. Stay with us..."

"My Fire?" she asked in a tired voice.

"Yes, mother?"

"Promise me...that you will have Nico...Nicodemus train you... Like he trained your father..."

The boy held onto his mother tighter, closing his eyes through the tears.

"Can you do that for me?"

He only nodded his head, before another fit of shaking and tears washed over him.

"There, there," she cooed. "I'm going to be with your father now...I'll tell him of the strong man you are becoming...I need you to be strong for me..."

"No...no. Stay here!' the boy pleaded, pulling on her dress. "Don't leave me!"

"I'm sorry, my Fire. But it's my time."

He felt her hand, weak as it was, grab him and push him back a little so they were eye to eye. "You remember your promise?"

A slow nod was all he could do for a moment. Composing himself before speaking, he wiped a tear from his cheek with a sniff.

"Have old man Nicodemus...train me like father."

Behind them the sound of the guard scraping around and then walking back. Then, the sudden eruption of orange light sprung up. The boy looked up to see the man had found a stick of some sort and had set it ablaze, holding it with one and dropping the opposite hand that had a glowing red ruby ring on it. Thankfully, the light illuminated the space, and the boy turned his teary eyes back to his mother, who held a weak smile, but to the boy, her smile was the source of the light. New tears formed.

"That's my boy..." She brushed a strand of his hair from his face before catching a tear from his cheek. Her skin was so soft but cold now. The boy could see her skin growing white as the light from the soldiers now lit torch illuminated the alley. The boy reached up and held her hand as she spoke her last words. "I...love you...my little Fire..."

As he watched the light fade from his mother's eyes, muffled silence was all the boy could hear. Her smile on her face as she left him...alone. He gently let her limp hand down to her lap. Seeing the blood, upon her hands and now his, for the first time. The red made him stop.

As he stared at the crimson upon his hands, his eyes bloodshot no longer able to shed any tears as he had shed all he could have. The emptiness was all he knew. Numbness as he stared at the red upon his hands.

There were sounds of heavy footfalls and the sudden scrape of metal on rock as the captain appeared at the corner of the boy's vision. The older man leaned down saying nothing as he tried meeting her eyes.

After a moment, the man cursed and stood up. The boy didn't know if it was to him or someone else. There was a shout that almost brought the boy back but then his mind seemed to dismiss this as he sunk deeper into that abyss.

In that moment, the boy did not care. Stuck within this state, the boy sat there as the guards spoke in angered tones, staring into nothingness.

Until a tiny spark within him lit, deep within he could feel the empty void within him being filled with that heat.

The *flames* within his heart steadily beat in their rhythm of Fire.

A slow beat, like that of distant water dripping into a still pond. The beat slowly gaining in volume as the Fire seemed to grow. Consuming all within its wake, like a glutton beast on a rampage. Not caring for anything, the Flames swallowed anything within its wake.

"Let the Fire rage!" a voice bellowed as the feeling overwhelmed him. A power so overwhelming it would take him until the end of

all days to crawl back to the gates of reality. The rhythm reaching a crescendo. Then the Fire seemed to wait. As if waiting for its cue. But none came.

How did I get here? The boy thought as he let the world fade away, the body of his beloved mother at his feet. *How can I go back?*

But he knew his answer. He knew the answer as if it were his own name. Like the blood running through his veins. Like the blood-stained hands before him.

There is no going back... No going back to simpler times. When he had watched his mother smiling as his sister laughed spinning in one of her new pretty dresses. He would never again see his father's proud smile as the man praised him on his progression in elemancy. Times of blissful ignorance, where all he wanted to do was be with the ones he loved.

Then there was a calling sound, like that of a crow, from above, towards the gray sky. When the boy looked up, he saw that of a large black bird, maybe the size of a house cat. It was a Ravin. The bird was looking down on the scene with something the boy could identify as sadness, how he felt in that moment. Then the bird blinked, cocked its head, and sat up on its perch straighter, like some majestic stone work of pride. Of power...

"...a *strong young man...*" the words echoed in his mind He needed to become stronger. If he wanted to protect the ones he loved, he needed power. And not some small little Fire that he could only summon and then move around, he needed the raw power of an Elementalist...

To do that, he would need to move past that horrible night of screams, smoke, and blood. Past the broken throne. Past that horrible war. He needed to become the Blue Flame. The strongest Fire to burn anything that wished to harm him or those he cared about.

If he wanted to do that, if he wanted to become the strongest, he would need to be more than he was. More than some poor, weak, lost, helpless little…

2

BOY

"Boy!" barked the bald man from where he stood on his old doorstep. The boy flinched a little as he felt the man spit in his face. The dust swirling up and into his face from the surrounding plains only added to the boy's annoyance on top of his fouling mood. "You're still just a little runt, look'n to get himself killed as soon as possible!"

The man was only half wrong. Seven seasons. It had been seven full season rotations since that day in that alley. And for the past season, Hagitan Ignus the forgotten prince of a broken nation, has been living in back alleys like a street rat, attempting to get himself to where he stood now.

Tan, as his family and friends always call him, had ran with other street urchins for an entire season until some of the older kids, sixteen to eighteen seasons old, and who knew better Fire skills, beat him to a pulp and kicked him out. Even at fifteen seasons old, Tan had the disadvantage of not having the knowledge or understanding of elemancy. He needed more.

So that was why he was now where he stood, standing there, and taking this verbal abuse. He was familiar with it. Beaten to mush every day, for the past season. Stolen of everything he held dear, except for the ring upon his right middle finger, still too big to where but he did anyways.

Compared to all of that though, this was nothing for Tan. Having lived in one of the most hostile places on the continent, the ruined country of the Fire Realm, this was just another day. And the old man was only the latest to add to it.

The Realm had once been a world power. One of the six great nations of the continent. It used to be the most popular and beautiful place to visit in the world with three world treasures within its borders. That was until the Purge at the end of the Great War.

Now it was a desert that harbored only the remaining clans, thugs, outlaws, and mercenaries left in this mostly barren land. And this dump was now what the once great Clans of Fire and broken citizens called home.

Tan stood in his stained, and tattered shirt and trousers, and with nothing on his bruised, and calloused feet as he let the old man rave on about how much of a "hopeless pipsqueak of a runt" he was.

"Please—"

"You're as small as a toothpick, boy! You'd never last a day under my training! Much less a lesson."

It wasn't entirely true. Yes, Tan was small by a fifteen-season-old boy's standards. He was of average height of just around five feet tall. Five feet one finger to be exact. But even with his smaller stature, he had made sure to keep up with all the other urchins and could run for a long way without tiring. His dirty, finger-length brown hair blew into his eyes, and he raked a hand through it to keep it out of his face. His eyes were piercing ice blue that always made him stare at himself in the mirror, as well as those from the clan. It was odd for someone of the clans to have blue eyes.

A strike contrast to the usual brown, golden-brown or dark red of the clans. He stared at the old man with those eyes.

Even though Tan had a few scars, bruise on his left cheek, and tanned pale skin courtesy of the weeklong trip to this forgotten shack. He glanced past the old man to the shack that looked like would fall over if a strong breeze pushed it. And then to the solen tree just to his left.

A knot of a tree with lush green leaves stood just taller than the shack at maybe thirteen feet. But thankfully it protected him from the harsh sun beginning to make its rise into the sky. Still, a good bit of sweat beaded his forehead as the blazing hot of summer was still a burden to any out at the peak of day. And since Tan didn't have a dragon, much less a horse to ride, it had limited him to moving at the beginning of day and towards the edge of night to get to this place.

"And, on top of that," the old man went on, "where are you goin'a stay? Because you ain't staying with me! That's for dang cert'n! Ain't have'n no stinky kid in my house..." the old man spat. Tan had to force himself to not raise an eyebrow and glance at the shack he called a...house. Instead, he attempted to answer the man's question.

"I have a place!" Tan spat out, even though not ten heart beats earlier he had thought he would just stay with the old man. He hadn't really thought that far ahead. In fact, Tan now realized that he had put too much assumption on whether he should have planned for this and many other factors. Like food or water. He wondered how this old man survived out here in this barren land after looking the shack over. Another thought popped into his mind that he quickly cast aside as he watched the old man raise an eyebrow at his statement.

"Oh *really*? Where?" the man huffed back. He made a show of looking around with a curious eye.

Thinking fast, Tan remembered seeing a cave in the hills before he had arrived. Yes! That's it! That would be a good place to stay. If he recalled correctly, it was on high ground, so he would stay dry. There had been a stream and a thin patch of woods near the cave. It was far, Tan admitted to himself, but it was close enough that he could get to the town or to the old man's... *house.*

"There's a cave back the way I came from near the mountain. I can—"

"Ha!" the old man's sudden outburst cut Tan off. "I hope it isn't that dragon den up near the stream. 'Cause *that* dragon will eat you alive!" The man's face contorted as if contemplating something. "On second thought, you *should* stay there." He cackled manically, slapping his knee at his own joke.

This made Tan's stomach fall and did nothing for his spirits, but he wasn't done yet.

"What if I proved myself?" he rebutted. He was desperate after coming all this way. He wouldn't allow a simple thing as shelter to keep him from learning everything he can from this man.. If this man was whom everyone said he was, then he was by far the best person Tan could have asked for, and the only one. "What if I... I can... prove that I'm worth it?! What if I show what I can do?"

The old man thought for a second. Then looked Tan straight in the eyes and said, "No."

With that, the man turned and began hobbling back towards his shed of a house.

Tan felt crestfallen. All this way and for what? After leaving his Gran, and the rest of the Clan. Defying the Elders in coming here, living like an urchin for several moons on end, they would cast him aside like an afterthought.

No! I won't let it end here!

"I thought you were the Captain of the King's Guard!?" Tan called after the old man. The old man stopped but did not turn as Tan continued. "I thought you were the greatest Fire Elemental trainer of the Nation, or was that someone else? Was my mother wrong in telling me to ask you to train me?"

"That was someone else." The man did not turn as he spoke. "That man is dead."

"So, the Royal Guard meant nothing to you?" Tan asked. The man whirled on Tan, a tempest behind his eyes as he roared. Tan winced and shied back, realizing he had might have gone a bit too far.

"It meant *everything* to me!" The old man seemed to gain a burst of energy as he stomped up to Tan, finger pointing in his face a mere hair length from touching his chest. "I gave my entire life to the Guard!"

"But you're still here," Tan pointed out, "And they're all gone..."

The Fire behind the man's eyes dimmed, and the strength seemed to fade. Then his vigor came back with a vengeance.

"How do you know that? Who are you?!"

The man's eyes squinted as he searched Tan's face. Tan felt his face go red at the thought of the man not recognizing him as the prince heir. Literally the last charge this man had before his mother's death and the old man's subsequent self-exile.

"*Ashes and smog,* you can't be..." the old man's face went pale, eyes wide as he took a step back. "Who—? You can't be—?" but the man never finished the sentence.

Tan's heart was racing now at the thought of someone finding out he was the prince after a year of hiding that fact, in fear of them sending him back to clan Ignus. If the old man turned him in...

"Why are you here, *boy?*" the old man demanded, face going red. Tan could see a muscle twitch in the man's jaw.

"My Trial is in only a few moons away. It's at the Red moon solstice. And I need a teacher, a *proper* teacher. Not one of those clan elders that deal with tame Fire. I need a master in *Fire*."

"And you think I'm a master?" the old man gave Tan a raised eyebrow. "You know how many people would kill to train you? Hundreds. You really want me, a washed up, old, and broken soldier, to train you?"

"If you're half the man I think you are, then yes," Tan said, raising his chin.

It took the old man a while to respond. Tan watched as the man's face went from confused and too mad to warn out. He was worried the old man would just spit in his face and kick him out on his tail. But the man's stutter cast that fear aside.

"Err-Fine...*maybe*! *If* you pass my test, I'll consider it," the old man finally got out. "But if you lose, you leave me alone, *forever!*" he pointed a finger in Tan's face for emphasis.

"Dea—"

"*Before* you decide," the old man held up a hand with raised eyebrows, interrupting Tan, "You better know your test will be to face one of the vilest beasts in this here broken kingdom. *And* trust me when I say, 'many a man have wet themselves at the sight of this beast.' Razor-sharp claws and all. It's the size of a building and can melt the meat off the bone with its breath!"

The old man looked Tan up and down then, clearly waiting for him to answer. Tan took a single heartbeat, glancing down past his bruised and callused feet to the dirt and sand he stood upon as if it had the answer he already knew. He had promised, hadn't he? And he would keep that promise. Not only that, but training under a man as strong as this bald one before him. If he had even a shred of the old Red Dawn, it would be worth it. To have the strength to protect those he loves. To do what he could not, what his father could not, he would do anything to make that possible. Setting his jaw, Tan met the old man's gaze and spoke.

"Then I'll face it!" Tan stated, straightening his back, widened his feet, and clenching his fists at his side. Rigid attention, like the Ignus Huntsmen, had taught him. "Whatever I have to do, I'll do it!"

The decrepit man grunted, but Tan couldn't tell if it was a good grunt or a bad one. The old man shook his head and stepped back up to his porch. He examined Tan again, crossing his arms in a disgruntled way, before speaking.

"I'm goin'a hold ya to that," the old man promised. "But I highly doubt you'll pass, being in the state you're in. The beast will probably just swallow you whole."

Tan stood straighter at this.

30

The old man sighed, shaking his head, "Ah, well...I warned ya." He then spoke low, as if to himself, but Tan could hear him well.

"... hope the old slug ain't in one of his deep sleeps. He really needs to get out of that stoking cave more often. Ashes and cinders, where did I put that smogging thing?" The old man stepped just inside the door to the shed, reaching around for something.

The old man sighed, peeking back to peer at Tan with the rest of his body still inside the "house". Tan only raised an eyebrow at him.

Was the man even sane enough to teach? The thought grew. Worry swept through Tan's thoughts. Had he made a mistake? Was this the right thing to do? But before he had time to act on any of these thoughts, the old man stepped back outside, messing with something in his hands.

"If you happen to actually pass," the man spoke, not looking at Tan as stepped out from under the porch untangling whatever was in his hands, "I'll think about training you. *But* I think that's highly unlikely." He gave Tan a stink eye up and down as he stepped past.

"I'll pass your test!" Tan answered in response, straightening his shoulders even more, as the old man brushed past him. "You'll see!"

The old man grunted again, and Tan guessed that was sarcasm in his tone.

"Wait there," the old man called over his shoulder. "I don't want to have to explain to your grandmother that you were smothered by the Regal. That woman would have my head if you died from just being squashed like a melon."

Tan blanched at this. *A Regal?! There was no way! How does he have a Regal out here?*

If Tan was correct, Regal's tended to eat a good amount of food. When he glanced around, he saw neither vegetation nor livestock. But Tan had no time to respond to the old man's statement as the bald ex-soldier took what looked like a fighting stance.

The old man turned away then, facing the distant mountains with the rising sun to their backs. Tan watched the old man as he took in a deep breath, composing his body, and then he took on a stance that Tan had never seen before. He knew a good many of the Clan Huntsmen fighting stances, Gran making sure he studied them, and the clan dancing stances as well. But this was none he had seen before.

Then the old man began to perform a sort of dance, but it was like nothing Tan had ever seen before. It was far different from the Clan's ritual dances, with a lot of skipping, spinning, and clapping. This dance had a fluidity to it. Tan was also impressed that the old man could even move in some of the ways he did with how old he must be.

Then a flash of red and orange erupted in a trailing Flame that followed the old man's hands as he spun and wove them in the air, every step calculated, every movement measured. The Flames looked like that of a tail flapping in the wind as the old man seemed to paint the air with it.

Finally, the man's dance reached a climax as he spun out of a strange sequence of steps and threw the tail of Fire high into the air. It was only at that moment that Tan saw something burning within the Flames as it was thrown into the air. At the top of the arc of the throw, the trail of Fire erupted into an explosion of sound and color. As if a giant had taken an iron hammer and slammed it down against the metal anvil. The resounding explosion echoed over the vast distance of empty dirt, sand, and dead grasses.

Then, off toward the hills, Tan heard a roar. And not just any roar. No, this was the roar of a great beast, a war cry for beasts of Fire and scales. Behind the roar, a clap of thunder that shook the very air in a shockwave made the very leaves upon the tree rattle next to him.

Tan took a step back as he watched a dot on the horizon slowly growing bigger and bigger as the dot came more into focus. A loud screeching roar bellowed from the winged creature as it grew closer at an alarming rate. Tan taking an unintentional step backwards as he gaped at the approaching beast. From that loud bellow, Tan knew he had probably made one of the most irrational decisions of his life. The old man looked back to Tan, and Tan attempted to hide his fear by straightening his posture to stop the trembling, but to no avail.

"You know, you *can* still opt out," he called with a smirk, his bald head shining in the sun.

Tan stared at him for a breath. To think that he would be trained under Master Nicodemus Hellfire, the most legendary Fire elemental teacher known to the Realm, and last Captain of the Fire Realm Royal Guard, after what happened within the past season, would be foolish. But one would also need to be a fool to train under him. And Tan guessed he was a fool. He was in this until the end. He *needed* this. And if he died, the world would keep spinning. So, he turned around...

The hurricane could be heard coming as the dot in the sky grew larger and larger. And then the sound of large wings was the only thing Tan heard. The visual details of the dragon slowly came into perspective as it made a pass around the small shack-like house. With its snake-like neck and head, it apparently observed the two ant-size humans below. Its piercing snake eyes never wavered. Large, dark red and black wings propelled it forward. Frills ran from the back of its head to its shoulders, like a lion's mane. The dragon's two hind legs curled up under its sleek black body.

Not as terrifying as a Blood Thorn Regel, but close enough; Tan knew that from just staring at the beast. He would never win. Its razor-sharp talons, the hooks at the end of its wings the size of his arms. The dragon circled once and then landed with an earth-quaking *thu-thud!!* upon the ground in front of the two tiny humans. Tan felt like he jumped ten feet in the air when Nicodemus spoke, as he had forgotten the old man was even there.

"Last chance, boy," he offered, no sympathy in his voice.

Tan looked from the old man to the magnificent beast before him in awe. His mind went blank as he gaped at just how *big* the dragon was. The hot panting breath of the beast washed over him as he took the creature in.

It sat back on its hind legs, with its clawed wings supporting his front like a bat, and exposing its armored chest. The creature's head reached as high as the surrounding trees. Tan had heard most everyone call them Dragons. But in his opinion, they were more like large wyverns. Actual dragons have four legs and two wings, like the smaller green and red scout dragons the clan hunters liked to use. But since this type of wyvern was so much bigger, and a more sought out and preferred breed, they took on the name Dragon.

However, the clans always classified this larger species of wyverns as Regals. Which was always made Tan think these creatures were so immense, that the power of the winged reptiles were such that they needed to add an entirely different subspecies. Which Tan would agree with being able to see a live specimen up close and in person,. He craned his neck back to look up at the massive creature's gigantic head...

Tan tried to build his courage. *It was just an animal. Right? A very dangerous animal, yes, but an animal nonetheless. But it can be beaten, outsmarted. Yes! I can do this!* With his courage restored, Tan took a solid step forward. Toward a beast he believed had melted down an entire city before...

Nope! No! Stop that! Don't think of that.

"I'm ready," he stated as bravely as any fifteen-season-old boy could. He looked at the old man.

The corner of the old man's mouth twitched upward ever so slightly. Then the old man's face went stony as he looked to the dragon and called to it in a language Tan had only heard on very rare occasions. Some of the clan riders spoke a little of the ancient tongue, but Tan had no clue where it came from or how to speak it...yet.

"Tyrone," Tan watched the beast turn its enormous head towards the old man, cocking its head to the side in a very humanlike gesture, *"In puer facile rapiunt illud... sicut terrent eum."*

Tan became even more puzzled when the dragon snorted in response. *The dragon can **understand** him?*

The dragon narrowed its eyes towards the old man before focusing back on Tan.

As the dragon huffed out what Tan could only assume was an annoyed grunt, Tan now had a deeper understanding of what stood before him. This was not a wild untamed beast, but a creature of intelligence. One that understood some of the world around it.

As Tan seemed to lose himself within the dragon's orange flame eyes, he could tell that this creature held secrets far beyond what he could hope to understand. And yet there was still the underlying hint of an animal, the king of the Flames, held deep within.

Then the dragon brought back its head, similar to a snake, ready to strike.

Tan realized what it was doing and prepared himself. The dragon's chest began to glow a slight orange, as did its mouth. Tan looked about himself and only saw the tree behind him. Too far away for him to reach in time, as he turned back to the dragon.

Flames erupted from its mouth as it stuck out its neck towards Tan. He was too far away for the beast to *physically* touch him, but its Fire reached him with ease.

Scorching hot and burning the air and ground, Tan could imagine himself erupting into burning agony and pain. But he knew what to do.

Searching within himself for the part that was consumed with anger over the loss of his mother, father, and sister. Tan had already resolved to become stronger. He will pass this test!

With a roar Tan pulled the built-up energy and flung it at the oncoming Flames. He watched as what looked like heat waves left his body and ignited into a wall of Fire. The feeling of power flowing from his chest, down his arms and out his fingers as the dragon's Fire met his own.

After a moment, Tyrone's Flames subsided, and Tan dropped his hands. Panting, he wiped the sweat building on his forehead and met the dragon's eyes with a smirk. The beast stared at the boy, blinking in what Tan could only assume was confusion.

"Didn't think I could block a puny Flame like that?" Tan taunted. "Watch this!"

Tan adjusted the slightly big metal ring set with dragon sapphires on his middle finger, before taking a breath as he gathered the energy into his fist. Focusing on the ring as he did, before he thrust his clenched fist at the dragon as if he were delivering a punch.

A Fire ball blasted towards the dragon, though the dragon merely lifted his wing like a shield and the Fire ball harmlessly splashed against the leather scaled wing. Tyrone peaked out, looking from its wing to Tan and then to the old man. Tan watched as his hopes dissipated when the dragon seemed perplexed at the fact that Tan had just attacked it.

The dragon then brought its full height as it tilted its head up, sucking in a large lung full of air. The orange light building within its chest. In three consecutive fire bursts, the dragon spat out concentrated Fireballs at Tan's face.

Tan took a ready stance, thanking his Gran and a few of the elders for teaching him the basics of elemancy, just as the first fireball reached him. He produced his wall of elemental Fire again and all three Fire balls impacted the shield wall, dissipating after each strike.

Hearing crackling noises behind him, Tan quickly turned to see the tree behind him ablaze with its leaves on fire before slowly snuffing out. Smoke rose into the air as he turned back to the dragon. And then he realized he had just withstood the attack of a full-grown Regal. A *regal*! Maybe he could do this!

With his courage and arrogance overflowing, Tan decided to do something even more foolish. He held his hands before him as if he were holding an invisible ball and focused the energy within this space. The air between his hands seemed to warp into a small Flame that grew into a large ball of Fire the size of his head. Tan had taken a basic course in Fire when he stayed with his uncle after his mother's...death.

Tan had quickly outpaced all the other kids within his group, who had been at it for two more years than he. Having been on the run for a good two years hadn't helped his training any. And then, after just a few moons of training, he set out on a year-long journey to find the man his mother had asked him to train with. And Tan would fulfill that promise.

Tan took a deep breath to calm his nerves. Then he launched the ball of energy at the dragon. The missile headed straight for the creature. The dragon did something different this time, surprising Tan as it let the fireball impact the dragon's chest.

The force of the explosion hitting the dragon created a shockwave that pushed Tan back. He stumbled backwards before looking up and see the dragon stumble back with a roar of surprise.

When the smoke from the explosion dissipated, the dragon was shaking its head as if clearing it of water. The dragon turned to the old man and Tan followed to see the older man with one hand stroking his chin and the other supporting it in the ancient 'I'm thinking' pose.

Then suddenly the man's eyes went wide, and he spun to point and shake a finger at a large black bird perched onto the edge of the shack Tan hadn't noticed until that moment.

"Only that pesky birds might keep their minds to themselves!" the old man shouted at the large Ravin that had been sitting on the roof of the house, watching them all. The bird cocked its head to the side and ruffled its feathers.

"Well then, don't interrupt me when I'm thinking!"

Tan swore he saw the bird roll its eyes at this. But that was dumb. The dragon Tan could understand, but the bird? He wondered if the old man was going crazy and had begun talking to his pets.

Then a reverberating sound that would make any small creature tremble had Tan slowly facing the source of the noise. And watched as the dragon, staring at a black smoke stain on its shiny now matte black scales. The growl intensified, almost making Tan's skin tingle as it slowly looked up to meet Tan's eyes.

Tan watched as the dragon made a hissing noise, as if he were sucking in a large amount of air. The dragon's chest began to glow from the heat it was accumulating again. Tan's eyes widened as he realized the dragon was taking way too long with its build up this time.

As if it were gathering a storm within itself that it could barely contain. Tan met the creature's eyes of rage and anger and thought for the briefest of moments before a torrent of Fire raced toward him.

I want that type of power.

Hastily he gathered his own power and threw up a Fire wall just as the dragon's Flames reached him. He held his arms up as if to hold the Flames back with his physical strength and elemental power.

Gritting his teeth, Tan held the wall up as long as he could, but he was too weak. His power to small. Then he watched as his orange Flames seemed to shred like cloth fabrics being ripped apart by a jealous suitor before his wall dissipated to nothingness. Tan felt his heart fall at this thought. Was he going to fail? If this strike reached him, would he fail? Never able to fulfill his promise.

No! He would not let that happen. He had come too far already. He would not let it end here! But what did he have left? He had given it all, hadn't he?

Then, for the briefest of moments, he felt this tug within, the smallest of hopes. The light deep within that shown as if to say, *you still have more to give little Flame.*

Tan reached within himself. It was so far, yet so close. With a cry, Tan felt the briefest of brushes of this inner light. And before him, a small spark the size of his thumbnail appeared between his warding hand and the dragon's red Flames.

The explosion that came from this phenomenon was enough to that it launched Tan back in the direction he knew the tree was and only had one thought before the world went suddenly dark…

What was that power?

Nicodemus da Haliken had watched the boy's eyes during that last attack Tyrone had thrown at the boy. Nicodemus thought it was over the top for the dragon, but since the dragon's scales had been matted, he considered it somewhat fair.

But all he could think of now was that light, that glow within the boy's eyes. Just like his father when he had been that age. It was a look he knew all too well, with his vast history and understanding of fighting, had seen only a few times he had seen that look, but he would never forget it.

That bit of power just beneath that wished to rage out and consume. That need for victory over one's enemies. He had seen it within one man in the old guard he had trained. He had seen it in the face of a silver-eyed princess and the eyes of her trusted silver masked bodyguard.

But most notably, he had seen it in the eyes of one of the most tried-and-true men he had ever come across in this world. And he had been the King of this once great nation in ruins, and if his conclusion was correct, which that annoying bird assured him it was, this boy was that very King's orphaned son. Prince heir to the broken throne.

'*So,*' Corax asked Nic within the private confines of his mind, '*will you train him?*'

Twisting the metal ring on his finger, which enabled him to speak with the creature telepathically, Nic cursed the bird and its timing.

'*Shoulda got rid of this thing seasons ago,*' Nic thought in spite.

'*So, you would toss aside Aideen's last request then? For you to keep me company until he is ready?*'

'*If I would have known it meant you can hear my thoughts when I wasn't focused, and not stoking shut up for more than ten minutes...*' That insufferable bird was going to drive him mad, even more so than he already was.

'*It was twenty minutes, and you know it,*' The bird corrected smugly. '*But you still didn't answer my question...*'

Nicodemus rolled his eyes and turned to watch the now sleeping boy. After the boy had bonked his head against the tree, Nic had bandaged the bruise, put a small rag tied with ice inside on the bruise after placing the boy on his bed. The sun was high in the sky now, almost time for the mid-day meal. Curses and it was supposed to be onion soup night too! Well, he won't be able to have his favorite meal for a while yet now.

'*Yes, you stoking bird. I will. Now let me be.*'

The bird didn't say anything else as Nic watched the boy's slight frame. Chest rising and falling in its slow, sleepy rhythm. That's when he truly took in the boy then.

Nic studied the boy's face. He could see the boy's father in his jaw line, the way it set, and the round bulb nose. The same messy brown hair, though his hair held a bit of Lady Silf's black raven hair, as well as her freckles sprinkled lightly across his nose and upper cheeks. Nic noted all these similarities that hadn't been there when he had last seen the boy at Lady Silf's funeral.

For failing her then. Allowing that scum of a man to kill Lady Silf, his charge and one of the kindest people Nic had ever known, a person kind even to a gruffy old soldier like him, to allow that scum to kill her was unforgivable. So, he would train her son to protect himself and protect those like her from scums like that stoking Imperial weasel.

It still irked at Nic how easily the man had taken Lady Silf out from under his watchful eyes. But after the uproar made by the innkeeper, Nic got too distracted to monitor Lady Silf and the young prince. Letting his age get to him.

With a sigh, Nic pinched the bridge of his nose to forget those memories. He needed them to settle so he could focus. If he was going to do what he had now set his mind to do, he had no time for self-pity and over analyze the events long since passed.

The boy stirred then. Moving about and bringing a hand to the icepack on his face as he leaned up with a groan.

"Finally up, are we?" Nic asked the boy.

The boy made to swing his legs off the bed, but Nic placed a hand on the boy's shoulder, preventing him from pivoting off.

"Oh, no!" Nic moved to push the boy back down into the bed. "You don't need to move for another few minutes. You hit your empty skull a little too hard; good thing there wasn't anything important inside."

"What happened?" the boy croaked out after adjusting himself to sit against the wall Nic used as a headrest with his very thin and comfortable pillow.

"Tyrone, the little princess, he got mad that you scorched his scales, so he tried to burn you to ashes. Ended up just knocking you out instead," Nicodemus stated. "That overgrown lizard is a pridefully petty princess in a beast's body."

'Because you spoiled him too much when he was a hatchling,' Corax pointed out.

'Shut up bird, that was fifty years ago and don't mean squat now,' Nic shot back.

The kid seemed to have to force his eyes to open. After blinking the several times, Nic watched as the boy looked about the tiny room Nic called a bedroom, with only the bed and a single chair as furniture. No decoration except for a picture of the Golden Palace set on the wooden wall above Tan's head.

"Where are we?"

"My home," Nic answered, glaring at the boy, "you empty-headed numbskull. When the blast hit you, you flew ten feet back." Then added, "You know you can't fly, right?"

The boy didn't laugh at the joke.

"It was quite peaceful until you started snoring."

"I don't snore," the boy argued.

"Mhmm. I guess you're gonna say it was me then? Snoring, sleeping, *and* awake?" Nic picked the hot bowl of onion soup he ended up fixing while the boy was cold from the small chair in the room's corner. The boy's eyes followed the soup like a starving buzzard until it was placed into his hands. Nic chuckled at this.

"Boy, you look like you hadn't eaten in days," though Nic had looked the same way when he had had a bowl of his own earlier, he figured.

'*You did.*' Corax took that opportunity to point out the obvious.

'*Stay quiet, bird. Make sure that dragon ain't eat'n my onion patch again. You know how it makes his breath stink.*'

'*Fine. But only because his breath does really stink after he has a few.*'

The boy gripped the bowl as if it were full of liquid gold before grabbing the spoon and shoveling a mouthful of the soup into his mouth.

"Eat it slowly!" Nic warned. "I don't want to be changing any bedsheets of onion soup bile."

The boy only nodded and gripped the spoon and slowly, wincing a bit, he took a sip. That turned into a loud slurp that just made Nic's toes curl. The sound was like some tiny thing, with many legs crawling up and down his ear as the sound passed. A revolting sound that only people with no manners ate like.

"Argh! Stop that *disgusting* sound and eat it normally! You are not some rat in an alley. If you don't remember at least some sense of decency, then I will have to change my mind." Nic reached for the bowl, but the boy shrank back, curling around the steaming soup before scooping another bite into his mouth and, thankfully, not slurping this time. "It's such a fingernail-scratching sound. If you can't eat properly, then…"

"No! I'll stop!" Tan promised. The old geezer gave him a look before stepping back.

The boy ate it as if it were the best soup in the world, which Nic highly doubted was true. Queen Silf had made a mean vegetable soup… Nic cut that line of thought short as he watched the boy finish the rest of the bowl in under five minutes.

With a sigh, the boy sat the bowl in his lap. Then Nic watched as the boy's eyebrows furrowed together before speaking.

"Did I pass the test?!" Nic smirked at the boy's attempts to play off the question as something he knew the answer to already, but Nic had heard the slight quiver in the boy's tone.

Nic studied the boy for a minute before answering. Twisting the ring that he had been holding in his hand since he pulled it from the boy's finger while bandaging him.

'I should just kick the twirp back to the clans…' Nic glanced around the cabin. *'I am not a teacher anymore.'*

'And yet you'll do it anyways.' The bird called.

'Ha! Says you.'

'Says you.' The bird's tone held a smile. *'Wait till you hear what the boy has to say. Ask him why he wants you to train him.'*

"I'll make my decision," the old man began, "after you answer a few questions."

"Okayyyy…." The boy said hesitantly.

"My first question," Nic paused, attempting to sort out his first question.

The ring in his hand felt so heavy as he fiddled with it. Then he steeled himself and brought the ring up between two fingers for the boy to see.

Holding up what he had in his hand, he asked.

"Are you really prince Hagitan Ignus, boy?" Nic looked the boy up and down with a raised eyebrow for emphasis. "Because you sure don't look like a prince. More like ashes and smog to me."

The boy went still, staring at the ring in between Nic's fingers. With no answer, Nic nodded.

'You know he is,' Corax pointed out.

'Better safe than sorry.'

"I'll take that as a yes," Nic stated as he palmed the ring. "Next question, why are you here, other than the obvious fact that you are here to kill me with your annoyance?"

"I promised Mother," Tan answered.

Nic felt his skin go cold at this. The image of the young woman laying in a pool of her own blood. He blinked the memory away.

"You...you promised little Silf what?"

The boy narrowed his eyes at Nic, and Nic cursed himself for falling back on that nickname he had given her. Nic raised a hand in defense of the glare.

"Apologies. What did you promise *her majesty?*"

Satisfied the boy answered, if not a bit hesitantly.

"She...she made me promise that I would have you train me that day in the alley. She said that you would teach me like you taught my father. And that..."

The boy's words drifted off as Nic's mind took him back to the past. When a boy that looked eerily similar to the one in his present day bed had stood before him, requesting the same thing. The boy's red eyes had met Nic's, and the clearness of them struck him. Slowly returning to the present, those eyes shifted to the crystal blue of the boy still speaking.

"...and I *need* to learn all that I can about Fire Elemancy..."

Nic felt all of those screaming memories attempting to come back all piled together to weigh him down. Then when his eyes met those crystal blue again, all he could see was the young lady that had married into a family that hated her and she still had that warm, motherly smile. She nodded to him, as if encouraging him. And the image faded back to the boy sitting in the bed.

Nic cleared his throat as he felt a tear attempt to build in his eyes. "She was a right good twirp, your mother was. Better than any person I know. The best pick for your father, Aideen. She was a fighter, in her own way..."

Then paused as he remembered his first encounter with the little lady, that seemed to try to wash his loom and gloom away whenever she saw him. It brought a smirk to his face before it turned to a sad frown at the thought of her light being snuffed out.

Should have done more! I'm sorry Silf...I let you down... he studied the boy, still holding the bowl, twiddling his thumbs and looking around with that nervous twitch the boy's father had at his age. ... *But not anymore.*

The words seemed to settle his mind a bit. The racing thoughts slowing to a crawl. Nic sighed inwardly, visibly relaxing as he did.

'I guess you aren't so bad,' He said to the bird.

'A compliment? From you?'

'You better enjoy it. Because you won't get another today!'

'Beggars can't be choosers, I suppose,' the bird said in reply.

Nic nodded and then spoke after clearing his voice wouldn't crack from the emotions that had just racked his psyche. "My final question is 'what is the ranking of the Elemental class Fire and what is your general knowledge of Fire?"

The boy steeled himself, clearly rehearsed this line before as he spoke like someone giving a brief report. "Spark, Ember,

Blood Born, and Fire Born are the four class types, with Fire Born being the last *evolution*. Fire is the process where rapid oxidation of a material in the process of combustion release to create heat, light, and other various...stuff. And is also called plasma. We as Elementalists control this state of constant combustion through our powers and through an elemancy glen. Some crazy, evil scientist had discovered this much during the Great War when he did...tests on captured Elementalists.

"Only one in every five clan members has Elemental powers. Fire is the second most powerful elemancy in terms of raw power. Lightning beats it in that field. But Fire can sustain for longer periods than lightning, but we lose out in endurance to an Earth and Nature elemental. Water elementalists are our greatest weakness, with Wind being a close second. Fire Elementalists can use their powers in more ways than just what people typically consider Fire."

The boy's eyes grew bright, and his arms became animated as he spoke on this next bit. "I've heard that some can make themselves fly. " He shot a hand up like some bird climbing into the sky. "*Or some run really fast, like you.*" The boy smiled at Nic then, the first smile he had seen the boy make sense arriving in this dump Nic called a home. "Oh! And I know the basic forms and stance."

Nic nodded in affirmation as the boy sat back. So, the boy at least had a rough entry into the schooling aspect. It was also interesting that the boy even knew about Flash Step. That would make this a lot easier. Especially if they only had until the Red Moon Solstice. It was only...what? Five weeks away? Nic didn't know, as he didn't really keep up with the time out here in the middle of nowhere.

Two and a half fortnights,' Corax piped up.

I didn't ask you!

And I didn't tell you to be a pain. But here we are,' the bird shot back.

Why you-!

46

'Are you going to tell him you'll train him?' the bird interrupted. *'Or are we going to wait until the Red Moon Solstice for you to answer him?'*

Nic blinked and then, returning to himself within the room before turning to look at the window the stoking bird was now perched on.

'I'll deal with you later,' Nic promised the bird.

"I've reached my decision," Nic said it so suddenly that the boy jumped visibly. "But before I finalize it...answer me this." The boy looked up.

"What?"

"Is this about revenge?" Nic held his breath as the boy looked down for a moment. It got to the point where Nic thought he might need to check and make sure the boy hadn't hit his head hard enough to rattle his brain. Finally, the boy lifted his head with eyes that seemed red, but Nic saw no tears.

"No." The boy said it so fast that Nic thought the boy would protest the issue. Nic raised an eyebrow but, after a moment, shrugged. *Better that he didn't go looking for revenge anyway.*

"Alright then. You'll be my apprentice then, as your mother wanted."

The boy's face visibly rose from worry to hope, to a contained joyful, yet silent, "Yes!"

Nic rolled his eyes at this. But inwardly, it gave Nic a small thrill of his own. As if the boy's youthful energy seeped into his own a bit.

"I will take it as a royal order," Nic continued, "in case that crazy woma— erhm. I mean...so that your *grandmother* doesn't eat me alive when she comes to check on me, got it?" the boy nodded aggressively. "And from now on you will address me as Master, nothing else. You will do *what* I say, *when* I say, *how* I say," he held up a finger for each point. "Understood?" he shook the three fingers at the boy.

"Yes." The boy said after a brief pause.

Nic raised an eyebrow. "Yes…*what?*"

"Yes, Master." The boy straightened on the bed, his whole body going to a strange sitting attention.

"Good, we start tomorrow. Today you rest. But come sunrise, your stoking rear better be up! We've got a long way to travel."

3

TRAINING WITH
AN OLD MAN

"Within the time span of me training you, you will have lived through Hell Fire," his Master said, before cursing his sore leg as he limped towards the large black regal.

Tan followed behind the old man. His eyes were clear, and everything came to him as if he were in a dream.

"It will be the worst experience of your life," the old man was saying, "and there will be no way out except to finish it. If you want out of the training, all you have to do is say so."

The gigantic dragon snorted as Master Nicodemus gripped the saddle and swung himself up and onto the beast's back with a grunt.

"There will be no breaks, no off time, and no whining *I'm sorry,*' if you mess up, understood? It's annoying when people do that."

"Yes, Master." Tan watched the old man strap himself in from the ground.

"As for food, water, clothing, and a bed, you will not need to worry. I will be making sure you are provided all of that," he said and stretched an arm down to him.

Tan grasped the old man's small hand, wandering if the man could lift him, until he was hoisted up onto the dragon's back. Set within the settle behind the old man he was about to ask if he needed a strap when the old man spoke over him.

"Hold on tight. Or you can find out just how flightless you really are."

Tan white-knuckled his master's shirt, as the dragon rumbled with a glint in its eyes. Nicodemus flicked the reins, and the dragon shook beneath Tan. A low vibrating hum sounded from deep within the beast. Extending his wings, they gained altitude. It still impressed Tan with the size of the beast's wings, the size of ship sails, propelling the beast through the air.

Tan knew what it was like to fly on the backs of dragon's, he had ridden with his father upon Freis. But every time he was about to take off, he felt that jolt of adrenaline.

That next morning had been a little better. Tan no longer felt the pounding in the back of his head. And thankfully, he didn't get nauseous whenever he rode now. But the number one thing he was grateful for was that the old man, *Master* Nicodemus, had told him they would leave that afternoon. He would not be training Tan here.

So, for what felt like the longest flight of his life, they flew toward the mountains in silence. Tan let the rushing wind hit his face. The sun's rays sliced through the clouds that Tyron would weave in and out of. Tan loved this feeling as he looked across the landscape, seeing how small everything below looked. Like miniature-scale versions of everything. He laughed at the thought of playing with a small version of Tyrone.

Glancing off to his left, towards the south, he could see the beginnings of the grassy plains of the Lightning Province. The vast open fields with patches of trees along the small hillsides looked as if they went on for miles. At one point, Tan saw a large city with a massive castle. Being able to see the structure on the horizon, it had to be a castle. With what looked like a large white spike rising into the sky just to the east of the city. Tan wondered what it was like to live in a country full of armored knights, Lords, and Ladies.

Tan knew he had when he was younger, before the Great War and the Purge. But that was so long ago that he barely remembered. He had been to Central City and Reed City, two of the neutral sanctuary cities that allowed for trade, commerce, and connection between the countries that overlapped these cities. Like Central City was at the center of the continent where the Fire Realm, Lightning Province, and Dark Lands all connected like the four pieces of a board. But those cities were always...different to one of the country's veritable cities.

Tan wished he could just be in one of those cities, though. Being a normal boy doing normal boy things with his normal family. However, the title of Prince Heir, and a Fire Elemental of the Ignus clan, would never allow him to be *normal*. Instead of lingering on that, he focused on his task. To train under Nicodemus and be the strongest Fire Elementalist. He could do it. If his father had been considered of the strongest in the world when he was alive, then Tan could be even better!

With renewed strength, he sat up and peeked around his master. The sun was falling in front of them faster now as they came close to their destination.

Master Nicodemus directed Tyrone toward the mountain that had smoke rising from it. Tan was so intrigued by the amount of smoke that emanated from the partially active mountain...and how close they were getting! *No way...*he thought. *Why are we this close to an active volcano? I think he has gone mad. Talking to birds and dragons. And now he's brought me to this place to sacrifice me, or something.*

"This is where you will be for the next month," Nicodemus shouted over the wind, breaking into Tan's train of thought. "So, best get used to the smell."

As he said this, Tan took a whiff of the air and felt a disturbing clench within his stomach as he gagged. The smell was almost as bad as rotting corpses. The thought of being in a place like this made the idea of being Nicodemus's student slightly less pleasant.

Tan wiped his forehead, and sweat drenched his arm, and his clothes slowly became damp from the humidity in the air. He removed the piece of cloth from his waist and tied it around his forehead to keep the sweat out of his eyes.

"We're landing near the base of the volcano." Nicodemus pointed toward a wooden cabin roof with a chimney far below them at the foot of the mountain. "Hang on!"

Tan scrambled to grasp onto anything as the dragon took a sudden dive vertically toward the small dot on the ground. Eyes watering from the wind, Tan did not know what was happening until suddenly, he felt intense shaking beneath him and then a sudden stop.

"Your death grip is a bit much, kid." Nicodemus patted Tan's white hands, gripping the sides of his master's shirt.

"Yes, Master. Sorry." Tan released the man's shirt, his knuckles turning normal again. Tan slid down to the ground with an "oof," clothes sticking to his flesh now as he peeled his thin, once white shirt, now gray from the sweat his body was producing. The heavy air around them was intense, like the atmosphere seemed to be closing in around them. No escape anywhere, Tan stood.

With a grunt, crash, and curse, Tan turned to see Nicodemus rubbing his bottom, standing up from the ground. Tan smiled at this, but noticed something about the old man's clothes that made him scrunch his face in confusion.

"Why aren't you sweating?" Tan asked. "It's so hot I almost can't breathe.

"Because," his master smirked at him, sticking his chest out, "I have mastered the ability to control my environment. Which will be your first lesson." He jabbed a finger at Tan's chest.

"How do I do that?" Tan rubbed his face with his shirt, but it only added to the sweat.

"How?" The old man laughed. "You think I'm going to just tell you? No, you're going to have to find that out on your own. I set the stage, and you play it out. Life gives you a test so you can find the answer. Schools give you lessons to know the test. You're not in school with them Elders that know stoking nothing about the real world. I do. So, figure it out yourself."

Tan groaned and kicked dirt as he walked toward the cabin.

"And where do you think you're going?"

"To the cabin?"

"You *are* a dull one." Nicodemus shook his head. "You think the day is over?" He looked up at the sky. "I still see daylight." Then held up a finger and then a second, "First rule, the day is not over until the sun is down. Second, you do as I say, how I say, when I say. Remember?"

"Yes, Master."

"The enemy won't care if you are tired or exhausted when they come. They will give you no mercy, no time for a rest. They will kill you. The Trials are almost a joke. You will go through a staged task that you will have to perform in a controlled environment. Though I said, 'This is a joke', you *can* still die in them. But you will be fresh and well rested with a proper weapon. *I* will train you to fight life and death at *any* point and time. Understood?"

"Yes, master."

"Now, the first order of business...there is a stream that way." he pointed off into the thin line of trees. "Take the pail from the side of the house and go fill it up and bring it back to fill the trough on the side of the house. But don't let your disgusting, grubby hands touch any of the water. I do not want to taste what the slums are like."

"Yes, Master."

Tan couldn't keep the drone from his voice as he went to the side of the building, grabbed the pail, and walked in the direction in which his master pointed. The heat never subsided, and Tan almost didn't know what to do except move forward. He did not know why they had come to this place of uncomfortable heat.

Finding the small stream took time, as it was about a mile from the cabin. It felt so much farther than that, with the heat and sweat covering his body. The water looked so clear and crisp, and Tan could see the small pebbles and sand beneath the surface.

About halfway back to the cabin, he panted almost uncontrollably, to not spill the water, Tan only filled the bucket halfway. He could feel the wire handle of the bucket dig into his fingers as the weight grew heavier with every step. But he made it to the trough, moved the lid, and poured the water into the metal can.

With a bemoaned sigh when the water didn't even make it to the first marker at the base of the tub, he let his head fall back and stared at the blue sky. Glancing towards the enormous mountain where the sun was sitting just high and to the left of the great volcano.

A groan escaped him then at the thought of there still being a few hours left in the day. But he would do as his master ordered. And so, until the sun set upon the mountain's shoulders, Tan walked to the stream, to the trough, and to the stream, and back to the trough, drenched in sweat and dirt the entire time.

Tan finally finished filling the trough, the sunlight nowhere to be seen as he wiped his forehead for the umpteenth time since beginning this job. Then he walked toward the cabin.

"I filled the trough, Master," Tan announced at the entrance, waiting for permission to enter. Tan stood at the entrance, not daring to enter without permission. He felt good at having finished just as the sun was slipping behind the volcano.

"Good." Nicodemus stood from the chair at the small table in the dining area. The entrance led to a small sitting area that opened to a Fireplace and kitchen with a table in the back. A door was closed in the back of the building that most likely led to the bedroom with the window Tan had peeked into when he had been on his third trough run. And with a glance to the left of the entrance, Tan could see stairs that led up to what he assumed were more rooms.

"Now," the man held out a wooden cup, "go fill this and bring it back. And don't put your filthy, disgusting hands in that water. That's what that stream is for."

Tan did exactly as instructed. On his return with the cup of water, Nicodemus took it and drank most of the contents. Tan watched the old man drink the crisp, clear water through dry lips and a sore throat, and he could only dream what that cup of ecstasy tasted like.

"That was good. Now fill it up one more time."

Tan returned with another cup of the god's nectar. Tan's annoyance with the old man growing a bit as he replaced the cork. He had wanted to be a student of Fire elemancy, not to be a personal servant.

"Now, tell me," the old man began as he held the cup of water. Not drinking from it yet as he addressed Tan. "What is something Fire produces?"

Finally! Tan thought. He was tired of playing master and servant. When the man asked Tan this, it gave him a boost of energy. But the question stumped him.

What is something Fire produces? Tan repeated in his head. *Light? Smoke? Ash? Heat?* Tan knew they were all correct, but he assumed that the old man had more of a meaning behind the question and went with what he assumed would be the best answer.

"Heat?" The hesitation in Tan's voice was clear, but he was pretty sure he was right.

"And what are you?"

"A Fire Elementalist?" Tan said. Then winced as he realized he sounded like Lighten Ignus, his bratty cousin, when he said it like that. Thankfully, Nicodemus either didn't seem to notice or just didn't care.

"*So,* if Fire can produce heat, and you can use Fire, what also should you be able to control?"

"Heat!" The smile on Tan's face was genuine, but the pain he felt in his chapped lips cracking hurt enough to keep him from doing anything too childish. Like jump and punch the air or run around like an idiot at the sudden realization of what his master had revealed.

Tan felt so dumb that he hadn't made the connection. Now he understood what Nicodemus was trying to teach him. Hitting him like a breath of fresh air.

"And what does that mean?" his master asked. "Or do I need to spell it out further?"

"I'm guessing that the reason you are not sweating is because you're controlling the surrounding heat?"

Nicodemus smiled. "Maybe there's still hope for you yet, *boy.*"

As a reward, he gave Tan the glass of water and a slice of jerky leftover from Nicodemus's trip bag. At least that's what the old man said. The jerky was so dry and had what looked like a layer of dust on it, as if it had been in this cabin for years. Tan did not care. He was so low on energy he would have eaten his shoes…if he had any.

After eating the tough jerky and still sweating, only finding out that he had the potential to control heat but could not do it yet, he sent Tan on another chore of collecting more water.

"Until you can control your environment, you're not allowed to bathe or touch water except to drink. Until that time, you will sleep under the stars, where I won't have to smell your stench along with that smelly dragon outside." The sound of a large huff from outside indication that Tyrone had heard. "For now, I will begin with teaching you two things. First, I will teach you the *forms* of Fire that you will need to know and use for training."

This last part made Tan smile, remembering how Nicodemus had used a dance to call on Tyrone.

"Yes, Master."

"Second, something you brought up earlier. The thing you had mentioned about me being able to move really fast? I call it *Flash Step*. I will begin with teaching you how to do this."

The excitement welding within Tan at this suddenly wonderful news had him sounding like some over excited child, as he pumped a fist in the air.

Was learning that move something he was considering? Tan couldn't believe it. Master Nicodemus had used it only twice, as far as he knew. He had seen Commander Dex use it in a duel once and on the night of the Purge as well. But to be learning from one of the best users of it? He had only thought it was something unique, not a skill that someone could learn.

"Before each drill, you will run to prepare for situations when you can't use your elemancy because of breathlessness, not for exercise."

"I wouldn't be able to control my breathing?"

"And what do you use your breathing for?"

"Heat."

The connection made Tan's eyes widen. "So, it's like endurance training with the Dragoons?"

"Y-yes. In a way." He glanced at the sky. "But since it is dark, consider the day done with. We will begin in the morning."

"Yes, Master!" Tan was so excited that his exclamation echoed through the silent forest around them. He didn't care, though. Tan was going to learn one of the coolest techniques ever!

Sadly, it did not go as Tan had envisioned it would. For the next several days, Nicodemus taught Tan the first five forms of Fire. All this while, Tan's clothes continued to stick to his body. During portions of the day, Tan would strip out of his shirt to let it dry and practice bare chested.

Tan wondered if he would pass out from heat exhaustion, but he never did, for Nicodemus constantly had him drinking water and then order Tan to fill the trough up with more.

"If you are worried about the heat, that is the least of your problems," Nicodemus remarked as Tan performed the fourth form for the third time that day. "If we were any closer to the volcano, the toxins and smoke would get you before the heat would, and if you thought *I* was going to send you up the mountain soon, you will be happy to know that will not be happening. Your grandmother is far less forgiving when I am too harsh on a student."

Tan continued through the form, trying his hardest to keep the feeling of relief from his face and make his master change his mind.

He learned the first five forms through sweat and tears. When he took breaks, his Master would give him a stick and tell him, "With how hot and dry it is, lighting is easier, but controlling the *strength* of the Fire is key. Light the end on Fire but keep it contained to the very tip."

At first, Tan would take the stick and go to the stream, and when the Fire would become too big, he would toss the stick in the water and start again. Keeping the Flames from expanding and consuming the entire stick was hard. He went through eight of them before he was just able to keep one from coming halfway down the stick. For the rest of the day, he practiced this until he could finally contain the Flame to the very edge of the stick.

When he showed his master, the old man nodded with appreciation.

"Good. I'm glad that didn't take you long. Your father did it in about the same amount of time."

At that, Tan grew angered. Hadn't he already proven he was above average? He was the only one he knew of that went searching for the best teacher. Why was he always compared to his father? A man who failed his kingdom, and his family. Tan hated that feeling, but it was how he felt. He knew his father had been a good man, his mother always had said so. But his father hadn't been a good king, *or* father, in the end.

With this sudden anger welled up within him. The small Flame grew so large that it made Nicodemus jump back. It was the same feeling he had when he had been fighting Tyrone. That well of power that he was just able to lay a finger on and let the power flow through him and into the world. Then a shout brought Tan back...

"Hey!" the old man exclaimed. Tan turned to see that the old man's face had gone red with anger as his master shoved a finger at him. "Watch that! Who told you to make it a stoking bonfire?!"

"But you said to just keep it at the edge of the stick, not how big it needed to be..." Tan pointed out.

"I told you to keep it to the point of the stick. Not to encompass the entire area around it! Bring that down!"

"Yes, Master," Tan didn't argue further as he brought the Flame to a small flicker again. But that feeling he had felt before was still there. Just beneath the surface. If he reached out and touched it now, he knew he would feel that rush of power and strength again.

"Have you heard of *Ferox Fire*?" his master asked.

"N-no, Master."

"Ferox Fire was named after a warrior before the Fire Realm even existed. Back when we were only clans and tribes that were more barbaric in nature than today. This was around the time your great, great, great grandfather, the first king of the Fire Realm, was gathering clans under Clan Ignus and creating the nation we call the Fire Realm."

"Ferox was a warlord that had profound influence and power. He was a king in his own right and ruled with Fire and fury. When he stepped onto a killing field, friend and foe ran from him. For his elemancy was a beast ravaging anything in its path. When the last battle between your ancestor and Ferox began, Ferox's Fire became erratic and uncontrollable. When it was all said and done, Ferox was destroyed by his own Flames."

Tan had read a little about the founding of their now broken nation, but had read nothing as interesting as this. It never occurred to Tan that Fire could not be controlled. *How would you lose control of it?*

"The name Ferox means cruel, wild or ferocious," his master continued. "We give the name Ferox to the Fire that cannot be tamed," his master explained. "If you allow yourself to be enthralled by your Flames, let it consume you. That is what it will become."

Tan nodded. He had felt something like that when he had used his elemancy just then. Maybe that was what his master meant?

"Your job is to know when to use your Flames, and how much to use. No one else will help you out there in the real world, not even me. Remember that."

The old veteran was right, Tan knew. He would be put in situations that required his judgment. He couldn't incinerate people simply because it "felt good". To prevent ending up like Ferox, he needed to maintain control over his reactions and himself.

"Yes, Master," he answered reverently.

And after a week of training in these forms and mastering his powers of control over the Flames, Tan was beginning to understand what he needed to do in order to put his master's words to action He was finally beginning to control the heat around his body.

Tan realized that by focusing on his breathing, and controlling his breath he could regulate his body temperature, more and more, to where he only took his shirt off during the hottest portion of the day and only because he was attempting to gain a darker tan to his skin.

The thought made him think of his uncle, Orion Ignus. A large man who was the head of the Ignus Clan. Which made him think of the clans and all those he had left there. He missed being with his cousin, Dancer. But she was most likely training with her father to become a Dragoon, something she said she always wanted to be, and probably didn't think of him very much.

Then there was Gran. Though Tan knew his grandmother would more likely skin him alive for leaving home. So, it was probably best he actually stayed away until she calmed down... she was always trying to set him up with girls around the camps. Some were okay, but most were just...bland. Lackluster and had none of the kindness or beauty his mother had had.

There had been one or two other girl's he had had a crush on, but he only knew they were of other clans, and it was a fleeting feeling, anyway.

When they talked, it always made Tan just want to puke. He was always so self-important because of what clan they were with, even though they didn't do anything to achieve it other than to be born into that clan. At least the boys did stuff, like become warriors. But Tan couldn't deny that he wanted to have a woman, as did any young man. Being out in the middle of nowhere dashed any hopes of those aspects.

Though there were no girls to impress out here, Tan felt good with his toning body. At fifteen, coming up on sixteen-full-seasons now, he was filling out in all the right areas.

With the constant work his master kept him at, there was no wonder that he was becoming stronger with every day. Thankfully, his one year of being on the streets had eaten away the residual body fat and all he needed to do now was added on the meat and muscle. Though he wished his height would improve, he was content for the moment with his now five foot two fingers.

Come the middle of the second week, Tan was on the verge of mastering the first five forms of Fire. And with that, Master Nicodemus introduced Tan to the various forms of hand-to-hand combat of each form to better visualize what he would be doing.

His master was really in-depth in his teachings, and he would run drills during the beginning and end parts of the day with Tan personally, and during midday, when Tan had his small break, Nicodemus would teach him various tips and tricks he had learned over the years. There was also schooling, from arithmetic and reading, to combat skills and techniques.

At the end of the last day of week two, another rigorous day of combat arts training, Nicodemus tossed Tan a towel. He hadn't sweat like those first few days, but he worked up a sweat when he was doing his forms.

Tan was proud at the fact that only when he was doing his forms did he ever sweat. So, with a raised eyebrow, he looked to the old man, who only stood there with same *I don't give a smoking care in the world*, look. The old man raised an eyebrow back.

"What?" he asked.

"Why do I need this? I'll dry up in a bit..." Tan pointed out, about to toss the towel back.

"You stink worse than the volcano does," he stated. "Go take a bath. But make sure it's further down the stream from where you get our drinking water! I don't want any of your mud-caked sweatiness in our drinks, ya hear?"

Tan smiled at this. A bath? He couldn't believe it. Wait! Did that mean he passed the first lesson?

"Well?" the old man placated.

Tan took that as he had and took off running. "Thank you, Master!" he called back over his shoulder.

Nic watched the boy lope away, shaking his head with a smile he only let slip once the boy was gone. "To think he learned it at such a young age... He is definitely your kid, Aideen."

'Are you only just now accepting that?' came a voice in Nicodemus's head. He turned to the Ravin sitting atop the cabin.

'Now listen here, you bird! I thought I told you to go watch the town?' He turned to face the bird as it fluttered down from where it had been circling the trees. It landed on a broken stump at the edge of the small clearing.

'I did.'

'And!?'

'*You were right,*' the bird confirmed. '*There is a watchman in the mining town. As well as a group of bandits on the east side of town, along the traveling road.*'

'*Then let's do our best to avoid them, shall we?*'

'*Oh! And I found this left on the cabin roof,*' The bird flapped over to him. Nic glared at the bird, wondering if it was a trick, but his curiosity got the better of him and he held out his hand.

The bird dropped a small letter it had been carrying in its talons into Nic's waiting hand. There was a tiny wrinkle, but other than that, the letter seemed undamaged and untampered with. What had Nic staring at the letter, however, was the insignia placed on the wax seal. That of a burning phoenix.

"Ashes and smog," Nic cursed as he opened the small letter. He scanned the message quickly, then crumbled the paper in his hands before tossing it up and letting his Fire consume it to ashes.

'*Wait! What did it say?*' the bird protested.

"It said that trouble is coming."

'*What?*' the bird sounded perplexed.

"That woman is sticking her nose in my business again, that's *what*! She's coming here to check on the boy."

'*Lady Abree is coming here?! How wonderful! I haven't seen the matron in years. I have missed her deeply. She is a gem.*'

"She's a pain in my side is what she is," Nic retorted. "I hope that they can't stay long..."

'*They? Who else is coming?*'

4

TINY RAZOR

Dancer Ignus sat within the confines of the Dragon Reserve incubation chamber underneath Central City. A large underground world lit by glowing rocks that shone brighter than a full moon. The cavern was large as it needed to be to hold the great Regals and other enormous dragons. She sat in the small, warm room where all the dragon eggs were stored until they were ready to hatch.

The warm elderly woman caretaker stood at the door of the solitary room. The room itself was only big enough to be considered a large closet. And thankfully the old woman, Granny D, as everyone called her, had made sure that Dancer and her would be the only ones in the room. Her father, the head of the Ignus clan, had protested before Gran had given the man an arm slap which stopped his overprotective protests.

I'm not a child anymore, you oaf of a father, she thought to herself. Which was almost true. She was only a moon cycle away from becoming a grown clanswoman in the eyes of their law, and on the verge of taking the Blood Trials. She hoped that it would be the same one that Tan would be attending. Her cousin had promised that he would try to finish in time before then, but that had been nearly a season ago, and word was that he hadn't even made it to that old hermit yet.

There was a cracking noise, and Dancer blinked as she remembered where she was.

"Oh!" she exclaimed with a smile. "It's- Granny D, it's—"

"Calm yourself, girl. Or you will scare it from coming out."

Dancer winced, forgetting that she was working with a baby after all. Regardless of how exciting this all was.

"Sorry."

"Focus, or you will end up burning the shell."

"Right! I mean — yes, Granny D," she said, lowering her voice.

With her attention back upon the egg, Dancer could see a good many more cracks along the top portion of the egg growing like a spider web as she continued to keep the Fire as it sat upon a blaze. It was really difficult, as she hadn't practiced much with temperature control. Her Master was always so slow with her lessons. And Dancer was becoming worried she might fall behind. She was learning the forms easy enough, but her master kept with the same slow pace. It was annoying. Unlike what she was doing right now.

Dancer watched as a piece of the opal blue and red powdered eggshell broke from the top and a cute little snout pushed its nose out to sniff the air. With a sneeze of Fire, the egg exploded. Dancer flinched away, raising her arm as shell pieces shot everywhere.

Being so close to the egg, she knew she would get dirty, and with a groan she felt the disgusting feeling of slime on her legs where she kneeled before the pedestal.

It still covered the tiny sky-blue baby dragon in the slime from the inside of the egg. But Dancer didn't care as it watched her with large doe-like eyes. That's when Dancer remembered she was supposed to give the cute thing food.

"H—here, try this." Dancer picked up a piece of small fish and held it towards the baby dragon in her palm.

The small thing chirped and cocked its head at the meat before sniffing it tentatively. Dancer watched openmouthed as she studied the creature. It was smaller than the Regal babies, but that was good, for a scout dragon needed to be small and fast. If Dancer wanted to become a part of the Dragoons, she needed a good mount. The long thin membrane of the small dragon's wings came to a point that looked like a swallow tails wings, without the feathers obviously.

The dragon sniffed the meat again before perking up and then licking the meat with a forked tongue. Satisfied, the tiny beasty snatched the meat with sharp teeth, nicking Dancer as it did.

"Aw!" Dancer gasped, but attempted not to pull away as she gripped her hand tight. When she opened it, there was a bit of blood where the dragon had nicked her.

"Ah! Them teeth are already razor sharp, aye? That'll be good for you," Granny D noted. "Will make it easier for feeding time."

Dancer watched as the dragon finished gulping down its small portion and then sniffed at Dancer's hand. A small sound, like a dog whining, came from the tiny creature as it nudged her head with a lowered head.

"Oh, it's not your fault your teeth are already razor sharp," Dancer comforted the small dragon by petting its head, which the creature clearly liked as it did that weird thing cats do when you pet them from head to tail. She felt small ridges along the thin spine as she continued to pet the dragon. The small thing chirped with a content purr with closed eyes before climbing into her lap and curling up to take a nap.

"Somebodies tired," Dancer commented as the dragon shrugged into a comfortable position before closing its eyes. Sharp teeth, fast, all outstanding characteristics of a good mount. "I think I'll call you Razor."

The dragon continued to sleep as she pet him.

"That is a good name, young lady. I'll let you two be for a bit and be back with some more food for the little beasty."

Dancer nodded and watched the woman leave, shutting the door behind her. Dancerthen shifted her attention to the little creature and imagined what it would be like to ride him once he grows up. It wouldn't be long.

Dragons grew rapidly and were adult size within two moons of growth. She had heard, or maybe read, somewhere that it was because they grew like the Fire within them. And Fire grows as fast as it can. Dancer smiled as she felt the rumblings of the purring dragon through her clothing and hand.

"You and me, Razor," Dancer decided. "We'll be the best Dragoons ever."

5

VISITORS

As Tan washed his clothes in the river, he listened to the birds and insects of the woods, the rushing waters, and the wind that gently rocked the evergreen trees around him. Letting the sounds whisk him away as he worked. It had been a refreshing and good first two weeks of training.

Not only was he now able to control his output of Fire, but he was also beginning to understand how handy it was to control his own body temperature. The Forms were coming much more naturally, and he was already seeing the little imperfections in his forms compared to his master's like being unable to finish the last subtle hip and shoulder movements of form three. But he knew it was only a matter of time.

He was just laying out his extra shirt. Nicodemus had finally gone and bought him another two pairs of each item of clothing, except socks and boots, of course. *"You buy them expensive things with your own money,"* his master had said. Tan just chuckled and shook his head, surprised the old soldier had even bought him a shirt, underpants, and an old pair of working shorts a size too big, but he wore a string to keep them up.

There was no one to really make fun of him out this far in the woods. When he went into town that one time, he had worn his more fitting pants, that he rolled up to his ankles. He wore those now as he stood in the refreshing waters, bending back down to scrub said to large work shorts into the water and scrubbed the dirt stain out with his brush.

Then a gust of strong wind whipped through the trees, causing the large evergreen to bend and shake as an enormous dragon flew just over the tops towards the cabin. Assuming it was Nicodemus and Tyrone returning from some errand, he bent back down to finish up his...

That's when he remembered. And slowly he turned his gaze over to see that a large black form of Tyrone was sleeping soundly under a dark shaded area of trees.

Sooooooo, if Tyrone was here, Tan thought, pointing at the dragon, *then who was that?* He turned towards the cabin.

Then, he burst out of the water, throwing the item in his hand into the pile of clothes he had been working on, and dashed towards the cabin. Following the path he had made over the amount of trips he had made to the stream, he was within sight of the cabin within six heart beats.

Through the trees he could make out the enormous form of a Regal, one with more frills than Tyrone had, redder and more maroon than deep black, green. It was definitely bigger than Tyrone and took up a fourth of the cleared field around the cabin. Tan slowed as he came to the edge of the tree line and stopped when he heard a voice call out.

"*Hagitan Ignus!* Where are you?!" called a voice so familiar to Tan it made his heart stop, flutter, and panic all in one instant. He felt sick at the emotions that ran through him and almost turned to walk back to the stream when the dragon's wings relaxed to show the two riders slide off its back.

Tan smiled when he met his cousin's gaze before she rushed over and almost talked him into a hug. His cousin, Dancer Igrus, squeezed him so tight that he felt like his ribs were bruising. "Tan-! You're okay!"

He crashed into the small girl and crushed her in a bear hug.

"Uh-eh! Not...for much longer—" he choked.

"Sorry," she said, releasing her death grip.

"What are you doing here? How did you know I was here?" he asked her.

She was wearing the cloth of the children of the clans. A stylized version of the woman's clothing, which was made after the Huntsman's furs, and leather and metal armor. A new, small dagger was strapped to her leg, which was shaped like a dragon tooth and probably was one.

She gave him a look as if to say, "are you serious?" before speaking.

"What? You think we didn't know where you went off to? We've been checking in with Captain Heilken every two weeks to see if you had arrived yet. What took you so long?! It's been almost a season!"

Tan was flabbergasted at his cousin's vagrant use of arms and facial expressions ranging from worried to mad to concern. She finished with hands on her hips before crossing them over her flat chest. She was a season younger than Tan and still hadn't hit puberty yet and raising an eyebrow at him.

"Oh...uh..." Tan felt his ears turn red as he rubbed the back of his head. "I ended up taking a...detour." He settled with that as explanation enough.

"You got lost, didn't you?" she stated bluntly.

"What?! No, I didn't!" Tan argued. Then felt his cheeks redden a bit and caved. "Fine! Yeah, a little, but I was on foot, so it was bound to take me longer."

"Yeah, yeah. It still doesn't change the fact that at no matter what age, men hate asking for directions. It just took you a full season to finally break down and ask for some."

Tan had no comeback to this and instead shut his mouth and crossed his arms.

"Is the only reason you're here to scold me?" he finally asked. "Because if so, then—"

"*You'll* do what, Hagitan Ignus? Hmm? Run off again?"

Tan visibly jumped, having forgotten the voice that had called out to him just moments ago. He slowly turned with a wince on his face to meet the Matriarch of the Ignus Clan. Tan wanted to run into the woods and do just what she said as he met the old woman's hard eyes and set jaw.

"Hey, Gran..." Tan attempted. But his grandmother was not having any of that right now.

"Hagitan Ignus!" Tan flinched and watched helplessly as his grandmother marched up to him, not breaking eye contact the whole way until she was right before him. Tan almost blinked in surprise at the fact that he was now as tall if not a little taller than his grandmother. He hadn't realized he had been gone that long.

Gray hair braided into a bun to keep out of her eyes while flying, Gran wore dragon riding pants under a split skirt dress that looked like a normal dress when she wasn't sitting or riding. She wore a long sleeve shirt Tan had thought she would sweat in, but apparently she knew how to control her body temperature as well.

As the woman stood over him, Tan shied away from her scrutinizing eyes.

Then, her face broke into a warm smile, and he swore he could see tears welling up in her eyes.

"Oh! I can't stay mad at you, my grandbaby. Come here and give your Gran a hug." The worried feelings built up with in Tan broke at this and he felt a sadness wash over him as he gave his Gran the biggest hug he could manage.

"I missed you, Gran."

"I've missed you too, child."

He stepped back then, and she had to look up just the smallest bit, but noticeably, as she smiled and laughed. "Oh! And look how tall you've become! And you are gaining some good muscles as well, I see." She poked his exposed chest. "That will definitely get the ladies fawning over you."

"Gran!"

"Sorry, sorry! Slip of the tongue. Now where is that old fart at?"

Tan raised an eyebrow at this. "You mean Master Nicodemus?"

"*Master* Nicodemus? Is he making you do that silly Master apprentice thing, too? My ashes, that man!" she turned to walk towards the cabin then. "Come along, children. I need to speak with an old, stupid soldier."

Dancer gave Tan a questioned shrug towards their Gran, but all Tan could do was shrug and shake his head as they followed her into the cabin with a shout from deeper inside.

"Ow—! Stoking woman! Don't—ow! Stop smacking me! Bree, listen! I didn't do anyth'n wrong! It was—*Hey!*"

After the two elderly adults finished their...*greetings? If that was what old people considered a hello,* Tan thought as he watched his Gran still glaring at Master Nicodemus from the chair she sat in. *Yeah, I think that will be the best they give each other, for now.*

He sat next to Dancer along the table awkwardly between Gran, who sat at one end, and Nicodemus, who sat at the other. Gran still glared at the old man, while the veteran nursed a reddening hand mark upon his cheek.

"...As I said," Tan's master was saying, "He came to me, and I tried to tell him to leave. Didn't I, boy?"

Tan nodded his head dutifully, yet quickly, not wanting to be in his Gran's ire any more than he already had.

"See?"

"Despite this, you still accepted him as a student?" Gran inquired as her face turned red and her voice grew heated.

Nicodemus's face fell into that of worry again as Tan watched the man eye Gran's hand near a plate on the table, probably wondering if he might get hit by a flying plate, and with the tone she had taken on, Tan thought she just might.

"W—well," the old man stuttered.

It baffled Tan, the fact that the hardened veteran was stumbling over his words. Tan had never seen this side of the man before. It was...entertaining, to say the least. Tan had to keep a smile off his face by putting a hand over his mouth. He glanced to his side and saw Dancer attempting to force her face not to smile but failing miserably.

"'Well,' what? Spit it out!"

"Well...when you have a royal prince give you the last dying orders of the queen, do you just ignore it?"

Gran frowned at this. Tan knew his grandmother and mother didn't get along well when his mother was alive, but Gran, Tan had noticed, had attempted to never slander his mother's name. No matter the situation.

"No..." she finally said.

"Then you understand then?" the old man pointed. "I had no choice but to train the boy!"

The room went silent at this for a moment. And Tan didn't know if that was a good thing or not. He knew that his grandmother only had Dancer and him there to add pressure on Master Nicodemus. The old soldier couldn't lie in front of witnesses now, could he?

"What about his studies?"

Tan felt a smile creep onto his face as his master stared blankly at Gran.

"What about them?" Nicodemus had an eyebrow raised in confusion. Tan's breath caught at the realization of the trap his master had just stepped into. And when Tan slowly turned to his Gran with wide eyes, it did not surprise him to see the elderly woman's features darken.

"Let me get this straight," his Gran stood and began circling the table. Tan had to turn in his chair to follow her until she came to stand behind his chair and grip the chair's back. He kept his eyes forward as he heard the wood groan under the stress.

"You haven't been teaching him any of studies? His political studies? What about his studies in world history? His royal studies?"

Tan inwardly groaned at the thought of having to return to those studies. It had been so long, and he was enjoying his practice and elemancy studies with Master Nicodemus just fine. In fact, he had just begun his first true Flash Step training by practicing making tiny leaves explode. He was pretty sure he almost burned his hair with one of the attempts.

"Well?" his Gran's voice brought him out of his thoughts.

Tan watched as his master looked like a fish struggling for air before deflating.

"No," the man admitted. "I have not."

The man looked like a beaten dog in that moment, which made Tan angry, but then again, his master had neglected to do his full duty, according to his Gran at least.

"Well then," Gran said, walking back to her chair, "it seems I will need to send for some writings and books for you to get on with that. I will have a messenger deliver them upon our return tomorrow."

"Tomorrow?" Tan asked, turning. "You're only staying one day?" He didn't want them to leave so soon.

Gran gave Tan a sad frown but nodded, giving his hair a loving pet.

"I'm afraid so, child. There are duties for me to attend to and Dancer needs to get back to her own studies, *as well as* Huntsmen training."

"Oh…"

"Now, now. Don't look so sad. We'll be back right before your trial. Don't you worry."

Tan nodded. Accepting that for now.

"How about you and Dancer go to town and get a treat? Me and this old brute here need to have a meeting without little ears nearby."

Nicodemus looked to Tan like he was about to protest but caught Tan's grandmother's eye and the old man's face softened as he spoke.

"N-yes, and with your latest achievements, I believe you have earned yourself a little reward." Tan turned and watched as Master Nicodemus placed a small bag of what sounded, and felt, like coins into Tan's hand. "Go to that place I showed you when we visited the town. The one with the nice hostess lady."

"Yes, master. Thank you!" He waved Dancer to follow him out. She stood and followed him to the door. "We'll see you later, then!" he called over his shoulder as they exited the cabin.

"Be back by nightfall!" Nicodemus called after them.

Once the sound of excited voices had faded into the trees, Nic turned ever so slowly to the woman within his house he least wanted to be there.

"Now, Abree, don't go and—"

"O! Just shut up, Nic." She said it so bluntly that he did just that. He waited like a student about to be reprimanded for some ill deed he didn't recall doing. "You're such a pain."

He opened his mouth to protest, but she met his eyes, and the worry in them made him falter.

"Yeah, maybe I am," He admitted. "So, what's the problem?"

"You need to train him better!"

Nic raised an eyebrow at this. "Train the boy better? *Better?* Ashes and Smog, Bree," he slipped right into calling her that old nickname as if they didn't have those vast years of not seeing each other. "I can barely keep pace with the boy. He is following the lessons so well and at such a pace that he might well hit a mastery level before his eighteenth season!"

"Not possible. No one, not even Aideen, mastered the Blue Flames that fast." She said as if it were fact and not open for revision.

"Tell that to the boy." Nic swung his arm to where the kid had sat. "But when I say that boy is a force of nature, I mean it. I was teaching him the first lesson for the Flash Step, you know? The lesson to keep the flame on the end of the stick without burning the rest of the stickup."

She nodded.

"He did so in *one stoking day*! And on top of that? Bree, he showed me he did and then made the Flames the size of my head, *while* keeping the stick from burning to bits in his hand! He has also developed his heat vision. And it won't be much longer before he has his first Burning. That'll be a rude awakening..." he said the last bit more to himself.

"But he hasn't even completed the trials yet..." she protested.

"In my opinion, he will most likely take the test and throw it in every single one of your faces. The trials happen in three weeks, right? He thinks, and fears that he won't be ready... *I* fear that he will just run through it and wonder what the point was."

Abree gave him a look that said otherwise.

"It won't be as simple as that, Nic, and you know it."

"Why do you say that? He'll be facing some thug and it'll be—"

"He'll be facing Kill, Nic!"

Nic froze. That name was a name he thought would be dead and gone by now. He eliminated an entire clan that "knew too much," and as a result, they jailed him after the Purge. Wasn't that man sentenced to death last season?

"And the council agreed to this?" he finally asked, aghast at the fact that they would even consider this.

"They finalized it two days ago, with me protesting the entire way. They argued since you were training him, and he is the king's son, that he needs to prove himself."

Nic sat back down slowly, bringing a wrinkled hand to rub his bare head. "They *want* him to fail..." was all he could say.

They were spineless cowards that only wanted to further their own power within the clans after all. He huffed out a laugh at the realization. "They want the boy's cousin to take the throne. Is that it? They think the boy will fail like his father? Don't they realize what the king did for them?! He didn't fail!"

Once Nic finished his tirade, he laughed out loud at the ignorance of the elders. If they were making a play for this now, then how come they hadn't just outright killed the boy? This was so blatantly obvious to anyone that had eyes and two ideas to put together. He could only assume that they were ignorant fools.

"In the end he didn't. But Aideen did fail, in the beginning. I know," she held up a hand, holding back Nic's protests, "He was a good king. I know that Nic, and you know that there is a faction that still supports Naiveen within the clan elders," Abree seethed.

The way she talked about her own daughter was worrisome, if said daughter didn't happen to be a narcissistic sociopath named Naiveen Ignus, with an even more of a brat son Lighten Ignus, Nic could understand the bitterness. How that crazy woman was ever a part of the Ignus house was beyond Nic.

"My daughter," Abree continued with a pained look in her eyes, "has been after the throne ever since Aideen took it from his father and hasn't stopped. Even after she almost brought about the civil war after Queen Silf died. But I guess you wouldn't know that. Stuck all the way out here after she died."

Nic knew he deserved that one. He had self-exiled himself after the funeral and as he had he received word that the clans had gone into a brief civil war before a third of the clans broke off and fled to Central city and along the river Stix that ran from the Northern

Sea all the way down and through Central City. Nic hadn't heard much but had heard that there had been a scuffle at the Blue Moon Festival. After that, nothing. And so Nic remained where he had for the next year. Until that boy showed up.

"I'm sorry, Bree...for not being there." The pain he felt. Of admitting he had failed, tore him up inside. He clenched his fists, his jaw twitched.

"I know, Nic," she sighed as she reached into her dress for something.

Nic eyed her for a long moment. Watched how she looked like someone on the edge of a cliff preparing themselves to jump. Tight posture, set yet distant eyes, clenched jaw. There was something else, something she apparently needed to tell him. That much was obvious. But she hesitated. Her toes were just at the edge of the cliff. And he knew that he would have to shove her over the edge if she were ever going to do it.

"*Bree*," he warned. "What is it? I know you didn't come all this way to see the boy, or to have a good laugh at scolding me."

She half smirked at that bit, but then her jaw flexed again.

"Bree?"

"Oh—Fine! Here!" she took something out and slapped it onto the table. "He came by yesterday and told me to give this to you. Then asked for an invitation to the trials at the Red Solstice."

Nic stared at the black envelope for a long time. A black envelope with a black wax seal with a swirling vortex for an insignia. Something that very few people had ever received, and those that do, usually were not in the best of positions. And sadly, Nic knew who that letter was from, and he knew the dangers it held if he didn't read it.

"He said you needed to read it by the end of today," Abree said as a last thought.

Nic took in a deep breath before reaching across, slipping his fingers gently underneath it and sitting back. With a sigh, he placed his thumb upon the wax seal. The tiniest of pricks nicked his thumb and when he drew back, his red blood seeped into the crevices within the seal's swirling insignia. Then, like some strange magic, which it was since Nic had only seen a very specific group use this, other than the Wraiths, the wax seemed to decompose to a black smoky mist that evaporated, as did the top layer of the envelope, revealing the letter beneath.

Nic silently read the letter, his jaw tightening and his lips pierced together as he gripped the black paper written in what looked like white ink.

"To the Drake of the North,
Nicodemus da Haliken,

My dear friend, I know it has been a long time, and now I seem to be short of it. I will get straight to the point. I am sending a correspondent to meet you at the base of the volcano the day you receive this letter at sunset. Why you choose to train in such revolting smelling places and eat that revolting onion soup is beyond me. Oh! And don't worry, he is a friend you will remember. He has something he needs to discuss with you on our behalf. He also said to come alone. Not even your birdie friend. He wants to discuss something with you, but he requested to do it in person. He is concerned that letters might get torn. I hope to hear your reply soon, old friend.

Respectfully,
GrandMaster Arien de Traès the Owl Legion,
of the Shadow League"

After Nic finished reading the last line, the message dissipated in his hands, as if the thing had known he had finished reading it. He blinked in surprise, only then remembering that they did that. Stoking Shadow magic! Nic had no taste for it but was a walking contradiction as he messed with the druid ring that allowed him to talk with Corax, who was probably the only reason Nic hadn't gone mad alone in the wilderness, or at least more mad.

'You're welcome, by the way,' the bird finally piped in as he flew in from the open door to land on the table in front of Abree, who seemed stunned for the briefest of moments before smiling and then giving the bird a pet. *'Oh yeah! That's the spot.'*

Nic gave the bird a glare and was about to tell the thing off when Abree interrupted him.

"What did it say?" she asked with worried eyes.

Nic met her eyes before sitting back in his chair with a very improper slouch that made the woman frown at him. He ignored that and answered her question.

"I'm going to meet someone later today, and before you say anything, the letter said to come alone." She made a strange pouting face that almost made him laugh before composing himself and finishing with, "You know how cautious they are. If they get spooked, they are gone even before I show up."

"Fine. Just...be careful. They may have been friends in the past, but they are still assassins, thieves."

"When am I ever not careful? Don't answer that! Either of you," he pointed from Abree to the bird.

The bird cocked its head as if to say *'Who, me?'* and Abree only gave him that stoking smirk that drove him to want to throw something at her.

"Ugh, whatever! I'm going to make sure that lazy dragon of mine is ready to fly me there. I'll be back."

6

REWARD

It wasn't the first time Tan had been into the local mining town. Just called Town by most. It was only five streets with four overlapping alleys. The mine had the west half for housing, the north side for the minor's guild, and the rest were goods, services.

Tan had asked Nicodemus about the town when they had visited it to get supplies at the beginning of his second week of training. His Master had told him it being a small town, there wasn't need, nor want, for much after a hard day's work in the mines than to get some food, a couple of drinks, and to be with some friends and company.

The mine was a simple iron and steel ore mine that was sold to make items ranging from simple armor and swords to horseshoes and metal chains.

Striding into the local tavern with Dancer, Tan smiled at the scene before him. Most of the usual drunkards were in that Nicodemus had pointed out to him last time. Master Greg, who often sat outside until they opened, was in his usual seat at the bar, tankard in hand, and a half-eaten meal of steak and beans in front of him. He was laughing and talk'n it up with some locals and merchants looking for an escape from the day's hard and hot work.

Tan waved Dancer to follow him as he walked past the bar and went to the back corner to observe everyone within. As he passed one of the younger barmaids, she gave him a blushed smile that made his cheeks go red. He glanced over and caught Dancer rolling her eyes at him.

"Let's keep it moving, lover boy," she ordered, giving him a playful shove in the back, which only made him blush even more. He knew as his ears grew red as they attended tables and ran back and forth from the kitchens.

"Why hello there, young Mister Tan! And who is this here?" said a very broadish woman with strawberry-red and hair wearing a barmaid's uniform. "That old geezer finally letting you of fun, is he?"

"Lady Renewed," Tan answered in greeting. His squeaky, chipper voice sounded funny when he tried to talk formally. "This is my cousin Dancer, and we have come to eat at the best place in town. Can we get two of your best meals at your fine tavern with this..." He held up a silver piece.

The woman's eyes sparkled at the coin. Being the owner of the fine establishment, she was always in need of some coin, like every place in this town, and this was more than enough to cover about an entire night's worth, Tan knew.

"Aye! That we can do that for ya," she remarked with an even brighter smile. He flicked the coin to her, which she caught before examining the shiny piece with the eye of one who had been fooled by a hustler before. Then she put it between her teeth as if she were going to bite it before looking at it again. Smiling in satisfaction, she gave Tan a wink. "I'll be back with a hot meal and a tug of Honey milk for ya."

"And could I get some sweets with it? The red pepper candies!"

"Oh, you rascal! All that sweet stuff will make your teeth rot out..." she half-heartedly chastised. Then she smiled with a mischievous glint in her eye. "I'll be right back."

"Thank you, Lady Re," he called after her as she disappeared behind the bar and into the kitchen.

"So, you've been here before," Dancer remarked with a knowing smile. "Has that old man got you drinking now?"

Tan glanced at her but didn't meet her eyes. Then peeked back to see her eyes had gone wide as she gasped in shock with the hint of a smile in her eyes. "No way! He has?!"

"No. I still hate the taste, but he said if I could drink an entire tankard, he'd leave me alone for an entire day and would never pressure me to drink again."

"AND?!" she was practically at the edge of her seat.

Tan tried to keep the smile off his face, but failed. "I drank an entire tankard, and then the rest of the establishment chanted for me to chug one more before we left."

Tan had been to this tavern a few times when his master wanted to wet his chops. But since they lived outside of town and there were very few young adults, much less as young as Tan was. So, Tan had been very noticeable to the rest of the establishment when Nicodemus had sat them at the bar.

"There is no way! Please tell me you were stumbling or said something stupid!"

"Nope, was as sober as when I entered," Tan tried lying through his teeth.

"Oh yeah, whatever. I bet he had to carry you."

"He didn't. He only had to keep me from running into...several trees." She burst out laughing at that. "What?! It was dark!"

"Ha, ha! Yeah! And you, as a Fire Elementalist can't just produce your own light or anything? Dad and the other huntsmen would have loved to see that! I can just imagine you." She then took on what Tan assumed was an impersonation of him, lowering her voice and talking sluggishly. 'Oh, I am so sowy misteh twee. I di'n see you vere.' Or how about, 'Hey, Who put thif twee here?' Ha, ha, classic..."

Tan just smiled and sat back in his chair, letting her calm down from her laughing fit, and watched the people move around them in the dance only referred to as... a night out.

People all around the room were toasting and drinking, bellowing in laughter, and scoffing large portions of food into their stomachs, while stories of recent events were passed around like trading cards. Tales of far-off lands. Of adventurers scouting out a new cave to be mined by the dwarves just north of Central City. Some griffins were harassing the border towns south of them. Some merchants were bringing in new farming tools this week for the mines.

Tan tried to catch a bit of information as conversations came and went. He turned to see across the room where a man that sat two tables away was speaking with two others, most likely all merchants passing through, dressed in half-decent clothing as they were. A tankard each sat between the lot of them on the table.

"... Yeah, apparently they had hired one of the Shadows to assassinate a member of the old Fire Realm Royal Guards. I believe the knight's name was... Sir Guildred?"

Tan froze.

"Now who would want that?" one man at the table asked.

"Apparently the dead King's sister, Princess Naiveen, is trying to put her son, Lighten Ignus, on the Broken Throne... and Guildred, that fool, was trying to oppose her, in the open! He be saying that the Royal heirs still yet live. So, the bastard got himself killed for trying to not let that tyrant of a witch seize control..."

"Hey, are you listening to me?" Dancer said pulling on his arm.

Tan blinked, then said. "What? No. Shoosh! I'm trying to listen to this..." he thumbed over to the table of three men.

"If you ask me the Wild Prince," one of the other men was saying, "what's his name? Orion?"

"My dad?" Dancer whispered. "Is he talking about the clans?"

Tan nodded and brought a finger to his lips. He loved Dancer, but sometimes she could be a bit of a chatter lizard.

"...Yeah! That's his name, Orion. Well, he should just seize control. Ain't he head of the Ignus clan or someth'n?"

"Well, apparently the man is to honor-bound and won't take the heirs' throne. That and since he had forsaken it years ago to become the Ignus head, he has no claim for the throne unless the heir defers."

"Well, if someone doesn't take control, some outsiders will just step in and take it over."

"The clans would never allow that," stated the first man. "Even if they are just nomads right now, they wouldn't let any outside party take control of the Realm."

"I heard that old Captain. What's his name...Nicodemus? The Drake of the North or someth'n? Someone was looking for him around these parts. If he stepped in, I'm sure it would all get straightened out."

"Stop saying, 'or someth'n.' Makes you sound stupid."

"Sorry..."

Tan sat up straight at the mention of his master's name. Apparently, the old court still recognized the power of Tan's master as his influence was felt even here. And with a broken system as it was, someone definitely needed to come and fix it up, especially since the system was still trying to right itself after the great war that had been fought almost ten years ago now. And Tan did not want to do that, because if he took control, then he would just end up failing, just like his father had.

The Gran, along with a few of the elders, always pressured him and told him he needed to learn all this stuff, like what she had told Nic to teach him from now on. But Tan wasn't sure he wanted that. Didn't he get a say? And if he had a say, he would choose to be just a huntsman. Not any special or important. That way, he wouldn't have to have what happened to his father happen to him.

"Well, I for one am glad that my business doesn't go into the heart of the Ruins. I've been hear'n stories of bandits on Wolf Trail along the east side of the Fire Realm, attacking anyone who tries to settle in the old cities."

"Well, I heard that some of the old court, led by Councilman Dreg, is trying to rebuild the Golden city... but them bandits keep harassing them and they are unable to get a strong foothold to start up. No one wants to support a losing fight."

"Can you blame anyone?" chimed in the third man, "If them bandits aren't dealt with, then nothing will get done..." At that, the discussion went on about the trade through the Realm and the deals they were working out for the Northern Lightning Province.

Tan stared at the table, unblinking as he processed this. If aunt Naiveen was trying to take control of the Realm again, Tan hated the thought of that woman in some kind of position to ruin not just their family, but an entire nation, was worrisome.

As Tan admired the wooden furniture, a young waitress arrived with their food. Setting the two small tubs of Honey Milk down, with a steaming chicken dish and a bowl of grath. He waved down the maid and handed her a silver piece and was about to dig into his food when Dancer's voice stopped him.

"What is this?" Dancer asked in a stage whisper. She eyed the bowl with a scrunched-up nose.

"This," Tan exhorted as he stirred his own bowl, "is grath, the best stew ever to be cooked this side of the volcano. A savory liquid of milk soup, with small, cubed griffon thigh meat chunks simmered in, with golden potatoes cubes, a dash of mushrooms, and a diced onion. Cooked to mouth-melting goodness that anyone would die for, and many do since they have to hunt griffons around the south side anyway. It's *really* good."

"If you say so," she quipped sarcastically.

Then she took a small bite and seemed to melt into her seat with a funny smile on her face. "Wow! That is soooo good!"

"I told you so," Tan remarked, as he dug into his own bowl.

As they continued to eat, the barmaid returned and set down a small bag of red pepper candy. Tan thanked her and tossed her another piece of silver. He was about to go back in when he had nearly two, maybe three more spoon full of soup left, when he realized his mistake. He had gotten so comfortable in their corner that he hadn't been keeping aware of his surroundings and what exactly he had been tossing.

Tan watched the coin he had given the stewardess as she turned. The light of the hearth at the other end of the tavern flickered off it as it tumbled through the air before landing in her hands. She beamed at him before thanking him and dashing away behind the bar.

Tan hadn't paid her any mind after she had caught the coin. He was focused on the several pairs of eyes in the opposite corner near the door. Several eyes that had watched this young, small boy toss a lot of very shiny coins at the maids. Not only that, but this boy was with a young woman but no other supervision around, and with all that money he was tossing around like bird feed for the ducks, he was attracting the wolves, and they sat just on the edge of the water. He recalled what his master had said. *"Your job is to know when to use it and how much to use. No one else will help you out there in the real world."*

Being in the slums had taught Tan a very important lesson that he had just forgotten in his moment of showing off for Dancer. A lesson in prying eyes.

All the greedy and desperate eyes would focus on food or money whenever it was passed around near any ally, if they knew where to look. They would then trace it back to where the bigger pile was kept.

Silver and gold in these parts were uncommon, to say the least. There was more bronze and copper than anything. So Tan, still somewhat looking like a slum-looking brat with his young female clan friend, looked very unusual, tossing this type of cash around.

"Hey? Are you okay? You look upset," Dancer noted. She placed a hand on his.

He flinched away at the touch but attempted to hide the fact by answering. "No, I'm fine. But I need to do something really quick so don't mess with me, okay?"

"Oookay..." she didn't seem all to convinced but Tan didn't mind.

Taking a deep breath, he closed his eyes and focused on the flow, the heat of the room, as his master had taught him this past week. Heat vision, it was called, allowed Tan to see the lights and mirages that Master Nicodemus liked to call heat waves washed across his vision. Tan saw yellow and orange of delight from a majority of the pub. A little standard orange of the hearth warming the room.

This was definitely not something you would normally use in a fight as it required too much concentration for Tan. Master Nicodemus said he sometimes could do it while fighting, but that had been a rare phenomenon. But in situations where Tan wasn't in any immediate mortal danger, he practiced. And it was paying off, he hoped as he looked over the room.

There were a few colors he had rarely seen before, like the brown and green of some kind of negative energy that he had seen come off his master sometimes whenever Tan messed up a pose while using it or wasn't listening very well with a lesson. Disappointment and disgust, however, was not what he was looking for...

Then he saw it. Toward the table with gleaming eyes was the red, black, and dark purple flow of energy. It gave Tan a small tinge of anticipation.

Opening his eyes, Tan took a last gulp of the very delicious golden milk and stuffed the bag of treats in his pants pocket before slowly standing, telling Dancer to follow, and walking toward the bar. He stood at the bar till Lady Renewed came out of the kitchen carrying a tray of hot food and drinks.

She paused with a raised eyebrow as Tan waved her over. The noise of the tavern drowned out what he whispered in her ear. But she nodded, then turned to her bouncer, Big Dave, and nodded her head toward the men near the door.

The large brute of a man stood with a grunt from his duty station next to the bar. Adjusting his leather guards and light armor, the large brute of a man stood up from his duty station next to the bar with a grunt. Tan thought he was fit for a fight. A metal baton dangled at his side.

Stalking to the men in the corner, Tan watched as the men had a softly spoken yet heated discussion. There were several men. One, a scrawny weasel of a man that squeaked when he talked and seemed to have a nervous habit of twitching his hands. Another was a large burly man that when he spoke, his deep voice seemed to vibrate around the room. A few other fellows unworthy of mentioning sat or stood around the boss man.

However, the man leaning against the wall at the head of the table wore a blue jacket of an Imperial Noble. He was a decent-looking fellow. White hair that parted down the middle a thin layer of stubble, gray-blue eyes and a pale complexion that gave him an almost permanent light blush. He had that smug look of a cat that had a tiny bird in its claws and was playing with it. And there was something about him that set Tan on edge as he spoke to the bouncer.

After the Bouncer replied, the man cocked his head and stood from his spot at the center of the group. He scratched his chin with a look even a fox would call conniving.

The man took a quick glance towards Tan with a smirk before the disgruntled and cursing men around him as he stormed out the front door. But not before a quick backward glance at Tan. The blue-robbed man sneered before disappearing into the street with his goons, the light of dying day casting their shadows long.

"How about you two leave with my bouncer?" Lady Renewed suggested. "That way you can get back to your master safely?"

Tan smiled at her with gratitude. But thumbed at himself and Dancer.

"It's okay. We are stronger and faster than we look. We should be fine. Could we just use your back door?" Thw woman gave him a questioning look.

He gave her his most convincing smile that few could resist. All someone needed to do was ask his Gran.

"Okay, but you be safe now, ya hear? Straight back to your place." She tossed her head behind her. "Go through the kitchen."

The alleys of the small town were all cut off by fences and walls that were run down but were difficult to climb for an average-size adult. Whenever Tan had gotten caught stealing an apple for a snack from the local stand, he would dip behind the buildings and disappear into the garbage and ruins behind them. He and Dancer should have no problem.

Tan thanked the kind tavern lady, and he led the way into the kitchen, but not before stuffing a handful of rolls in his pocket with a raised eyebrow from Dancer...

7

WILD FIRE

"That was some good food, though." Dancer said as they left the small town behind and entered the small bath next to the main road that single travelers liked to walk under the trees and was a bit out of prying eyes. This road will lead them to the creek, which they will then follow back up to get to the cabin.

As they walked and talked about the tavern, they spooked a White Thorn Deer, easily identifiable by their white-tipped antlers that the male and female deer both adorned for most of the year until the shedding season. This one had smaller antlers that were just beginning to just gain their white tips.

Dancer and he had peered through the trees after it in wonder. And then agreed to keep their conversations lower and see if they could come across any other animals along the way without spooking them.

Tan loved evergreen forests, he loved the smell, and he liked the way they looked, on top of their needles possibly saving his life. But as they grew more distant from the town, the forests "mcod" shifted.

As they came to a bend in the path that would lead them up towards the creek, the woods about them grew silent. There were still bugs about, but the sound of the birds' chirping slowly faded, and the deer they had occasionally seen were now nowhere to be seen. The stillness and near-silence as they neared the intersection was palpable.

Tan moved to the just the edge of the tree line to peer down the road in both directions. It was all but deserted. Even though the hour was growing late, and Dancer and Tan were near about late to return to the cabin. There should have been one, if not a few, people traveling the road to the fields and farmhouses at the edge of the forest after visiting the town. He moved back to where Dancer was crouched and whispered as low as he could.

"Something isn't right."

She nodded in affirmation, electing not to speak. Tan motioned for her to follow him and lingered a little deeper into the woods. He opted to stay off the path now, a ways into the woods, but followed the main highway toward town. He didn't wish to be caught in a thief's web, where a band of thieves usually set up a trap that unsuspecting travelers would get cornered in. Tan hoped to avoid such a nuisance as he and Dancer needed to get to the cabin before nightfall. He so wanted to just run and get there with all haste. But he followed his master's advice of, "better to be cautious than dead, don't be a wuss." His master wasn't wrong; being a simple man tended to make lessons easier to explain. This memory brought a smile to Tan as they maneuvered through the underbrush and shrubs.

Then there was a snap, like a tree limb breaking. Tan and Dancer froze where they stood in the brush. Tan didn't want to attract any eyes with excessive movement, so he slowly crouched in the shrubbery around him Dancer following his lead.

Being off the path definitely saved them in the long run as he peered up through the brush up ahead, back towards the main road and spied a group of people off to the side of the road.

There were three on the side of the road that Tan and Dancer were on, and peering across to the other side, he thought he could just make out three more.

They were a mix of both burly and scrawny men, dressed in strange garbs, garbs similar to a merchant, but with darker colors that mixed with the foliage better. They held a mix of weapons between them. The bigger men had hammers or clubs, while the smaller men had long swords, daggers, and one had a spear.

The closest group was a mere five large steps away from Tan. And yet, thankfully, none of them had seen or knew that Tan or Dancer was so close to them. He kept it that way as he crouched behind a bush that kept him from their sight. Another blessing in disguise were the pine needles on the ground, which silenced their footfalls. That was another reason Tan loved evergreen forests.

The group of men were all relaxing under the pine trees, either napping, snacking, or conversing softly. Across the road, the two larger men were sleeping and snoring loudly with their weapons in their hands, curled up like a baby holding a rattle. The two men in front of Tan were busy talking about something. Tan stayed low as he attempted to listen to their conversation. He hoped to glean some information about how long they would be, the band would be there, and what Tan might need to do if they ended up staying the entire night. Or if there were more bands of thieves around.

If this turned into a fight, Tan wasn't sure how many he would be able to take on and he was unsure at what level Dancer was at in her training. So, he waited and listened.

"... all them cowards up at Mist Mountains are stupid, though. All they want to do is hide in their mist castles and do raiding parties on the stupid clansman in the valleys. They focus on that ruined country and then only talk about messing with the Provinces like it holds all the keys to the plan, and only talk about taking the Nature Forests as if it were an afterthought, yet they still haven't done anything. Why don't they?"

"Probably because we aren't strong enough yet? Or it isn't the right time?" Tan peeked through a bush at the men and watched one chewing on what looked like a piece of jerky, but it was hard to tell with the sun just about to set. The man pulled it out of his mouth to speak again. "They probably want us to work on espionage before trying to amass our forces instead of just charging headlong at them like last time. Imagine what the knights would do to us if we tried to attack them now? You think we would stand a chance?" the other man shook his head as the man continued. "No. Not until we get those dumb tree huggers under control. Until then, we will not be able to do anything."

Tan glanced over to where Dancer lay. Her eyes met his and held a thumb up. He returned the gesture before turning back to look over the men, and then Tan finally registered what was around the men.

The pile of money in the bags was not what made Tan want to just curl up into a small cubby. It made Tan's stomach churn as he stared at the bloodstains on the bags, and he followed a trail of blood to a pile of bodies... that were still. Bodies that looked frozen, stacked off to the side under a dark top that probably held the smell within from reaching far.

Tan knew they were dead from the amount of dried blood underneath the pile, and the pale white color of the skin that showed. But Tan froze at the sight of the one face staring lifelessly from beneath the pile of human remains. Tan felt empty as he stared into the empty clouded eyes of the once-kind merchant.

Tan didn't know the man's name. He only knew that he was the merchant that sold the candy goods from a stand at the edge of the market for the kids, and fancy-looking jewelry and silverware for the adults. The man always had a smile on his face, a rounder-set man with red cheeks that gave him such a warm personality, someone you always wanted to be around. Now that jolly man lay lifeless at the bottom of a pile of dead, innocent travelers.

"It's sad that we need them now," the other man commented. Neither of the men seemed aware that they had blood on their hands, but as Tan took in the scene, the sounds of the men's voices faded away.

"And strange, since them nature freaks were so against us in the beginning. Now a few of their own council on our side, and a small chunk of their army now too, I bet..."

They went quiet for a bit as they nursed on their jerky. One pulled out a small pipe and stuffed it after scraping the burnt stuff out and flinging it to the ground. Tan's eyes traced the bile until he saw the coin bags in a pile next to the thugs.

All the while, Tan's blood boiled, and a fire deep within him lit beneath a furnace that would engulf them all. They were murderers, and they needed to be stopped.

The local town guards wouldn't be able to. They only stayed near the town. And there were no soldiers or Huntsmen out this way. Tan couldn't sit around and do nothing.

Then his mental image brushed against that wall of power. And he was there, as if floating just above the surface of a glass wall. He felt the heat, the power could feel it just close enough to reach now.

The wall reflected and showed him an image that—

Forcing himself to come from that place, Tan glanced back to Dancer and met her confused eyes. She made the universal gesture for "What?" as if to ask what was going on until her eyes seemed to find his and she grew really, really still. Tan mouthed and pointed for her to, "Stay there," and she nodded her head slowly, eyes growing wide, face growing pale.

Tan turned to glance over at the scene again. And felt the rage waiting there for him. He was back in that mental landscape of the glass wall. Reached out this time, taking a deep breath, he plunged his hand into the wall, and it broke like ice up to his forearm.

The feeling, like freezing water hitting his body, washed over him. An involuntary gasp escaped him as he attempted to put on his ring, that now was glowing soft blue color as he reached deep within the well. It was like reaching into a deep sack and pulling out a long piece of rope from that pool of Fire. Sweat beaded his forehead as he drew upon the Flames within.

The men had gone silent, Tan knew, when he had gasped. But it was not until Tan stood and his almost glowing eyes met theirs did the men in front of him stir into any sort of action.

They were too late, however, as they brought their small useless weapons up to point at Tan.

"What the...?" They seemed utterly baffled that Tan was standing there watching them.

"Where did this kid come from? Did he sneak past Randle?"

"I don't know, but it's just one kid. He was probably sneaking around in the woods. Let's just kill him and be..."

And that's when the beating furnace within Tan erupted.

8

SHADOWS AND BONES

Nic hated this. He gritted his teeth as Tyrone landed on the volcanic rock, the shelves breaking loose under the dragon's weight. They slid into the small valley where a cave he knew was and where he assumed the assassin would be most likely waiting near.

"Alright, Tyrone, *hic est bonum*," which translated to *"here is good."*

The dragon snorted and crouched down. Nic tossed a leg over and slid from the dragon's harness to the rocky ground. The crunch of rocks and the dragon noises echoed throughout the empty space. Every step Nic took over to the cave made a sound. He cursed his heavy footedness as he reached the cave. The shadows hid everything within it a mere two steps in. He lifted a hand and called upon a small Flame to light the area. The day was growing late as the sun was almost behind the volcano at this point, making the shadows even longer still.

Waving the Fire over his head, the light illuminated the empty cave and its vines that were creeping up along its sides. Nic sighed, wondering if the old assassin had just played a nasty jump scare trick on him as he turned to wait for the supposed *friend* he would meet. And nearly stumbled over a man in black and gray assassin robes.

"Drake of the North, of clan Lupus."

The proximity of the man and how loud and firm his voice was scared Nic so much that he nearly stumbled back, assuming a defensive form.

With the practiced hand of a soldier, Nic drew the dagger from its holster, leveled the tip at the man with the other arm out, legs spread for balance. After a brief pause of the man standing with his arms crossed in front of him with a raised blonde eyebrow, the assassin's eyes and forehead were the only bits of skin showing.

Nic relaxed slightly before altogether shrugging off the fright. It was probably a good thing that the bird or Abree hadn't been there. They would have just laughed at him.

He studied the assassin for a moment, noting the wrinkles that hadn't been there upon his brow eight seasons ago. The dark blue eyes and the blond hair were the same, if not firmer. With this and the designated small patches sown onto the man's robes at the shoulder, an owl mask on his right with a white dagger on the left, Nic knew who this man was speaking with. He was indeed a friend.

Clearing his throat, Nic answered the man.

"Talibee White Claw, of the Owls."

"Captain Heilken, Drake of the North."

The assassin bowed formally to the warrior, who returned the gesture. Then the robed man dropped the extra formal formality and held out a hand to Nic.

They clasped forearms and gave a warrior's side hug. He met the assassin's now crinkled eyes and knew the man was smiling. Nic smiled back as they separated. The assassin looking him over.

"Goodness Captain," the man's thick accent still made him sound like that of a true Nature Forester. The man's smile was audible, but he spoke like a warrior, controlling his emotions. "It is good to see you. It looks like age has not treated you to poorly, with moves like that."

"Ha, ha. You got me, finally. That better be the last time you tried to do that."

"Doubtful," the man gave a light chuckle.

Nic watched as the assassin crossed his arms again.

"Talibee?"

"Captain…the old Dark Lords' Seats are now filled," the assassin announced. Nic froze at the man's words. "The *Rău Council* have returned…"

"The Lords? They have returned? As in, we didn't kill all the stoking turds?"

"One of the Dark Lord's sons, who is calling himself *Dark Lord Alaris,* has taken his seat as head of the Lords, after re-founding of the *Rău Council* while Dark Lord Obsidian remains in hiding. And he is in the midst of starting a new campaign."

"Another war?" Nic felt sick to his stomach as he brought a hand to rub his forehead. "Even after that defeat we gave them? I thought we destroyed most of their forces?"

"It will not be the same type of war, captain," the assassin stated. "It will be an altogether different war at first."

"Meaning?"

"They wish to destroy the very structure of this world and step in as the usurpers. According to our sources who have infiltrated the highest level, their plan seems to be already in progress in the Lightning Provinces. Our sources have informed us that they plan to give an address to the king that will spark a civil war. As well as the Bandit war that is going on in the southern province right now. They have hired bandits as well as mercenaries to disrupt the structure in the south and west provinces on a local level. With an infrastructure bill, to pit the north and east against the king on a governmental level.

"And what? You want me to help you with espionage or the like? I'll have to warn you that the provinces know my face and would be all too happy to kill me if I step foot in their lands."

"No. We wish for you to help on a different front. We believe that, at some point in the future, the Clans will be put in a position of civil war. With the Lady Naiveen and her colleagues as the catalyst of this movement. There is word they will begin soon, and we believe it to be the similar tactics they are using in the provinces."

"And what would I do?"

"Be the military figure to step in and rally your country. There are no huntsmen that wouldn't follow the legendary Drake of the North. They would rally behind you with banners had, and passion strong."

Nic tightened his jaw. They wanted him to play politics? They needed someone within the Clans strong enough to oppose the crazy woman's movement.

"I'm sorry, Talibee, but I can't..."

"Why? ...Because of the prince?"

Nic eyed the assassin for a long moment.

"I guess you would know where he is, wouldn't you?" Nic said it more as if it were fact than a question.

"We make sure to keep tabs on all of our potential clients." He paused and Nic caught the glint in the man's eyes. "And promising prospects..."

The openness to the statement only allowed Nic to assume one thing, and he would not allow it, not while he lived.

"No! He is not a part of your little cult of assassins, or whatever it is you call it. You know what that would do to the clans."

"All the same. We watch out for *any* potential. Friend or foe. For now, we will only watch and wait."

The silence of the valley encased itself around Nic as he swallowed this lump. What if the boy joined the Shadow League? Would that be something that would aid him, where his father could have used aid? No. That wasn't what the boy needed right now. Nic needed to train the boy so the boy can do what he needs to do. Become king and protect his people.

"Will you join us?" the assassin asked again. "There are plenty of-"

"My answer remains the same," Nic cut the man off. "The boy is still unrefined and needs boundaries and a steady hand to guide him down the path he walks."

"And what path is that?"

"The path of kingship." Nic said it like everyone should know this.

"Oh. You believe that is where the boy's path leads?" the assassin inquired, the hint of elaboration on his tongue. "Because from what we have gathered." The assassin looked towards the direction of the town, "is that his motivations and drive turn him elsewhere? At least for the time being."

"What do you..."

A great boom cut Nic's words short. Glancing in the direction the assassin had been looking. Light reflected off the darkening sky.

"What—"

When he turned back, the assassin was gone. Nic spun around looking for the assassin, then realized the man had probably left for good then.

Looking back in the same direction the sound had come from, Nic got the sudden impression that something was terribly wrong. He turned and scrambled up the valley mountain side a bit to peer over the tops of the trees at sea level.

Searching along the tree lines for the source was not hard as a bright orange light erupted in the distance. Fire. Fire that Nic had never wanted to see again. It shot into the sky a good hundred feet, he reckoned, and that was all he saw before he was scrambling back down the valley side towards Tyrone.

"That stoking fool is going to be the death of me."

Tyrone noticed Nic running towards him and thundered over and leaned down for Nic to climb into the saddle. Then they burst into the air with a fury towards the Fire ravaging through the forest between where the town and the cabin was. *Is that along the main road?* Nic prayed to whatever being was out there that the boy hadn't lost control yet.

9

BURNING

Tan's eyes glowed with a Fire, a Fire that built and built and built, welling within him as the heat gained momentum and swirling into a typhoon of wind and Flames. The beauty within the red, orange, and white light washed across him as he conducted the chorus of the inferno to a tipping point. Using the forms of Fire Nicodemus had taught him the Flames reached high above him, the pressure of the power, the weight of the devastation mounting.

It was amazing! The deadly elegance within the Flames alighting his eyes in such a way that left all to witness awestruck.

As the two men jumped back and attempted to run away, screaming, and shouting about a demon, as the orange, red, and now black Flames engulfed them, Tan kept the Flames well away from Dancer's hiding spot. He watched, however, as the Fire ate away the shrubs and underbrush in front of him.

The other men jumped and screamed as they took in the sight of the boy within the Flames. What stared back could almost be associated with a demon. For no person, much less a boy, should have that much power.

Tan smiled like a mad artist who had finished an abstract masterpiece, as the amount of power that he had pulled from the depths of the ring's well had been far more than he had ever dealt with in the physical world. His thoughts of these men burned away as the bodies all around him turned to ashes. The thieves hadn't stood a chance as the Flames turned them to dust within moments. Their screams snuffed out as the smoke engulfed them. And Dancer's cries of alarm seemed to drown out a bit as he took it all in.

Tan could feel the power all around him as he moved the Flames about. He laughed in delight at the sensation of power pouring over his nerves like lightning through a cloud. He felt like he could do anything!

And then he felt a hand upon his back, and he turned to find that Dancer had made her way to him and was now gripping his shirt with tears in her eyes. The fear, the panic in her eyes, scared even him.

What had he done? What...? And with that, Tan felt the spell break.

With sudden realization of what he had done and was still doing washing over him, he turned and reached out to the Flames. But they stretched and ripped themselves free from his control like a wild animal.

Swirling and tearing free from him and spreading around him and into the woods. Even the Firewall Pine trees, a wood that was not supposed to be able to catch Fire, were ablaze and crackling with Flames and burning all around him.

Tan realized what he had done in that terrifying moment, eyes wide as he watched the *Ferox Fire*, a Flame not to be tamed but by an *Api Biru* a true Blue Flame, ravaged the surrounding woods. The Ferox Fire grew and roared its fury at the ignorant boy who tried to control it.

A blast of heat hit the two of them, causing them to hug each other for protection from the powerful flames. Like a spirit dragon, the Flames twirled around them, jumping up and surrounding them before crashing down to the ground. The flames then enclosed them within a circle, much like a boa constrictor closing around its prey.

Tan as he realized he had trapped them within the wall of Flame. Why did he let this happen? Wasn't he stronger than this? Stronger than his father? But as he watched the Fire encircle them, he didn't know what to do. But before the wildFire could crash into them, another presence grew from the other side of the Flame. The Red Ferox Flames seemed to turn at the entrance of this newcomer. And a force that Tan would believe that could strike down mountains met it.

Blue Flames slammed into the head of the red heat with the power of a tidal wave. The Blue engulfed the Red and began swallowing the red snake within its own ferocity and silencing the wild Flames. But the heat of these Blue Flames gave off were even more intense compared to the Ferox. This was an *Api Biru*, a true the Blue Flame of the Blue Star.

And as the Flames consumed the last of the red Flames, it dissipated. Just as Master Nicodemus came striding from behind the dissipating flames with his expression set in stone. Jaw tight, face red, and knuckles clenched. His clothes were black with soot and his white beard looked slightly singed at the tips.

Tyrone stood behind Tan's master within a field...a field of ashes that Tan just realized he had just created. Meeting his master's face, he knew *this* would not be pretty...

Tan leaped from the dragon's back to the dirt ground. A small plume of dust rose in the moonlight as Dancer slid off Tyrone, landing next to him. Tear streaks down her soot covered face. And before Tan could take a step toward the cabin, he felt a sudden burning pinch ride up his back.

"What do you think you were doing, *boy*?!" Nicodemus marched past him with the intensity of a storm.

"I..." Tan began, but went silent. He hadn't really been thinking, had he? Ash and soot slowly fell as the smell of it wafted through the air.

Nicodemus turned and *slapped* him, stunning Tan. His master had never laid a hand on him before. Not even when Tan had accidentally burned some of his clothes one day while practicing; that's why he never trained near the cabin anymore. The booming voice of his master brought him back from attempting to avoid thinking about what he had done. The pain in his back was not subsiding as the man advanced on him.

"No!" the old man thundered over him with a raised finger. "You weren't thinking! You were digging your way into an early grave, your cousin along with you! And with *those* Flames? I would have been hard pressed to find enough to bury." The man shook the air between him and Tan as if it were a present. "*What did I tell you?!*"

"To be aware of my surroundings... but Master those men..." Tan was interrupted by Nicodemus's raised hand.

"Master Nicodemus," Dancer began, "It wasn't Tan's fault. There were bandits and..."

They stood outside the cabin, Tyron rumbling his cat-like purring as he slept next to the wooden box. It was amazing how fast the old dragon fell asleep. Ash on the wind fell all around them like snow as the sturdy wood sighed in relief from the heat. The smoke that had risen from Tan's "little" stunt had reached all the way to the cabin.

"So... do you think that means, uh? To go looking for a fight?"

"No... but they..."

"I don't care what *they* did!" The burning was growing up his spine now. He winced at the napping biting sensation. "You burned a fourth of the forest to the ground! Not just those brigands. You burned *everything* down! That is an abuse of power I cannot overlook, regardless of the circumstances. If you don't control your own power, you will no longer be my student. Am I clear?!"

"Bu-

"DO I MAKE MYSELF CLEAR?!"

Tan lowered his head. "Yes, Master."

"Your punishment will be to clean Tyrone of the stench of smoke, and I best be see'n my face reflecting off his hide or there will be coals to pay. And no supper! You can think about what you have done on an empty stomach. You're lucky I don't whip you."

"What is going on out here?" Gran's voice cut across the night like a knife through butter.

Nicodemus had moved to meet Gran now and was arguing with her about...about...something... Tan could no longer hear them as the nuisance turned into an intensity that made his ears ring. Burning Fire shot from his back down to his heel, making his body seize up before falling back in several spits and spasms.

An itching sensation that worked its way down his arms. He looked down to see feint glowing orange veins running down his skin. As if lava was flowing through his veins.

With a thud, he dropped to a knee. Tan Thought he might have heard Dancer call out. Then Nicodemus and Gran were above him, saying words that sounded distant or as if they were in a cave that echoed all around too indistinct to understand. Tan couldn't think straight as the feeling of a thousand needles struck his back, making him arch his body again. He clenched his teeth and fists to force the painfulness out, but to no avail as his body spasmed again.

Tears ran down his cheek as he cried out in pain. He screamed for what felt like hours until his voice went hoarse. He remembered being lifted, but then blackness swam in his vision as another fit of body-shaking seizures racked him.

Then, there was this feeling of cold ice hitting his body as water seemed to envelop him. The burning ache remained as finally, blessedly, he succumbed to the darkness.

Unconsciousness was the only respite as he entered the abyss of nothingness...

10

RITUAL

Three moons prier.
Lightning Province, Outside Titan City

Tom, Sir Thomas of Thundera, a yearling knight in the Tempus Knight Order, stood as the squires moved about, connecting his armor plating. The pearlescent silver reflecting the light. Oiled and polished the night before to prepare for this day.

With the last piece placed and strapped down tight, Tom let the energy pent up within him flow into the dark sapphire jewels strategically placed within the armor.

The feeling of power flowing from him into the jewels was a feeling Tom could rarely describe. The closest he came to best doing so would be if one was carrying a heavy load and then suddenly it was as if the load became as light as a feather. One could feel the heaviness, but it did not impact one's strength.

"Sir Thomas, you are prepared," said the young squire. Perhaps twelve seasons old.

"Thank you, Garth. Now, make sure my sword is prepared as well."

"Yes, Sir."

The boy went to the weapons rack where the sword sat to do his bidding. Tom called the squire a boy, but, in fact, Tom himself was only eighteen seasons old. Not much older than the boy attending him. Yet, here he was.

A full-fledged Knight about to be in a duel to settle a dispute between the Lord of Thundera, Lord Count Freighmin and the Lord of Titan city, Lord Lamprouch. What the dispute was, a lower knight like Tom wouldn't know. But he had been selected to duel on behalf of the Lord Count.

The thought made him raise his eyebrows and shake his head.

"Now, what's that face about, young knight?" a deep rich voice called as the tent flap before Tom fluttered open.

It startled Tom from his thoughts. Quickly looking up before he lowered his head, bringing his armored arm across his chest in salute, as the Commander of the entire Tempus Order stepped into the readying tent.

"Lord Commander, I — it's nothing."

As Tom stood straight again, he took in the tall commanding figure before him. Even when the man wasn't in armor, Tom felt a presence from the man. Whether it be from his enormous form or the sense of power that wrapped around him.

"Come now, boy. I know you better than that. There is something bothering you."

Tom closed his mouth and cast his eyes down to study the carpet. He could tell the Lord Commander what he was really thinking.

About how he was but an orphan that the very man before him took in as a squire and raised for the past ten seasons. What made Tom so special? Was there something that Tom was missing that the Lord Commander saw in him?

"If you are worried about the fight—"

"Why did the Lord Count choose me?" Tom asked.

Looking up, Tom met the man who has been the father figure for most of his life now. The man that he respected and would fight to the end for.

The dark, full beard crinkled into a knowing smile. The graying hair on top was the only indication of the man's age.

"Son, it is no mistake that the Lord Count chose you. He saw how well you did during the skirmish in the games and then how you helped down at the docs when that fight broke out. He knows the quality of man you are."

Tom nodded.

"Do you fear the fact that you are fighting the Fulman?"

Tom locked up a little for fear of his voice betraying him.

"I see."

The man crossed his arms, the dark gray uniform creasing and pulling taut as the man's muscular form took a very scholarly tone.

"Well, you have been keeping up with your drills?"

"Yes, sir."

"And you have been doing your meditations?"

"Every night."

"Then what is there to worry about?"

Tom chewed on that as the Lord Commander stepped up to him, clasped his armored shoulder, and with a stern face said, "Follow the code, do what I have instructed you, and you will have nothing to fear."

Tom nodded.

"Do a quick meditation and then join me. We head to the pit at the sound of the horn."

"Yes, sir."

The older knight gave Tom one last pat before saluting and turned to leave.

"Sir?"

The larger man stopped, his hand holding the tent flap up as he turned back.

"Thank you."

The Lord Commander gave a curt nod before exiting the tent.

Tom took a deep breath and let it out slowly before letting his armor come alive with power. Allowing the elemancy to flow through the armor allowed Tom to do what non Elementalists could not normally do in a full plate of armor.

Such as picking up a wagon. Falling from fifty feet without a scratch. Or even taking a knee or getting up from the ground.

Tom moved to the center of the tent where Garth stood waiting with the sword in arms, holding it by a padded cloth.

The long sword was made with bits of silver mixed in. Better for conducting electricity, but a softer metal over all. Tom's elemancy and constant upkeep were the only reasons the sword was not molten rock after each use.

The golden hilt, set with a large sapphire offset with two smaller diamonds, like a budding flower, was always captivating to Tom. No other sword he had ever held could match the elegance of this blade seemed to possess. The Anvil Crawler was the sword's nickname, but Tom had named it the Blue Flower once he had finished the blade not but a season ago upon his knighthood.

"Thank you, Garth," Tom said as he grasped the sword

Lifting it up delicately as the boy stepped to the lanterns and put out all but one near the entrance flap, before leaving the tent to allow Tom privacy to perform his ritual.

Standing within the dark navy carpet with the markings on the ground surrounding the center where a pile of rods sat. Tom studied it, where the points, each connected before sheathing his sword at his back and picked up the spikes.

Each spike was about the length of the bottom of the palm up to the top of the pointer finger. Too went to the first point. Using his armored forearm he lined up the spike to the ground, raised his arm, and brought it down like a hammer.

When the armor struck, driving the point through the carpet into the dirt, blue sparks and electricity scattered across, lighting up the partly dark room. Once the spike was halfway into the ground, Tom stood, moved to the next point, and repeated the process.

Nine times, Tom did this. Striking the spikes down, sparks flickering about. Once the last one was driven home, he took his position within the center of the circle again.

Grasping the hilt behind his back, he stared at the spot in the center. Eyes never leaving as he drew the blade, the silence cut but the ringing of steel. He twirled the blade point down.

He felt the electricity course through him as he raised it above his head with both hands before driving into the dirt.

The blade sank halfway into the ground, sparks shot forth, connecting to all of the spikes following the path of the lines until it faded away.

Kneeling next to the blade, he left one half grasping the hilt. Closing his eyes as he took a deep breath. Letting his body fill with energy on intake, and when releasing, letting the energy flow into the blade and from the blade to the rods and then back to the blade.

Once his breathing was in rhythm, Tom began reciting the Order's Creed...

11

LIGHTNING STRIKE

Standing at the edge of the arena, Tom listened to the crowd cheer as below two riders flew their pegasi towards each other.

Using a streamer across the expanse as a guide, the knights angled their lances at one another as their winged horses reached the point of no return.

The loud crack, wood and splinter flying everywhere as one knight fell screaming down the thirty-foot drop to the net farther below.

The victor paraded his pegasi around the circle, making his way up and into the sky.

As the knight passed, Tom recognized the silver winged helmet of the Winged Knight.

Tom raised a fist in salute as the knight dipped his head. And the horse winked before shooting up and out of the pit.

Tom turned back at the sound of the cranking wheels. The floor far below slowly began to rise and the knight in the net lay still until the platform slowly reached the net. The knight stood when he regained his senses, the platform still rising as he did, and began walking to the side where Tom stood.

When the platform became level with Tom's level,, the wheels stopped and the soldiers posted to the sides opened the gate.

"Ha! He did it again!" The knight roared with a laugh.

Walking towards Tom, the large knight ripped off his lion helm, exposing his lush red beard and long strawberry blond hair. His wide smile, electric blue eyes, and a bead of sweat on his forehead were the only sign he had been doing something exerting. Pegasi jousting was not the same as regular jousting by any stretch of the imagination.

"Ah! Tommy, lad! Did you see what that their shiny diaper did?! He done hooked me arm again! It was beautiful!"

"Yes, sir Drags. Marvelously done."

"Aye!" Tom had learned real quick when he had been a squire that sir Drags only had one volume. Loud.

The knight stepped from the platform onto the balcony gate. He was almost a head taller than Tom, already now at seven hands tall. Sir Drags seemed to notice as well. Looking Tom up and down with an even bigger grin.

"Well, color me blushed, Tommy! You've done had a growth spurt again! You'll be as tall as me before long!"

Tom smiled.

"An honor, sir Drags. It has been nearly two moons since my knighthood."

"Aye, and what a celebration we had, aye?! Oh ho! *That* had been a grand night!"

Tom laughed at the man's jolly nature, even at after losing his joust.

"Indeed, sir Drags." Tom's attention turned towards the gate as a horn sounded.

Sir Dregs looked to the far side as well, then nodded solemnly.

"Aye, got a hard match before ya, aye?"

"Yes, sir."

"Well, remember what me and Jonny boio taught ya. Keep it tight and don't overuse it. Got it?"

Tom turned back with a smile. All the knights had kind of taken Tom under their wing when he was called to be the Lord Commander's squire. They had all treated him like a little brother, and now he could call himself one of them. It was a dream come true.

"Yes, sir."

"Good, lad! Now go out and kick that sorry old bum's bum! There will be a new sheriff in town! And his name's Tommy of Thundera!"

Tom smiled, saluted, and marched onto the field.

The man's roar echoed in the back of Tom's head as he slowly made his way across the platform. He was about to be in a fight for the title of Fulman, as well as a fight for his and his Lord's honor.

The dark blue cape around his shoulders fluttered a bit from an updraft, not enough to kick up the dirt and sand thankfully. He held his helm under his arm, the other hand upon his hilt at his side.

Tom made it to the spot marked upon the ground, looking across to the other spot where a knight in full armor and a flowing purple cape stood.

Tom took a deep breath before sliding his helm smoothly into place, and belting the strap under his chin, a marvel that he was always surprised to do in the armor. Not only that, but when the helm sank into place and he began projecting his elemancy into it, the helmet seemed to glow on the inside and then it was as if his vision grew wider. He was able to see as if the helm wasn't even there.

When they stopped on their positions, there was a cranking sound as a chain met slowly encompassed the arena like a crab cage. When the cranking finished, the crowd mumbled.

"Who doth come forth to make the challenge?!" called the purple caped knight.

The crowd grew silent as the ritual calling of the challenger began.

Tom took a deep breath, relaxing, and called back, "I, sir Thomas of Thundera, of the Tempus Knight Creed!"

"The call is heard!"

"And it is answered!"

Gripping his sword with his gauntleted hand, Tom pulled the blade free, the metal ringing within the space as the blade hummed with power. The knight across from him drew his own curved blade and assumed a fighting stance.

Tom crossed around the space, his opponent mirroring as they circled each other slowly. Every step measured, every position noted.

Tom kept his sword between him and his opponent as the other knight held his blade low, as if ready for an uppercut strike.

"*Watch his waist.*" Tom could hear the lessons the Lord Commander would give him before he was a knight. "*Watch the way it tightens before execution...*"

Tom caught the slightest of movements in his opponent's waist, the scabbard bumping awkwardly against the armor as the men made a tighter side step.

Tom adjusted his grip as he gathered up the electricity. Feeling the familiar sensation of his hair standing on end. The power built in the moment between moments. The tensing of muscles, the building of pressure, with the exploding conclusion.

In a flash, his opponent exploded forward in a burst of movement.

Tom could see the individual motions the man made as he struck. Bringing his sword across to block the stab, then pushing off and stabbing back with his own burst of speed.

The armor and elemancy allowed Tom to move faster than normal. The electricity ran through his muscles and enhanced his response time to almost double that of the normal man.

With speed and precision, the two knights clashed in a fury of metal and silver. Sparks of blue and purple zaps flickering with each strike.

The crowd roared in approval as the duel began in earnest. A few attempted to yell out corrections and encouragements, but Tom was in a different world as he and his partner danced around the arena floor.

After the first two exchanges, Tom could feel the duel was coming to a head. The Fulman came at Tom with a bit more fury, allowing a bit more Lightning to arc at Tom as they came in for blows.

Thankfully, Tom's armor and own elemancy absorbed most of the strands. Clashing again, Tom could tell his breathing was becoming labored. There were longer breaks between each combination of strikes, and the Lord Commander's voice echoed in the back of Tom's head.

"After the first round of attacks, when he becomes tired, that's when the real test begins..."

The knight attacked again with a blur of combinations. Gritted his teeth as he rolled from a side block to a parry, a down block, followed by a thrust that forced the knight back. Tom watched Fulman's shoulders rise and fall. His head bobbing with each breath.

Now is when he will switch. Tom took an extra step back. His opponent seemed to stiffen at the action, before growling and spinning his sword in an arc, electricity building with each movement. Tom could feel the air change as the electricity the knight built up created a bit of a magnetic pull.

The chain around the arena jingled as it seemed to be pulled towards the knight as the power built. The wind around him even stirred, bits of purple lightning building.

Tom pulled from the store he had built during the ritual, feeling his own field being made as the crowd cheered. But the only voice in his head was his mentor's.

"If you build up too much too fast, the elemancy might backfire. Lightning is not the same as all the rest. You are a battery and can only

constrain so much for a certain amount of time. If you don't release it, you may end up exploding."

The knight finished his movement, his sword aglow with purple light, and thrust his sword at Tom, but the distance was too great to physically touch Tom, instead a burst of Lightning leapt from the glowing blade.

Tom gasped as he let his own power flow into his blade, turning and slamming the Blue Flower's blade into the path of the lightning aimed at his chest.

The purple lightning hit the little field Blue Flower created, repelled and scattered in a web of light into the surrounding chains. Tom smiled from behind his closed helm. *That wasn't so bad.*

The next strike had enough force behind it to drive him back a step. Using both hands, he held the blade in place as a stream of purple lightning slammed into the field.

"Don't overdo it with a casting. If you do it for too long, you will burn yourself out. It's easier to hold a disrupting field than it is a casting bolt. Unless you are fighting the Fulman..."

Tom gritted his teeth as he felt his heels slide across the ground. *Okay...this is getting to be a bit much.*

Tom could hear the roar the other knight yelled as the power increased. Tom was already pouring a steady stream of energy into Blue Fire, but as the barrage of power continued, he could already feel himself coming to his limit. The tingling in his hands was sign enough, as his grip slipped.

There was a last roar from the old man and Tom was worried there was going to be another increase in power until the flow stopped.

Tom stumbled forward but regained himself enough to bring his sword up and diverge the blade aimed at his chest.

"I commend you, young knight..." The voice of the knight reverberated. Surprising Tom as they locked hilts and began a shoving match. "You—have lasted longer than most..."

"Thank you, sir..." was all Tom could get out before bringing his sword around, flaring his elbow to strike and pull his blade from the tussle.

Tom's elbow connected to the knight's shoulder, pulling the swords apart. Turning him about, the knight brought his leg up and connected to Tom's side.

Bracing it, Tom let the moment stumble him back a bit. And just as planned, the subtle charge up of his elemancy finally hit its peak when he gained the distance needed. He harnessed the power within him and swiftly infused it into his sword. Blue Flower's blade instantly glowed as he aimed it at his enemy. Dirt and sand swirled around him while electricity crackled with immense power.

The purple knight's eyes glowed from the light, wide as the blue lightning shot out, striking as a snake. The knight endeavored to disperse the attack, but the speed of the assault prevented him from mustering a response.

The knight was flung backwards by the explosion, crashing into the dirt.

Tom held his sword steady, panting slightly after holding that much energy within himself. If he had waited much longer, it might have backfired.

Tom slowly approached the knight, but the man didn't move for a long while. A gong sounded in the distance and a loud voice proclaimed, "The challenger is victorious!"

The sounds of the world returned to Tom as he made it to the now former Fulman. The man was groaning and beginning to move a bit, which relieved Tom he hadn't intended to kill the man. After another moment, the man looked up and noticed the hand Tom held out to him.

After hoisting the man up, Tom noticed the bit of crystal flakes from a shattered crystal, which if the knock out wouldn't have declared him the winner, the crystal shattering would have.

"OoOh," the man groaned as he steadied himself. "That was a mighty punch there, well met young knight. And brilliant. I hadn't expected you to pull a FullFrontal out of that slow build up you were amassing."

"Thank you, Sir Welsh. I wasn't sure you could tell."

The man popped off his helm to reveal a scarred face with a full gray beard. The man turned to Tom.

"It was subtle, but I could tell you were doing something. It wasn't until I kicked you away that I noticed it, too late."

"Congratulations, Sir Fulman!" a booming voice announced.

Tom felt his chest swell with pride as he and Sir Welsh turned to find the Lord Commander and the Lord Count Freighmin.

Tom gave the two men a slight bow, armor clanking. "Thank you, my lord."

"You deserve it, my boy," the Duke said with a grin. He turned and gave a slight head nod. "Sir Welsh..."

The knight bowed and then bowed to the Lord Commander before turning and walking towards the gate he had entered.

Tom couldn't believe it, as he watched the fallen knight, the man's burned purple cape fluttering as he walked. Tom hadn't thought he'd lose, but he hadn't thought he would win like that either.

"You performed your duties well, Fulman," the Commander said with a grin. "That last bit was well met."

"Thank you, sir. But it was your teachings that kept me focused."

"Oh no. It was you. You could have been doing anything else, but you took the time and dedication to learn this skill to the best of your abilities and applied it spectacularly."

"Indeed, which was the reason I took the Lord Commander's advice and chose you as my champion," the Lord Count said. "But now, I must call upon you again."

Tom bowed again. "I am here to serve, my Lord."

"There has been a disturbance within the woods between Thundera and Titan. Bandits are running amuck and attacking travelers along the road. There is a nest of them within the Great Pine Wood."

"I have already dispatched a company of soldiers to patrol the roads," the Commander added. "But they report that they are vastly outnumbered if the scouts are correct. I am sending a legion with a knight leading each company. I need a field commander that has a decent head on his shoulders." He raised an eyebrow with a slight smile. "Are you willing?"

"Willing and able, my Lord." Tom saluted.

"Good," the Duke said, directing them off the arena floor for the next event. "Now we will go and work over the details..."

12

THE COURTS AND
STATE ADDRESS

Present day,
Lightning Province Capital, Conductor City

T he noise of people chattering echoed throughout the chambers
of the castle. Within the Capital of the Lightning Provinces,
Duchess Nina Weinstein felt so small within her seat in the upper
levels of the parliamentary chamber.

The men and women of their respective guilds, houses,
and governmental bodies sat below and spoke across the council
chamber floor. It was just mingling gossip, pleasantries, and the like
for now. All the stuff that made the typical conversation flow into
the deeper issues that Nina loved. But for now, though, she found
herself studying the murals on the far wall of a depiction of a black
pegasus flying through the air with an armored knight upon its back
holding the king's banner.

The grandness of the space and the beauty and art within
always made Nina lose her train of thought whenever she didn't
have to focus on anything. And thankfully, right now, she was
only a spectator with her husband sitting beside her, speaking with
someone on his other side.

Nina was still lost in the mural and wondered what the knight felt while he flew on the back of such a creature. It always amazed her that men would dress in their full, heavy-set armor and then ride these winged horses into the sky without fear of plummeting to the ground.

"My good gentleman and Ladies!" A voice boomed through the chamber, drawing Nina's attention and quieting those within the room. A good two hundred bodies now.

Nina turned to look down upon the floor where a pulpit sat tucked between the council member seats beneath the royal throne. The bald head of the council speaker stood addressing the gathered nobles, merchants, Lords, and Ladies.

"Thank you," the older man continued. The man paused and leaned into his pulpit. Nina was too far away to see the man clearly. Still, she could imagine the thin man squinting at the paper in his hands as he spoke, "uh-Thank you for coming all the way here today for this annual meeting. I know it was a bit of a…walk for some…"

The group of merchants from the Northern Province chuckled at this. Nina guessed she should count herself lucky for only having to travel from Ore City, only a two-day trip northwest of the capital up the River Steps. Some, she had heard, had taken eight days to reach the capital. And there were still a few seats missing.

As she looked across the crowds, she saw a few of her merchants from the Gelding guild, as well as the Gelding's lord, Lord Pindle Wallus. She noted where he sat. She needed to discuss the prospects of a trade deal with a new griffin hunter from Spark City…

The Speaker's voice drew her back to the floor.

"Council and Guild members, Lords and Ladies, please rise for his Majesty, King Urith, and her Majesty, Queen Frem…"

Nina stood with the rest of the crowd, her husband scrambling up after her as if he had not paid attention to the Speaker, which he probably hadn't been. She watched as out of a side passage near the head of the chamber, the king strode to his highchair, wearing his

royal blue on white suit and crown. The queen trailed behind him
with her crown upon her braided hair, wearing a stunning white
and blue rose dress.

Nina glanced down at her own blue dress and had the instinct to
think she should have worn something more fitting, but reminded
herself that she was only there to listen today, not speak in front
of anyone. The following week will be filled with addresses and
complaints. Today was the governmental body's day of address.

Once the king and queen seated themselves, the crowd sat as
well. And Nina again watched as her husband seemed late on the cue
and quickly plopped into his chair next to him. She kept the small
smile to herself at his awkwardness.

Duke William Weinstein was a good husband. Nina knew this.
He was dutiful, and charming, and loved her with all his heart, as
she did him. But he was still a poet, not a politician, merchant, or
knight. No, not even this world she had brought him into five years
ago was able to change him. This world of politics, backstabbing,
fake smiles, empty promises, and backroom deals remained just as
foreign to him now as it had that first day.

That was fine with Nina. She loved that about him, loved his
quirks and strange mannerisms. It always gave her a laugh when he
did something, and it threw some of the other Lords and Ladies off
their game with a blunt remark he made.

There were times she had to keep him busy so she could
conduct business, but he was usually fine with that. He dealt with
the smiles while she dealt with the snakes beneath.

"Thank you," the Speaker began again. He leaned back into his
pulpit and Nina had to put a hand to her mouth to hide the smile.
She could not believe that they still allowed the man to do this. It
was a laughing stop. Though he did seem to enjoy it.

"Today, the head of the governmental bodies will read off
each of their addresses. We will begin with the Address of National

Defense and the Tempest Knights." The bald man turned to a row of chairs along the right wall. "Lord Commander?"

Nina wondered how anything ever gets done. So much bureaucracy and hurdles to jump through to even get an idea to the floor, much less propose that idea. Other countries with less infrastructure, like the Nature Forests. Or the Fire Realm, with their strange clan system similar to the province's noble Houses, had to have been less troublesome, right? Nina couldn't see how it could get any more political than this.

Though she knew they each had their own difficulties, when she had visited the Nature Forest city of Silva, their system seemed to pass senses within days of the charter or law being brought forward. The Nature Councilmembers always seemed far more understanding and cooperative than the province's politically violent arena.

"There is an increasing number of bandits and pocket thiefs along the roads and near the cities down in the Southern and western provinces that are being managed by the Fulmen and the Tempus Knights. We have found several nests near the northern mountains, as well as the Griffon peaks in the south. The border disputes have lessened this past cycle, and we have lost ground as we attempt to deal with this recent rise in banditry.

"Focusing our efforts on escorting and protecting caravans and merchant guilds. The Tempus Knights are spread thin, but we are maintaining order upon the road as best we can. If the Duke's of the cities would put their troops out to aid us, we will be better able to combat this threat while dealing with the Northern border."

The man paused and Nina noticed a group of the Dukes and Duchesses around her shuffling nervously at this last bit of news. Of course, they would be nervous, having to put their own troops into the mess and therefore have less protection for themselves and their cities. But Nina knew that was one of the many weaknesses of the city rulers within this country. They lacked spine. Nina had put a crackdown on banditry and robbers within and around her city the moment it arrived.

The brutes had attempted to set up within the forest upon the back side of the city and Nina had ordered her troops to go out, capture, and then kill every one of them by either the sword, or hanging. She would not let it infest her city or way of life. And thankfully, the Northern and Eastern Provinces were doing well in that regard.

"The training of new Tempus Knights this quarter is going well, but—"

"*We need more troops*, of course they do. They always do," a voice whispered into Nina's ear. She glanced at her husband, who seemed intent on the Lord Commander's speech, before turning to the other side to see that Lord Ttrist, a thin man with great taste in navy blue suits, sitting himself down next to her.

"Bran!" she smiled but kept her voice low. "I did not realize you would be able to make it."

"Just so, Duchess. I was able to make it in with the Duke of Mitrion. He was kind enough to let me travel with them in exchange for first bid on next season's crop sale from the Gelding."

The Gelding was doing good right now, in terms of a merchant guild. Nina's personal guild that she had built, despite her father's attempts to prevent or say otherwise. She had started the business at the age of sixteen and had hired Lord Bran Ttrist, the man beside her, as the Gelding acting head not three moons later and the guild had grown to four bases across the North and East provinces. It had been easy to hire him as they had been classmates when attending primary schooling and she knew he was an honest man.

Recently, Lord Ttrist had been away on a business trip to the Southeast City to see if he might gain passage through them and into the Nature Forests. Nina was still frustrated that even after eight moons of attempting to get trade to and from the Forests, every guild, lord, and trader from there had blocked or stonewalled her.

The Lord of White Tower, an older man with no children or heir to speak of, had died with all his connections lost as the man didn't keep any ledgers. The fool had died with such a wealth of contacts, tradesman, and brokers from across the world. Nina was still a bit perturbed by this act of spite the man had towards Nina. She believed it was the fact she had started her own guild, with no experience and got lucky with hiring a man competent enough to keep her new fledgling business a float, even threw all her plans, contracts, and schemes that had fallen through.

"Have I missed anything important?" Ttrist asked.

"No," she said with a sigh. "Other than the Speakers greeting speech. The Lord Commander is the first to make his address. It has so dreadfully boring that I caught myself admiring the murals."

Most of the attendees started clapping as the Lord Commander was finishing up. The speaker then addressed Mister Grigsby, the head of Trade, who was stationed in Nina's home city of Ore.

"So, I haven't missed the Foreign Affairs address, then?"

"No." she raised an eyebrow. "Why do you ask?"

Lord Ttrist gave her a look that seemed to say, *it's only bad news.*

"I fear it would be best if you heard it from the address. I am hoping that my informant is wrong, but..." he shrugged. "This may be why we haven't been able to make any progress with the Nature Forests."

"Your trip fell through again?" Nina's shoulders fell.

Lord Ttrist nodded, and Nina groaned as she sat back in her chair to watch the burly Trade Mister step up to give his address. The man's girth almost made it impossible to get into the podium, but he managed, clearing his throat as he lifted a sheet of parchment to read.

"Thank you, Mister Speaker. And thank you, good ladies and gentlemen. Now, I would like to address two developments that will be put through by the end of this moon cycle. Firstly, is the new tariffs that will be enforced upon the trade groups in order to pay for the safe passage across trade lanes through the North and Eastern provinces to help finance the trade in the Southern and Western provinces..."

The chamber erupted into outrage and shouting as a good many of the Northern and Eastern provinces Lords and Misters showed their discontent with this new tariff.

Nina almost joined in, if not for the fact that it would mean nothing for her to do so. It was like shouting at the wind to stop at this point. She would have to make a formal address during her speech of the City of Ore's report in the following days.

"Is that apart of what you were meaning?" Nina asked Lord Ttrist loud enough for him to hear over the shouting.

"'That is just the tip of the iceberg,' as sailors say."

Nina sighed as she set in for a long, *long* day of men arguing over these addresses.

Until her eyes met Lord Kremlin's. The man was smiling like a cat as the surrounding chaos ensued. Nina narrowed her eyes at the man before glancing down at the floor, hoping the Speaker would call for a recess to allow heads to cool. And as she thought this, the king stood and motioned for the Speaker to do just that.

"If you will excuse me, Bran." She stood.

"Of course."

Nina turned and her husband, oblivious as always, flinched as he watched after her in shock that she had just stood and started walking off. William jumped to his feet to follow her.

"Dear? Where are we going?"

"To speak with a certain Lord." Nina said.

"*What* in all of Helmite's name do you two think you are accomplishing?!?" Nina's voice was loud she knew, but it enraged her to the point that she couldn't care less in that moment.

TO BE K NG

The anti-chamber that she was now in held a fine desk, two chairs to sit at, a sitting area, and a fireplace. Nina stood just inside the closed door with William at her side.

"Why, Duchess Weinstein, whatever do you mean?"

The two men who lounged on separate couches smoking on cigars as they had the moment they had retired to this room. Master of Trade Mister Grigsby, the man who was giving that last address, with his round stomach as a sort of resting spot for his hands, sat with a bemused smile.

"Lord Kremlin, do you know of what she speaks?"

Lord Voss Kremlin, Lord of Black Spire, relaxed with a leg propped on one knee as he took a long draw from his cigar before slowly puffing the smoke out. The man's face looked like that of a snake, which he was for all intents and purposes.

"I dare say she believes that we were colluding together, my good man."

"Why that would be criminal, now wouldn't it Duke Weinstein?"

William remained silent as he glared at the two men, another reason Nina respected the man. He knew when to keep his mouth shut.

"I believe that you have the wrong idea, my lady. This was brought to me straight from the king himself."

She blinked at the man.

"What?"

These words struck Nina. Why would the king do this? There was no logical reasoning for this. Because of their upbringing, the king and queen favored the Northern and Eastern Province. In fact, the prince had just finished schooling within the City of Ore's academic arts of War and Trade. *Why would they apply pressure on them now when they were gaining traction?*

"It seems that he hasn't included you in on his council as of late," Kremlin observed. "I dare say that you should speak with him before you come barking at us."

"If you wish to twist my hand, Lord Kremlin..."

"I only say for you to watch where you step." The terse warning was evident enough that the Lord was not wanting to have this discussion with her. "Now, if you will excuse us... we were in the middle of something."

The man placed the cigar back into his mouth as he reached for the small table between him and the round Mister to pour a bottle of some dark electric whisky. The bitter smell of the drink washing over the room as the man poured the drink into a glass.

Nina took a deep calming breath, before she turned to walk out. As she opened the door and walked out, she could hear William giving the gentleman the proper goodbyes before following her.

She was so distracted so, that she almost ran into a blue-coated man. She pulled up short of running into him.

"Wow! Excuse you," the man's snob like face scrunched down at her. She was by no means short, at five hands and five fingers, but this man had to be at least six hands tall. The smug look on his face made Nina just want to slap him. "You best watch where you are going, lady."

A young Imperial man, maybe in his late twenties, was what Nina guessed him to be, wearing the identifiable blue coat, tan skin, and white-blond hair.

"If you hadn't been wrapped within yourself, *you* could see better," she shot back before pushing past him down the hall without looking back.

There was a mumbling from the man before he was out of earshot. William caught up to her and gave her a raised eyebrow.

"What?" she grumbled.

Both his eyebrows went up then. Which just made Nina smile. His animated facial expressions always cheered her up. He knew her too well.

"Oh, stop that. I know I was being a bit overdramatic. I needed them to think that I am angered with them."

"And you weren't?"

"*Oh*, I was. But I just needed them to give me the source of the issue so that I may address it. Calmly and more respectable, so that I might *actually* be able to accomplish something."

"Especially since it is the *King*, Nina. What do you think he is doing?"

"I'm not sure." They turned down the hall towards the King's chamber that he used when a recess was called. "But we are about to find out."

"Well, then... She was certainly upset," Mister Grigsby noted as he accepted a glass of the whisky from Kremlin.

"Indeed. But I do not think she was upset with us, per se. More at the situation. Which is good for us."

The door opened again and a man wearing a blue coat, white-blond hair, and a permanent look of snob all over his face walked into the room.

"Ah, Ice, my good man. We were wondering when you might show up."

"Mister Grigsby, Lord Kremlin."

The man gave a mock head bob that Kremlin knew the man gave as more insult than respect. The young man always had that superiority complex. But once you pointed out his flaws or stuck the man in a corner, he was like a crying child.

"I just arrived from Central. The Latest Race was a success, and I hope that my racer will be good for another season or two."

"That is good news! Congratulations." Grigsby lifted his glass in a toast, before waving the young man over. "Come, come, we were just having the discussion of our affairs here in the addresses. I assume you say Duchess Weinstein on your way in?"

The imperial man gave a half smile. "I did. She was a very... unpleasant woman, to say the least."

Kremlin rolled his eyes. The woman was sometimes difficult, but she was anything but unpleasant. The moment she had walked in, Kremlin had to catch his breath at her beauty. How that scholar of a man, William Weinstein, had married her, Kremlin did not know. And his hopes at claiming the White Tower had been shut when that marriage was sealed.

"But," the young man, the Iceman, as he told everyone to call him, kept speaking, "I am afraid that I will not be able to stay long. I have just gained news of a target that I have been hunting for, for a very long has reappeared and I intend to go settle some...old scores."

"That old hermit?" Kremlin inquired. Then he raised an eyebrow. "You think you can kill him? You?"

Kremlin almost laughed but caught himself when the Iceman's shadow began to ripple, in a way that Kremlin himself was familiar with. The shadow rippled and clumped up, before it grew solid and take on the form of a man's arms, head, then torso and the rest of a body that climbed out of the shadow to stand next to the young imperial. This man wore a hood and mask that hid his face. Vest, trousers, with a dagger and throwing blades strapped across his torso, but the exposed muscular arms of tattoos of unnatural design was what made Kremlin's heart stop.

This was no ordinary Dark Elementalist that can walk through shadows and cause black mist to kill. This was a Druid assassin of the Shadow League. *Only the druids were marked like that.*

Kremlin's own shadow rippled, but he put a hand towards it to stop his personal bodyguard from coming forth. Kremlin knew he was in no genuine danger. He hoped. This...recent development was only a shock.

"I do," Iceman stated. Then turned on his heel and walked out the door with the Wraith assassin following him out.

When the door was closed again, Grigsby let out a gasp, he had apparently been holding in. the man's complexion was turning back to a more normal color of peach as well.

"Dear Electrite and her holy powers," the Mister of Trade took a cloth and dabbed his beading forehead. "That man has a *wraith* now, too?"

"So, it would seem," Kremlin glared at the door the man had exited. "We might need to tread a bit more carefully when he is here next. For now..." Kremlin downed the rest of his drink to give his system a shock reset. "...let us worry about our situation and what we need to do for our next task."

13

A KNIGHT'S HONOR

"But your majesty," the voice of the noble woman reached the corridor outside the conference room well as she spoke, "you know how they would react. Especially when you had Mister Grigsby bring it to the floor. If you had allowed—"

"Someone else?" a man's voice interrupted. "Someone that they all appreciate and take seriously, who they would then despise because of this? No. His majesty chose Grigsby because a majority of the guilds already don't like him. So, it makes no difference to him, or the house, if he delivers the message or not. His majesty made the correct call in this regard, Duchess Weinstein."

"Lord Ahoa, the fact of the matter is not necessarily *who* gave the message, but *how* it was presented and what the message was in and of itself."

"Good Ladies and Gentlemen, settle down and allow his majesty to speak..."

The knight in polished Silver Armor relaxed a bit as the voices from the antechamber quieted down. For a moment, the knight was surrounded by silence, except for the soft hum of electricity that flowed from him and into the gem of his armor, as he channeled his elemancy.

According to the armor alchemist, who took the measurements for the suit, the armor resembled the exoskeleton of a shiny silver beetle. The...*technology*, as the alchemist called it, was remarkable and very useful, as the king's alchemist liked to point out whenever the crazed man saw the knight.

The armor suit not only did its job but exceeded expectations. Allowing the knight to hold his position of attention for hours on end if he focused his lighting elemancy into it. The armor was a perfect conductor for lightning elementalists, and Tom was grateful for it.

Because if there was one thing that Thomas Thunderian hated about his post, it was the fact that when the Lord Commander ordered him to sit at a post, it was usually the dullest post nearest the highest official or royal, and he would stand there for hours.

The upside was that he could practice storing his power within the gems set on the inside of the armor and infusing the armor with power. He was, however, most often privy to any voices or noises where he was posted.

Being the Fulman for the past moons after defeating Sir Welsh, the previous Fulman, in combat during a city Lord dispute that called on champions, has taught Tom the art of doing one's duty... even if it meant a boring station like this one.

The king was giving a speech now about why he added this tariff to the trade agreements and how it would help finance the war on bandits. A war that Tom had been fighting for the better part of a season. He had been pulled from the Southern Province amid performing a raid upon a suspected bandit hiding within a forested area at the edge of the Griffin Mountain range. Tom felt perturbed when he received the Lord Commander's order to attend the seasonal address.

"Now, there will be compensation upon the Northern and Eastern provinces. But they will be addressed at a later date..."

"Your majesty," the Duchess' voice was firm, but not authoritative, "some of the city Dukes and Duchess' have already left, and a good many of the Guild Lords as well. I passed Lord Greshim of the Winged Horse on my way to see you and he informed me that he would be leaving before the next session. The guilds feel betrayed by you not informing them beforehand. I was only briefly hinted at it by a colleague mere moments before it happened. Can you honestly believe that a warning was unnecessary?"

"Duchess Weinstein, you go too far!" Lord Ahoa proclaimed. The sound of a chair moving as someone stood. "His majesty does not need to—"

"Thank you, Lord Ahoa," the king's voice cut the man short, "but if the guilds want to play by these rules, then so be it..."

"Your majesty," a new voice cut in. Tom believed it to be Lord Count Freighmin, with his southern crisp voice of logic, "if you play them at their own game...there are whispers of them succeeding from the provinces. It would mean civil war."

The room went silent at those words. Tom was shocked as well. Not only would they need to deal with the Bandit War, but a civil war? The king assuredly wouldn't...

"If they do, it is treason." The king declared. "I do not deal with traitors."

"Father," the young man's voice belonged to Prince Frin, Tom knew, as he had attended a study in the City of Ore a few moons back. Tom was only one season older than the prince, but the lad treated him like some old knight general. "You most certainly do not mean that. You told me not two moons ago that if that happened, our country would be in ruin. Think of the economic collapse that would transpire. Not only that, but there are whispers that the Rau Council has returned—"

"Don't speak that name here! Those creatures were destroyed at the end of that war."

136

"Yes...sire, but your majesty, the prince makes a valid point. This is no time to be creating enemies when we need to strengthen our borders and clean up the rift within the provinces first."

Tom was drawn from the conversation by metal boots approaching from down the hallway. He turned to see the Lord Commander himself, Sir Tritin Ross, approaching in his own set of Silver Armor, a purple cape flowing behind him. The armor held a slight purple tint to it, whereas Tom's held a bluer shine that matched his blue cape. They both held their helmets, decorated after their own respective houses. A pegasi for Tom and griffin for the Lord Commander.

The Lord commanders broad chin scarred on the left side, shaved face, dark blond hair and blue eyes, one might assume him to be Tom's father. And Tom certainly viewed the man as one who could fill that role. Tom had a slightly more boyish face, bright blond hair, and crisp blue eyes that when he looked close enough in the mirror, he thought he could see blue lightning within them.

The Lord Commander came to a stop, and Tom gave the salute, left fist to right shoulder, and the older knight gave the salute back.

"Lord Commander."

"Fulmen." The older man peered at the door. "How goes it in there?"

"Not well, sir."

The commander grunted, his face growing thoughtful as a few voices grew louder from inside.

"Indeed..."

"Sir? May I be blunt?"

"As blunt as a training sword. Let's hear it."

That was what always amazed Tom about this man. He treated Tom as if he were just another man. Not some newly knighted kid that got lucky and beat the strongest knight in the provinces. No. The man spoke to him like a man. And ever since Tom had become Fulmen, the Lord Commander, who was probably the only other person stronger than Tom, had stepped in as the role of mentor and role model.

Tom's respect for him continued to grow by the day. Tom just wished he didn't have to play babysitter so often.

"If we go to civil war, would I be pulled to fight there? Or continue with the Bandits War?"

The Lord commander seemed to take this into deep consideration as he crossed his arms.

"Hopefully that will not be an option. If we were to go to civil war…I feel that the entire west side of the continent would collapse… I'm guessing that is what they are discussing in there?"

"Yes, sir."

The knight nodded. "Then I should like to help, no matter how much I despise politics. If there isn't a level head within these talks, their emotions would then lead us to the lines of war with our own countrymen…"

The Commander pushed the door open and walked inside. Shutting it tight behind him as he entered. Leaving Tom to wrestle with these new thoughts that were at odds within himself. Could he go to war? A civil war? He probably could. Especially if his duty required him to do so. To protect the provinces and its traditions, that was what the knights were for. It did not differ from fighting the bandits.

With that, he stood straight and attempted to not doze off, listening to the voices droning on and on about little political movements and backroom deals. Tom had to agree with the Lord Commander. He hated politics.

·+·+·+·+·+·+·+·

The meeting ended a short time later…well, Tom hoped it was a short time in between him closing and opening his eyes. As the guests filed out the doors. The Lord Commander stepped out and stood next to Tom as other guest passed.

"I will take this post for the time being," the Commander told Tom as they watched the guests leaving. "You will be on escort duty for Lord Count Freighman and his daughter, the Lady Rose."

"Yes, sir."

And just then, the young lady in question, wearing a red dress to match her namesake, stepped out with her father, a broad chested man in a black suit, whispering to Duchess Weinstein behind her. The duke Weinstein trailed just behind them, seemingly lost in thought as they walked.

Tom gave the Lord Commander a nod before stepping off to trail the four. He stepped up beside the duke and greeted him with what he hoped was a warm smile and nod.

"Duke Weinstein, it is good to see you again."

"Ah! Sir Fulmen. Why yes, it is. It has been some time since that duel you had with Sir Welsh wasn't it? How goes the adventures in Thundera?"

"Better than last we spoke. We believe that we have pinned down the bandits' main troop at the base of the Griffin mountains and hope to have them routed by the end of this Seasonal Rotation."

"Very good news, my good man. Good news indeed."

The man grew silent as the Duchess and Lord Count's conversation grew louder the farther they went.

"...I agree Duchess. We need to get the guilds together and show them the entirety of the tariff. If we don't do this, we may end up going to war for no reason."

"The only problem is that there is a division within the guilds that I believe is pushing for this. Those who are pushing for this have hired people like Lord James Toff and Lady Warren, who can be bribed, to create strife within the guilds so that we will go to war. The only problem is the division within the guilds."

"I will attempt to send you a copy so that you may address it to the them, duchess."

"Thank you, Lord Count," the Duchess curtseyed and waved her husband to take her arm and the couple walked towards the northern suites of the castle to retire for the evening. From what Tom had gathered earlier. They had to postpone the address because many Lords, Ladies, and Misters were 'summoned back' to their respective homesteads.

"Well, Sir Fulman," they continued walking towards the Count's rooms, "it seems you are our escort for the evening. Thankfully for you, I believe we have had a right long day as it is. I will be retiring for the evening..."

The Count looked pointedly to his daughter as they came to a stop outside a room where two guards in red uniforms stood post.

"I will be retiring to my rooms as well, Sir Fulman," the lady said in turn. "Our guards will be enough for our security." She curtseyed her head to Tom, who bowed.

"As you wish," Tom said.

"Thank you for the escort, my good man. I bid you a good evening."

"You as well, Lord Count, Lady Rose."

The two entered their room suite, closing the door behind them. Tom looked down the hallway and, in that moment, he felt his stomach rumble. He glanced at the guards, who stood awkward next to the door.

"Soldiers, I will return in three hours to relieve you so that you may eat and get some rest," Tom told the two guards. Tom could see the three bars painted on the man's shoulder plate. "Can you last until then?"

"Yes, sir. And thank you, Sir," the sergeant said.

This was always strange to Tom, only eighteen seasons old and a man that looked to be twice Tom's senior was calling him sir. It was strange.

Saluting the men, he turned to stride back down the halls, to the barracks to grab some food and a couple hours of sleep. Then he would relieve the Count's guards to allow them some respite. But after today? Tom had no clue where they would be after today's events?

"Sir Fulmen?"

Tom turned to see a page with a letter racing towards him.

"Yes?"

The boy held out the letter to Tom. Tom took the paper and opened it. His eyes scanned the paper and, reading the third line, he gritted his teeth and crumbled the paper. Another escort duty...

14

STORING HEAT

From the depths of darkness, Tan could just hear it, the faintest of voices, he could hear it distantly, the familiar voice calling to him.

"Tan? Hagitan..."

But Tan didn't want to move, as he was too comfortable in his enormous bed. He rolled over and attempted to pull the covers around himself tighter as the voice grew clearer.

"Hagitan!"

Wait a second, Tan knew that voice. Where was he?

"Father...?"

But as he attempted to open his eyes, he felt himself being dragged back down, back into the depths of the deep dark once again...

Suddenly Tan found himself within a different dream. One with a glass obsidian hallway that reflected light from the end of the corridor. Paintings decorated the hallway, but as Tan moved closer to inspect them, he couldn't discern their subjects. Every time he tried to move down the hallway to view the next painting, he felt as though he hadn't moved at all.

In frustration, he paused and stared at the painting in front of him. Focusing harder on the painting, he noticed it had a significant area at the center of the canvas, covered in blue paint brushed with a dark strip of green and brown around the edge. It was as if in a fit of rage. The artist had attacked the paint with white and blue lines that lit up the darkness and detail behind.

With more questions than answers, he turned to see another painting. But this painting was far different from the last. The last was a rage of blue, whereas this one was warm swirls of brown and tan colorings across the bottom half of the canvas, with a gray sky above.

But what threw the painting off the most was the black dot in the center of the canvas where the gray sky separated the grain-colored field below it. This painting was not harsh like the blue one, it was more abstract. But the way the painting left that one black dot that gave it an air of mystery around it, and made Tan wish he knew what the painting truly was.

Amid his pondering, he was pulled from the dream into darkness by a sudden jolt of pain in his back that grew all the way down his arms to his fingertips.

The ache was far from pleasant. Rippling needles up and down his body with every little movement he made. His eyes curt whenever he tried to open them, the light being too much for his eyes to handle for the first few attempts.

He felt something on his back, like rags or cloth, that stuck to his skin with sweat or some other substance.

The bed beneath him creaked as he attempted to roll from his stomach. The room was dark, so he could not see around him. Then a light grew in the hallway as Nicodemus walked in with a ball of Fire floating behind him. Or was that Tan's imagination? He blinked and the ball of light was gone. Tan tried to peer up at the man, but a hand kept his head pressed against the bed.

"Don't move," was all the old man said in a way that one warns someone before doing something stupid. The old man said, "I coated the cloth on your back with salve to ease the pain. If you're up to it, I can remove these and apply a thin coat of new salve..."

Tan nodded, though even that hurt as he lay on his stomach. As the pain in his body was making its rounds through his joints in waves that kept his teeth clenched.

The bed creaked behind him as Nicodemus leaned across it.

"It's best to breathe out..." was all the warning Tan received as the first piece of cloth was peeled clean from his back.

The sudden lack of substance from the cloth on his skin made him gasp and clench the bed sheets with enough strength to stretch and tear the material as the rest was pulled from his back. Four long white pieces of salve cloth in total.

Then he felt a cool brush across his back that was like a breath of fresh air that seemed to sap his pain away. Nicodemus slowly touched the soft brush to his inflamed skin, and wherever the brush touched the him, Tan could feel the pain dissipate. His body shuddered in relief, almost making him fall forward as if he hadn't braced himself.

"There." Nicodemus stood in front of him now. "That should last for a few hours. It helps absorb the heat that you have within you..."

"What's... ha-happening... to me?"

"You're going through what is known as the Burning. It is the downside of the power that we Elementalists wield. There is a price to pay for such power... especially the amount you can use. In fact, your father went through the same thing..."

It was then that Tan noticed the bandages wrapped around his master's hands and forearms. Tan noticed that the bandages on his master's hands and forearms. Had his master been the one to carry him to that water? Did he really get burned so badly?

Nicodemus noticed and nodded. "When you wield that much power, as you did against those fools, you have to build heat within yourself. Enough heat to be able to create that much Firepower."

"How do I—I get it to stop?" Tan shivered as he felt another small breeze come from the door. He definitely didn't want to go through this again.

"For as long as I have been training you, I haven't taught you where or how to store this power. And frankly, I didn't realize you had gotten this far in your training… So, the next lesson will be how to store and use this stored energy."

Tan groaned as the brush went over his back again. "But don't fret. I still haven't forgotten your punishment. This is pain here is just responsibility biting you in the butt." Tan moaned again, and not from the pain this time.

"Where…is Dancer?" Tan croaked out.

"Her and your grandmother left yesterday saying they had put off their duties long enough and needed to get back."

"How long…have I been out?"

"Three days."

"Three-?!" the sudden jolt through his body at even the attempt to rise had him crying out in pain.

"Wow! Easy there."

"But Master, I've missed three days and I only-"

"You don't think that as a teacher I don't know how much time you have left and how much you have left to learn?" Master Nicodemus bent down beside the bed to look Tan in the eye. "Trust me when I say this, boy. You will be ready if you *do* what I *say*."

"Y-yes, master."

"Good, because for the next day or two, we will be getting you back into working order. For now, you are to be bed sick for the next twenty-four hours."

Tan felt small spasms wash over him a bit as he took this in and thought, maybe his master was right. He could barely lift his head, much less perform any of the forms he was taught. So, he listened to his Master and slept.

Upon a broken and blackened tree stump away from the stream, Tan placed another small red crystal that reflected in the sun.

The gemstone wasn't that big, able to fit into his palm and close his fist around it. Not a true gemstone, but a crystal that had the same properties as one. A bag of them sat beside the stump... well, a bag that Tan had just gone through. There was the one he just placed on the stump and maybe two more in the bag.

Standing over the stump, he stared down at the rock pierced lips and a crease in his brow as he glared at the shiny thing. He wasn't sure what he was doing wrong. He needed to concentrate; otherwise, he would get knocked on his rear again. On top of this, his back was still tender. It would not be a good idea.

After three days of ordered bed rest, and two days of gaining his feet, Tan had felt surprisingly good. The seizers inflicted onto his body had stopped after the day he had woken up, and the after burns, what Master Nicodemus had called the strange red rash marking along his skin, faded away on the second day. And by the third he had been able to move around without wincing at every movement. Once he was up and about, however, Nicodemus kept his promise of punishment.

For the past two days Tan had scrubbed every black-green scale, every inch of the beast's wings, all the while the dragon napped away. Occasionally making a sort of dragon laugh whenever Tan couldn't reach an area before rolling to allow him to get it.

As Tan worked, though, all he could think about was that power that he had felt...and how much it worried him. He wasn't scared of it, well, maybe a little. But what he wanted to do was be able to control that power and not let it control him.

And that he had killed those men and felt no remorse was a bit of a surprise. From all the stories he had heard Huntsmen speak of, newly blooded throwing up, feeling sick, or putting down the sword for good after their first kill.

"Dat's how men get their first bleed," a drunken man had slurred one night at the local tavern. "Women have theirs and complain about it, while men go out and die of it..."

Another drunken man, on the same night, had walked by saying something that had caught Tan's ear.

"If you feel no pain or remorse, even the slightest, at killing someone, you're crazy."

Thankfully, Tan thought, have someone of that. It hadn't made him feel pleasant when he had.

"*And* had the justifiable measures, then a man shouldn't feel bad for cleaning the scum from this world."

Tan felt more at peace with that. He had rid the world of bandits that would have robbed, beaten, raped, and killed for who knows how long to so many people. Tan would do it again. Maybe with less emotion and more control, but he would do it again. He had a responsibility, didn't he? At least that much he could provide. That and the words of his mother echoed in his mind.

"*All ways try to be a good person.*"

Closing his eyes and taking a deep breath, he released a breath of steaming air as he slowly let the energy within himself flow out and into the crystal. The feeling of that power that sat and slowly grew within him begin to drain into the crystal at a very slow rate. Even so, it felt good to release the pent-up tempest within him.

Then he realized he had allowed the power to go unchecked, *again,* and the red crystal was taking the energy at such a pace that it began to shake, crack and it was like the energy within was forcing its way out from the inside. This sudden change made Tan grit his teeth as he attempted to shut off the flow of power, but it was too late.

The damage had been done, and the crystal began shining even brighter. Tan quickly took a step back and covered his face as the crystal exploded in a ball of red and orange light and smoke.

When Tan looked up all that was left was the stump, streaked with black burn marks from the explosion.

"Ashes and smog...not again..."

Tan winced as Nicodemus cursed, standing a respectful distance away from the stump and just in the shade of one of the tall pine trees.

He stomped over to Tan to tell him for the hundredth time...

"You need to focus! You're putting too much into it. If you put that much too fast, it will overcook the gem. I've told you this a hundred times before."

"Yes, Master." Tan felt the emptiness in his voice as he spoke the words.

"What was that about, then?" his master flung an arm to the side.

Tan lazily followed where Nicodemus pointed to the now entirely black tree stump that was a shattered splinter mess. He slowly looked away, scratching his cheek and not *really* sure if he should tell his master the truth, at least the whole truth.

"Well?"

Tan knew he should probably tell the old man and was just about to. But right before he spoke, Nicodemus sighed, rubbing his temple before turning away.

"The fact you can do it at all is...impressive." The bald man sighed as he rubbed his forehead. "I'm not mad at you. I'm just mad that if you could do this, maybe I should have taught you this sooner, and your burning would never have happened."

"It's not that, Master. It's that... It... it made me feel like a warm stream was pouring out of me...like a pitcher! And as it left me, I felt...lighter the more I put into it. And I didn't want to stop..."

Nicodemus remained quiet while he seemed to ponder what Tan had described. He scratched his bald head before squatting down at the tree stump.

"I see..."

He stood up and went to the edge of the stream and stared into the rushing water. The current wasn't strong, but it definitely had provided a refreshingly cool bath that morning when Tan had washed his morning exercise sweat from his body.

"We need to funnel the flow from you into the object," his master finally said. He turned to kick at the bag the crystals had been in. "Those cheap training crystals burst with even the slightest fluctuation of power level. And you are way above that level of power. Attempting to put your vast lake through a paper dam? Well, it does no practical good for you, *or* my limited supply of those crystal firecrackers." He hesitated for a second as Tan caught him reaching into his pants pocket. "So, instead of just using paper to plug a leak, we'll use a tank to drain it into..."

The next thing that Tan saw his master fiddle with something between his nugget fingers. The sight of his father's ring took Tan's breath away.

A black onyx frame with an intricate design that cradled a dragon heart sapphire. Tan hadn't seen it since his mother had stowed it in the letter for him to give to Nicodemus, and that had been years ago. Tan gazed at the object with the intensity of a great explorer searching for a majestic unicorn, a rare and beautiful creature that few have seen, but any sudden movements could frighten it away.

So Tan remained where he was standing as his master placed the ring on the blackened stump and backed away.

"This should be able to hold all that you have, and then some," said Nicodemus, who hadn't looked away from the ring. "No one has been able to fill it up yet, not even Aideen—I mean, the King, your father, wasn't able to reach the brim."

Tan hesitated, not sure if he should even look at such a precious relic. He would have been able to buy about five villages with the amount of money the ring was worth. It was a King's jewel, and an elemental crystal to boot. It should be with all the other royal artifacts the Elders kept in their hidden vault inside the Golden Plateau.

When Nicodemus saw the hesitation in Tan's gaze, he sighed.

"It's not going to bite you, boy. Take it." His master, impatient, pushed the ring into Tan's hand. "Now, do like you were doing before, but *slow!*" The old man emphasized that last word.

Tan nodded, staring down at the sparkling blue jewels, before stepping forward. He couldn't be afraid. If he wanted to be ready for the trials to come, he needed to master this, otherwise he would be a useless wreck, moaning in pain from another Burning.

Swallowing his trepidation, Tan set the ring down on what remained of the smoking stump, took a deep breath, and focused on the jewel and cleared his mind. The power within him was there, as it always was now. Swelling and swirling like a Firestorm that had sprung from a forest Fire and tornado. The well within himself was already beginning to fill again with power and it needed a place to go; if Tan didn't put it anywhere, it would just release itself within his own body.

He held out a hand and released a breath, allowing the heat to flow from him and into the ring, and he realized that the ring eagerly drank in the energy freely given to it, but it wasn't enough. Tan's well was deep, but the storm only took up half the space now. Tan focused on the ring's own well and realized that the amount he had put within it was minuscule compared to the vast ocean void.

Tan could barely see a small spark deep within its depths. But the amount that Tan was releasing into the ring felt like a clogged stream, like a beaver building a dam right in the way, but the closer Tan waded into the water, the more broken up the dam became.

Unknowingly, Tan had reached out and placed his hand on the stump, grasping the ring, and when he finally touched the ring, it was like his and the ring's wells collided. The tidal waves merging to become one as Tan poured the rest of his storm into the ring, all except for the smallest handful that he left kindled at the bottom of his own well.

When he peered back into the ring's well, he chuckled at the irony of what he saw. In terms of measurements, Tan's "storm" may have filled just about a teaspoon of the empty ocean.

"Good job," Nicodemus said from Tan's left, making the young man jump in surprise. He had been so enthralled with his task and with the ring that he hadn't known his master had snuck up on him.

Tan placed the ring back on the stump and felt a sudden loss when his connection to it broke and he stood back, blinking as if he had just come out of a very dark cave for the first time in years, the sunlight blinding his sensitive eyes.

"What are you doing?" Nicodemus asked Tan. Tan met the man's gaze. He looked like someone had just given him the rudest gesture ever. The man's nose scrunched up in what looked like annoyance.

"Master?" Tan didn't know what he'd done wrong. The old man praised Tan one minute, but became angry the next minute for something Tan didn't know.

Nicodemus looked to about bark something at Tan but stopped himself. Then Tan watched as the old man took a forced deep breath and said, in a gentle tone, or as gently as the old veteran could, "The ring is yours, boy. Put it on! Or I'll glue it to your forehead, so I won't have to worry that you got it."

Tan stared at his master with wide eyes before he looked down at the ring. Then he reached down and grasped the small cylinder, the metal band cool in his fingers as he slid it on his right ring finger. The onyx felt comfortable on his finger now. No longer loose with how much muscle he had been putting on. Tan admired the blue and black ring as it shone in the sunlight, feeling the wells connect with each other again with a satisfying motion of two waves slowly meeting each other.

"From your expression, I'm guessing it worked." Master Nicodemus noted. "If that's the case, good. Now we will be perfecting what you've already learned while you learn to use the ring, and one last *trick*," he turned to go but called over his shoulder,

Tan watched, wide eyed, as his master reached to the blade always strapped on his belt in the back. With a smooth motion the old man brought the dagger up to inspect before focusing on the bejeweled pommel. Tan watched as the red stone within began to glow, and surprisingly the blade itself began to glow before erupting into a Fire dagger. Tan had only heard about this, never seen it in person before.

"*Wow...*" was all he could think to say as he watched the flames while Master Nicodemus spun the blade in his fingers with a deftness Tan hadn't realized the old man had.

" Imbuing elemancy within a blade isn't much different from what you did with the ring. Energy flows in, but then you push the power up and into the blade itself."

Tan watched the blade, mesmerized.

"Hey? You listening?"

"Y-yes, master. I just thought it was really cool how you spun it in your fingers like that..." Tan's inner kid burst to life at seeing this magnificently hard task being performed with such ease. He knew he should control himself, but when his master did such cool things like this? He couldn't help himself.

"Oh..." the old man sounded genuinely surprised. Then smiled. "Well, thanks for the compliment, boy. Now...wait—" The man cut himself off so abruptly that Tan didn't know what was going on. Then the man was putting his dagger away and looking back at the cabin.

"Actually, practice with the ring, pulling some out and putting some in. I'm...need to go deal with something..." he turned and began walking away, still speaking increasingly louder the further he went. "Keep working on the forms, and work on the studies your grandmother sent. I want you to be able to tell me what three main properties a Nature Elemental uses, and how a Lightning Elemental typically uses their lightning within a civilized environment. As well as what the relations between the Nature Forests and the Lightning Provinces. You best learn all that by the time I get back!"

"Yes, master!"

But Tan knew his master was almost too far to hear him now. And he was now distracted by his...tasks. He was less than enthusiastic about the prospects of all that reading that he would soon find himself in. But with the foundations of command and obeying a part of his studies since he was a toddler, he would do as he was told. *A king commands and dictates, a prince learns and obeys*, as his father quoted once upon a time.

After the old man disappeared into the woods back towards the cabin, it was only a matter of moments before Tan heard Tyrone take off. Peering through the canopy, he could just make out the gentle flapping of wings as the dragon flew northward, toward the Ignus clan's main camp.

15

IT IS TIME

Tan continued pouring his inner Firestorm into the ring over the next few days. He had built up a good bit to store within the ring if he ever had to use a vast amount of power, but he'd still barely put a dent in the void of the ring's well. A small pond couldn't compete with the vastness of the sea.

And with his studies, all his master would say is, "Understanding not only your weaknesses but your enemies' weaknesses and strengths will allow you to go farther than those only focused on their own little world. That and your grandmother told me to tell you to do it."

Thankfully, Tan's studies of foreign elementals, their culture, fighting style, and powers, were coming along well even with Nicodemus's hands off approach, or lack of approach. Tan didn't mind.

It intrigued Tan that the Nature Elementalists and how they had so much more training. They went through many more years of training than Fire Elementalists. And their ranking system was unique.

Being plant based and expertise in a specific field of either Warrior or Nurturer. All started out Seed and went to Sprout, then Treeling, but after that it differs. If one was a Warrior, they would then go to Hardwood, then Conifer, and finally IronWood. But if one was a Nurturer, then they would go Softwood, Evergreen, and finally Agate. And there was so much that they could do. From making a plant grow faster and then making it move to using healing plants to heal a person's wounds.

He studied and studied all he could of the other elemancys. He studied until he ran out of resources of a particular piece and had at first asked Nicodemus questions that the books he had didn't have the answer to.

Like, *'How do Lightning Elementalists create a torch without Fire?'* or *'How do Dark Fire Elementalists pass through shadows and control them?'* To which the old man would just shrug and say, "Figure it out yourself, boy! I ain't no classroom scribe."

So, he had made several trips to the mining town and visited the local bookstore and used the allowance that Nicodemus gave him to purchase all the books he could on the subjects he had questions to. He kept his studies to himself mostly, especially when his master wouldn't answer something. It annoyed Tan, but at the same time he appreciated the tough love his master showed him. If the man hadn't had pushed him to go looking for the answers, he never would have learned the discipline to actually apply himself to study. A particular topic was a little intriguing to Tan.

Reading through Gahlin Quinn's book on *The knights of the old age and the Provinces of the new age.* He had moved into a portion that was talking about the country's infrastructure, in particular the trading system that the Lighting Province had and began wondering whether the clans might inter grade it into their own as well…

Tan shut that line of thinking down. He was toeing a very dangerous line of thought that would bring him closer to putting himself in his father's position. Taking on too much responsibility at once. And that was one thing that Tan did not want to do, especially not right now. With the trial literally a few days away, he had enough on his plate now.

Rolling the scroll up and placed it upon the stack of scrolls and books upon the desk. With a sigh he stood, extinguished his little Flame that he had floating next to him for light, walked downstairs, and straight out into the early morning air. The sun was in the sky, but it was still not up enough to wash away the purple on the opposite horizon.

Letting the morning fall frosty air fill his lungs before letting it out in a puffy, clear-white mist. His breath wasn't quite visible yet, but he knew it was only a matter of a few weeks. He stretched in an attempt to clear his thoughts that kept wanting to drift back to the province scroll.

Beginning his morning rituals of stretching and then forms, he moved through the motions of his day. The forms calmed him and reset his emotions as he let the power flow through his movements. Up his arms, down his legs, and across his back as he bent and twisted on the steps.

After Tan finished his forms, the sun was now well into the sky, and so he began his practice with the leaf. After four odd weeks of training, he could now bounce the leaf across the clearing, *without* burning it up, walking just behind it as he created tiny minor explosions that propelled the leaf through the air. Though, when he picked it up from where it had landed, Tan did note that the edges had blackened just a little. But compared to when he first started, and just incinerating each and every leaf for five straight days, this was a major improvement.

Tan enjoyed his studies. It opened the world around him that he hadn't known was possible. But it was nothing compared to being able to control his body and the power held within.

It was during his practice of meditating. He had done this as part of his training to clear his mind of distractions and storing his inner power within the ring, but it was in the middle of his session that he heard it.

The distant, "Harooffff! Harooffff! Harooffff!" of powerful wing beats that made him stop his meditating and smile.

With a bursting roar, Tyrone burst over the clearing, circling it before coming down with a ground shaking *"Thud!"* and the blackbird that always followed the old man glided down softly to alight upon the roof of the cabin.

Tan only shook his head with a smile.

"Don't give me that!" the old man said as Tan watched him hit the ground with a thud of his own. Perfectly stable and without a shred of the slight limp.

"What?" Tan tried to keep the smile off his face but failed to, and the old man pointed right at Tan's face.

"*THAT!* I don't need no one telling me to '*stop show'n off* or '*You're too old to be doing those kinds of stunts.*" The Old man shook his finger knowingly. "Wait till you get my age, and then say that!" he grumbled something about young people that Tan didn't catch.

It would seem his Gran had given the old veteran a piece of her mind upon his visit. She always seemed to be the only one to rile him up so much.

This only made Tan laugh, which granted him a right decent scowl. Though this caused Tyrone behind Tan to make a huffing sound, the closest thing Tan could describe a laugh from a dragon.

"Stoking overgrown lizard, half pints, and annoying birds..." Master Nicodemus muttered under his breath as he stormed towards the cabin.

"Wait-!" Tan called after the man racing to catch up to the man. Who did not stop and walked straight inside. For an old-looking man, he still could move, which always made Tan pause and remember what kind of man his teacher was. A soldier, a warrior.

"-Master." Tan added, even though the allotted time for formality was up.

The old man came up short and Tan had to back pedal so fast not to run into the back of the old man as he spun around. The intensity in the action had Tan pause, but the old man's face seemed...odd. But as quickly as it had come, it disappeared.

"How was the trip?" Tan asked, diverging from what he had been originally plan. But the old man seemed to not hear him as he spoke.

"We leave in two days..." the old man suddenly announced.

Tan cocked his head. "Tw-...To go where?"

"Your trial is in three days," Nicodemus reported, "And we are expected to be there a day early. There will be others taking the trial, but yours will be...special, to say the least. That was what I was doing while I was away. The elders are as stubborn as the day you left them, maybe more so since," His master smirked at this. "That seemed to tickle the old weasels the wrong way. You running off without their approval. Should have been there, boy. It was nice to watch them all squirm when I told them how far along you were."

The man turned to go in, but Tan began again.

"Soooo, am I not doing the trials? Or..."

Tan tried to keep his tone neutral, as he controlled the bit of annoyance that flared at the fact that the elders were changing things. Especially at almost the last-minute which perturbed Tan to the point that he wanted to punch a wall, or a face, or a...tree.

His master turned and raised an eyebrow.

"Oh, no. You're still doing the trials," his master turned to cross his arms and glare at the wall then, not that there was anything in particular that was on it, just that Tan thought the man was glaring through the wall, across hundreds of miles, straight into the elders' tents just to scowl? It gave Tan a little smile to see that he wasn't the only one who had qualms with the elders.

"The *elders*, not sure why *they* gotta be the ones in charge in the first place, but the elders say that you will be getting a trial unlike most. '*This is a trial through Blood, after all*.'"

Clearly, the old man seemed unconvinced.

"So...?" Tan hesitated before asking his dying question. The nervous energy welling inside his stomach at the cusp of asking the old veteran.

"Soooo...what? Spit it out, boy! Don't just sit there once you've started."

Again, Tan hesitated. Until he forced himself to spit it all out.

"Do you- do you think I'm ready? ...for the trial, that is."

There was a long pause as the old man took Tan in. with the smallest hint of a smirk, the old man said, in all seriousness, "Maybe..." and turned to walk towards his room.

Tan heard his mouth hit the floor at that.

"Maybe?!" Tan could hear the disbelief in his own voice. "Not, 'You got this, boy', or 'give it your all and remember what I taught you?' No pep talks?"

The old man scoffed out a laugh before he grabbed his door with a quick glance over his shoulder before shrugging.

"You either do it, or ya don't. It's up to you, not me. Besides, I'm not much for them officer speeches like your father or Commander Dex. You either take what I taught you to heart...or you die."

And with that second jaw dropping statement, the old man locked himself into his room.

Tan stood within the kitchen-dining area with what he guessed people would have assumed was shock, fear, pride, and various other emotions washing over his face. It made him want to just throw something.

All he knew was...he needed to keep training, which was also a way to "hit something". And with that, he turned on his heel and strode back out to the clearing. He knew what he needed to do, and he knew what he needed to do to do it. He would take in all his master's teachings and become stronger, more so even than his father.

With the rising of the sun on the following day, Tan had not tried to delve into the depths of his Flames since the...incident, but the memory of those Flames kept coming to him as he went about his routine. But after a strange visitor arrived, Tan's thoughts of those flames went to the back of his mind.

The sun had just passed midday as Tan was finishing his daily chores, and the sounds of heavy wings beats echoed off the cabin. He turned and looked up to see a small flyer, a scout dragon, descending towards the cabin. The yellow-green scales of the lesser dragon made the creature seem almost like a kitten next to a lion compared to Tyrone's monstrous form.

Upon the scout dragon's back, was a Dragoon, a Huntsman trained in scouting, information gathering, and occasional reconnaissance missions. He wore the garbs of the clans, tan and brown skins with leather armor strapped over them.

The Dragoon's armor was lighter than the average foot soldier's and allowed for better maneuverability within the saddle. And was light enough for the smaller dragon to be able to fly faster. If the man were to wear Dragon armor like what Master Nicodemus had in the past, the dragon would never be able to fly.

The small dragon fluttered its wings before landing, like a cat, front paws out and then bracing with the back legs. The rider rocked back and forth before hopping off the mythical creature and walking confidently towards Tan and the cabin.

The man wore a cap like helm and goggles to see through the wind as the dragon flew at top speed. He pulled down the bandana that covered the rest of his face and pulled the goggles down around his neck to expose a face painted with tattoos of dark, swirling patterns.

A strip of fabric held the man's long hair back in a bun that bobbed as he moved. His tanned skin matched his young, muscular features in a way that gave him power, yet the subtle hint of youth.

The young man looked not much older than Tan, maybe a season or two.

A newly initiated huntsman? Tan guessed. He was probably sent out to give Tan the formal invitation to the Trials. To fly all the way here must have taken a good amount of time. He must have left the day after his master, if Tan's math was correct.

Though he had been struggling in that area of his studies. He would probably get a scolding from Gran when he saw her next and she gave him a pop quiz. He hated when she, out of nowhere, would start interrogating him for information about his studies. Thankfully, her last visit hadn't been as bad as when Tan had been back at the main camp. His thoughts were trailing off again. And so, he focused on the newcomer again.

Searching for any recognition in the young warrior's eyes to see if he was from Tan's own clan. Clan Ignus wasn't a large clan, but they were the most powerful and sacred of all the clans, as they had been the first clan. Or so the Ignus elders stated. All the clans say their clan was first.

Tan didn't care much. The warrior appeared to belong to a different clan; a dragon head tattoo adorned his forearm, instead of a flame. The sign of Clan Dracus who were close allies of Clan Ignus.

Tan called for his master within the cabin, and Nicodemus grumbled about having guests and how they were *such a pain* or something as he exited the cabin. Tan tried to hide the smirk and realized he was copying the way his master seemed to think everything was a joke and smirk. Then he realized he liked it. That his master, one of the greatest warriors of this age, was rubbing off on him made Tan feel proud.

The Dragoon halted a short distance and saluted with an enclosed fist over his forehead, and Master Nicodemus returned the gesture. A very formal entrance. Tan hadn't met someone in the past few months that didn't think his master anything other than a hermit.

Tan would like to see a few of the minor townspeople's reactions if they ever found out who the man was. They would probably feint if they knew who Tan was.

"Graidus da Dracus, Blood Hunter Dragoon of Clan Dracus."

"Nicodemus da Haliken, Red Dawn, Captain of the Guard. of Clan Lupus."

Tan had to constrain himself from doing a double take. He hadn't realized that Master Nicodemus was a part of Clan Lupus, the dead Clan of the Wolf. The Clan of the Wolf was responsible for the Black Guard, as well as making up most of the Royal Guard members. The Lupus Clan was the first targeted by the Dark Lords during the Great Purge, if Tan recalled correctly. He hadn't seen these vicious acts in person, thank the ashes. But he had read about them from eyewitness testimonials that the elders had documented after the purge. Tan assumed he had never truly heard his master's full name before, either. But it made since that the Captain of the Royal Guard be from the Clan Lupus.

"How fare your travels, young Huntsmen?" His master had straightened once the young hunter had saluted, and now stood at a mock parade rest as he addressed the man formally, no hint of his normal complaining and mumblings. "And what brings you to my secluded homestead?"

The way Tan could hear the change in his master's tone amazed him. It was as if this were an entirely different man to the teacher he had grown to know over the past couple of months. He had never heard the old man speak so formally, not to anyone. Not even Gran.

"I have come ahead of the Elders, to inform you of their coming... within the next few moments." The warrior was a bit standoffish as he gave this message. Like one who knew they were about to step into a very stink mud puddle that there was no way around.

"Ah, I see. So, Fuma has sent you with just enough time to tell me that they are coming, and with only enough time to give warning and not allow for me to tell them they aren't welcome."

The huntsman tried to conceal his involuntary facial response.

"They were half a league behind me, Captain." The Warrior was defiantly trying to butter Tan's master with the added title so that the old man's wrath wasn't brought down upon him.

Nicodemus mumbled about a *conniving old silver tongue,* but Tan wasn't too sure as it was garbled.

Looking up, Tan squinted into the bright blue sky over the trees. The direction from which the rider had come from now had three dots growing on the horizon above the tree line. He could barely make out the steady flap of large bat-like wings. Two of the flying lizards were not as big as Tyrone, but they still made an impression. The other two mounts were as large as, if not bigger than, Nicodemus' mount.

The sound of mumbling behind him caught Tan's attention, but he didn't turn around when Nicodemus came up next to him.

"The smaller are...mmm, two Horned Backs. Most likely clan elders of other houses or clans and the larger two are most definitely Ignus, curse yall's Blood Thorns. Beasts are a different breed altogether in my book." His master's voice was distant, as if he were talking to himself.

Blood Thorn Regals were considered the king of the dragons. Tan was told once that the beast's Fire was to be the only one that turns blue upon maturity. And Blue Fire was the hottest and most powerful of all Flames. Everyone knows that. The Blood Thorn was the largest, and if not the strongest, the most powerful of all the dragons. Though they could range in size from that of the slightly but visibly smaller Horned Backs, to as big as the leviathans that flew towards them.

The Dragons grew closer, but it felt like ages to gain any distance to Tan. The young Huntsmen moved his tiny yellow dragon next to Tyrone and his shade tree, the dragon's favorite napping spot.

With a thunder crack, the ground shook as the four new dragons landed all around the cabin. The sight was a thing Tan would never forget. The beasts shook the ground in such a way that gave Tan a stupid child-like smile of glee at the event.

Upon the back of the two black-red, and Black-gold Blood Thorns were two riders and Tan could not look away from them as they looked over their beasts and checked their saddles, gear, and netting of supplies strapped to the dragons undersides.

Dragon Armor was something to behold. Tan hadn't seen a full plate of the armor since that time in the alley when Master Nicodemus had worn his. Well, maybe at the funeral, but that had been ceremonial, not training combat, or...this.

All dragon armor was collected from their respective dragon's and forged into Dragon Armor. Tan had little understanding of the technique, except that the elders knew how to do it, but it was limited. And the elders made sure of it.

The elders kept a strict registry of each armor plate set, bearer, as well as the weapon the bearer wielded. For the armor was not complete without a weapon.

The black and red armored rider, the same colors of his mount, had a wide, long sword strapped to his back. The weapon was not particularly large in terms of a long sword. But to be able to wield such a weapon while upon a dragon was something Tan could only assume the armor helped with.

From his limited understanding of what he knew, the user could use a form of melding and storing to push into the armor which causes the armor to glow its highlighted color, giving the bearer extra strength, the armor grew even stronger, and allowed the wearer to do inhuman things. The wearor could leap higher, run faster, and fall farther. And with dragon armor, unlike lightning knight armor, it was Fireproof, to a degree.

Other nations had similar armor, but none Tan knew of as strong as Dragon Armor. Maybe the Knights' shiny polished Silver Armor could, but Tan doubted that.

As he watched the riders move about their duties, sliding down the sides of their dragons, Tan finally noticed that each dragon had with them a few passengers behind the shoulder blades. The dragons crouched to allow their passengers an easier dismount.

The dark red and black dragon that landed closest to the front had a much different passenger. Tan slowly walked toward it until he was able to confirm it was who he thought it was. When he was sure, he smiled and raced toward the three people.

His cousin, Dancer Ignus, raced to meet Tan with just as big a smile. "Hi, Tan-!"

He crashed into the small girl and crushed her in a bear hug.

"Uh-eh! Can't-breath—"

"Pay back for the last time," Tan grunted before he released her. "What are you doing here?!"

Tan slowly looked her over. She wore a bit more fur and leathers now and was looking more and more like a real hunter. She had her small dagger strapped to her leg as always, but a twin was strapped to her other leg.

A grunt came from behind forcing her to hesitate before glancing back to the other two behind her.

"Maybe I should let them tell you..."

She turned and let a mountain of a man step up. Though, Tan noted, the man didn't seem as big as the last time he had seen him, he now reached the man's chin instead of his chest.

Tan nodded his head solemnly in greeting.

"Uncle."

The head of the Ignus clan, or Uncle Orion, was a muscular giant of a man that stood six feet tall, forcing Tan to tilt his head back to meet the man's intense eyes. The man had a well-trimmed beard, long hair held back by a strip of cloth in the Huntsman's style, he wore an open vest that exposed the profound muscles.

An Ignus tattoo marked the right shoulder and trousers and boots finished his clan like look for the day. The man didn't wear his Dragon Armor, something Tan had only seen in the man's war tent arrayed upon a mannequin. The man would rather his muscles and brain be what people feared most, and Tan had to agree with the man.

"Nephew." His uncle held a stern face and Tan was worried his uncle was mad at him still. Before it broke into the huge, warm smile that the man seemed to love to show off. "Now don't go treating me like your aunt, now! Come're!"

Tan smiled up at his uncle before giving him a big ol' bear hug. His uncle then held him at arm's length to look Tan over. The Chief's large hands gripped his shoulders as the giant manhandled him around, inspecting him for any signs of anything.

"You look good," his uncle said and gave his shoulders a comforting pat. "And you're beginning to fill out, not that little ember that left us for an old hermit. I see you've been working hard under captain Nicodemus..."

"I have. He's been a good instructor and-"

"Enough with you, Orion. Let me see my grand-babe!" An elderly clanswoman slapped the Ignus Chief out of the way. Being the Matriarch of the Ignus Clan, Tan guessed she was allowed to push him around, and being the chief's mother came with a few perks, Tan surmised.

"Hey, Gran," Tan said and smiled as he wrapped his arms around his grandmother.

"How are you, my grand-babe? Any more Burns?"

"No. I'm doing good, Gran."

"That old hag isn't giving you a hard time since I've been gone, has he?" She leaned back to look him in the face as Tan laughed at her calling Master Nicodemus a *hag*. He didn't know that anyone was allowed to insult the old veteran like that, at least openly. Though, he recalled her last visit and remembered the...sparks of that lovely chat. "Well, you aren't skin and bone, so I guess he's feeding you. And you've kept up with your studies?" She cocked an eyebrow.

"Every day after training." Tan smiled.

"Good lad." She patted him on the shoulder with an affectionate smile that seemed pleased and proud.

"What are you saying about me, you old witch?!" Nicodemus shouted from where he had stayed on the hill.

"We weren't talking about you, you old hag!" she shot back.

Tan watched as Nicodemus took a visible half step back at this, stunned at the audacity. Gran had taken his bloated ego and threw it on the dirt and proceeded to stomp on it. The old man was so stunned that it looked like he'd had an aneurysm before turning around and stomping toward the cabin.

"Can you teach me how to do that, Gran?" Tan whispered.

"I'll tell you if you don't figure it out after completing your training..."

She gave him a wink before she began the walk up to the cabin where the other clansmen and clanswoman were converging. Tan slowly walked to his master's side as the party formed a circle.

To Tan's left were two warriors in similar garb as the scout, with a well-dressed elder clansman between them. The elder had a disturbed frown on his face that gave him an unpleasant air.

To Tan's right were two other warriors and another elder clansman. This elder didn't wear a grumpy look, with more of the prideful, better than everyone else air. Tan didn't like any of these elders and they were a part of the group that had been trying to force Tan to stay with the clans. He remembered them both well, as they had been some of the most outspoken of the Clan Elders.

Elder Sage Fuma of Clan Treus and Elder Greyhart of Clan Herkin. All three of the major clans within the Fire Realm that always seemed to oppose the Ignus Clan and their allies, excluding the half of Ignus clan that attempted the failed coup led by his aunt, Naiveen Ignus. Those clans have earned the name Proditor, or Traitor Clan.

But who caught Tan's eye was the red robed old man still standing near one of the dragons and Dragoons. Tan wondered why the man was standoffish.

"Who's that?" Tan whispered to Dancer as they walked up the hill.

Dancer looked to where Tan nodded and nodded as if confirming who Tan was talking about.

"That's the mage that will be helping to oversee the Trial. Said his name was Abyos, or something? I don't remember. Father said that he was your dad's head advisor."

A mage? The Mage Association, after the Great War, had pulled their influence back in respect to let the countries they helped advise and oversee to recover without them trying to impose their will onto the broken kingdoms and people. They had been secluded to their hidden castle in the sky as far as Tan knew. Content to recruit new members and study elemancy away from the world.

In Tan's eyes, they somewhat deserved a rest after what they had done for the Alliance and neutral nations during the war. And felt like he understood the need to take a step back and take a breath.

Tan watched the old man, who stood with a content smile on his face as he brought a hand up to pat the Horned Back Regel affectionately.

The group gathered around, and Tan took up a position next to his master.

"Alright, you're all here." Master Nicodemus looked around the group. "Now tell me, *why* have you all come to my doorstep? I only just saw you and hadn't planned on seeing you for as long as I could. Better yet, how fast can I get rid of y'all?"

Tan observed his master had reverted to his condescending, rude, and ignorant teacher like attitude. If Tan had to guess, the old veteran still had a soft spot for the Huntsmen and Guard.

The group shuffled a bit at this harsh welcome. They had proabably been expecting a formal welcome like the Dragoon had received. But Tan realized that his master only reserved that for those who had earned his respect or didn't treat him like the warrior he was. The two elders gave each other a raised eyebrow before Gran spoke.

"Sage Fuma." Gran nodded to the old wrinkly elder.

"Hagitan Firebrand Ignus," the Sage began, "we have called for the Trail by Blood. You will be asked to take part in these trials. How you perform will determine if you are ready to join the clans as a member and Huntsman, and if you are allowed to take the throne as its heir. You turn Sixteen-Seasons in roughly half a moon cycle, therefore, this is your last chance to pass the trial before reaching manhood."

The old man stood erect as he gave this valuable information, like an old wooden post standing its ground against time.

"And what if I refuse?" Tan asked carefully. He didn't want to let his intentions come out just yet. But he was curious.

"It would mean," — Uncle Orion stepped forward — "you forfeit your right to the throne and Clan Ignus would most likely lose all power with the clans as the Clan Head. Thus, whoever becomes the new King would take control of the clans, and their clan would become Head."

What they did not know was that Tan did not want the throne. He hadn't wanted the throne ever since the day they had fled during the Purge. But if it meant that his family would suffer, he didn't want that on his conscience.

"What is my Trial?" Tan sighed.

"You, with fifteen other participants, will be given a...task," Orion answered, clearly not thrilled with being the one to deliver this bit of information.

If Tan wasn't the only one taking it, then did that mean that Dancer was taking it as well? They were both the same season, though Tan older by three moons, which Dancer always seemed to forget.

"Each task will allow the elders to judge your skill with your Fire and how adapt you are at performing your duty. Especially if you are to be king." Sage Fuma inserted himself into the circle. "But only if you pass, will you have a right to take the throne. And *if* we intend to put this child on the throne," he turned to the rest of the elders, "I fear that we would be severely weakened. An inexperienced boy, who has been living with a self-exiled hermit for the past few months and on the streets for an entire year before that? That would be irresponsible. *Which* is why I say that Prince Lighten should be the one we back. As he has been given extensive training and—"

"And I have told you," Gran spoke over the man, "that I will not allow that ignorant child to take charge. I mean that insufferable woman, not my grandchild, though he has become just as bad."

With Prince Lighten as a potential for the throne was worrisome for Tan's plans to step down from the throne. He had hoped Dancer would get a recommendation, but most seemed to think she would inherit clan head after her father.

With one of the great houses backing his cousin, more like his aunt, he knew it wouldn't be in anyone's interest. Thankfully, once Tan was chosen to take the throne, then he would step down, and hopefully give the throne to someone more capable. The Elders would convene to vote upon the next potential rulers, and they would then have the potential rulers battle for the throne through another Blood Trial. Knowing how his cousin was treated, Tan confidently believed that a true potential contender would outmatch his spoiled rotten brat of a cousin.

170

Tan did not know why the elder wanted to back his aunt, who was forming alliances with all Ignus clans' enemies. But Sage Fuma was definitely on the other side.

"That aside," Elder Greyhart turned to Tan and Nicodemus. "The reason we are here is to pick the two of you up and head to the sight of the Trials. There have been reports of bandits along the route and felt it best if you joined our caravan. Will you do us the honor of joining us?" For a glutton, the man seemed to pride himself on etiquette, Tan noted and appreciated. Despite his need to work on his girth, the man was charming.

Tan watched his master as the old veteran scratched his white beard, deep in thought. Tan wondered what the old man was thinking and why it would take this long to decide. Yes, Tan needed to train more if the other day's incident had anything to say, but Tan didn't think that his master would dare not show up for the Trial and Festival.

"We were going to leave tomorrow. So-"

"Good." Gran's sudden declaration made Master Nicodemus flinch slightly. When Tan turned to her, he saw his grandmother giving the old man a very stern look. *I was going to burn that stupid white beard off your face if you had refused,* that look said.

"With that, let us convene for the night?" Tan's uncle turned and addressed his Hunters and Dragoons.

Tan and Dancer were sent off to relax and play as the adults went inside to discuss... things. Tan didn't mind. He was just glad he finally got to see his cousin again since the Burning. Before that, the last time he saw her was just before he left to locate Master Nicodemus a full season ago.

They ran up a small hill to Tyrone's tree and sat down, leaning against the sleeping dragon, with a sigh. As the sun disappeared behind the mountain and the temperature decreased, the beast's warmth became incredibly pleasant.

As night approached, the huntsmen were setting up tents, and small fire pits to cook their food. The sounds brought a sense of home to Tan as they lay under the tree.

"It's nice here," Dancer stated beside him. Her eyes were closed as she relaxed against the black scales.

"Yeah. It gets too quiet though."

"I wouldn't mind that once in a while."

"Live out here for a month or two and you'll want to go back to the clans."

"Ha, probably."

"How is the clan?"

She leaned up to address him.

"It's actually grown. We had eighteen new Blood sworn and two Hunters this past year. And our crops and hunting grounds are growing back. Father says that we will need new houses on the outskirts of the town as well. Though Father calls the village a city now, with so many more people migrating back to us."

"Is that scary old house still there? On the edge of the camp?"

"Yeah, but the elders had some young Bloods renovate it and make it into a bathhouse."

"Aw... it was a cool hiding spot, though!"

"I know, right?"

They laughed at this.

She picked up a small stick and swung it in the air as she asked her next question.

"How long did it take for you to convince him, the Captain? I never asked."

"Not long. He made me fight Tyrone. And after that, he said he'd train me."

"What!?!" she gasped, jerking up to gape at him.

Her sudden outburst confused Tan.

"What do you mean, 'he made you fight Tyrone'? That dragon has to be as powerful as a Blood Thorn."

"It wasn't like Tyrone was going to eat me...I think." He remembered the angered look the dragon had given him when he had blemished the beast's scales.

"I'm surprised you passed," she admitted.

"Eh, technically I didn't. He just accepted me on a technicality."

There was a brief pause as she settled back down.

"I can't believe you left the clans like you did."

Tan turned to her. She was staring up into the canopy again.

"I'm surprised Gran didn't send a raiding party after me. And Uncle Orion's directions were kind of...unhelpful."

He had been on the verge of collapse when he had finally made it to his master's house, and it had taken him a season. His uncle's directions had gotten him lost, and he had wondered around for a season, a season!

"He can't find our own house without a map!" Dancer exclaimed. "You think he was going to be able to give you directions for someone who lived in the middle of nowhere?"

They both laughed.

"What was it like? Living on the streets?"

Tan looked away as memories of the dark allieys, gangs of children, and the underground attempted to force their way forward.

"Nothing much. Learned a good deal while I was out there, but it was...uneventful."

Lier, the back of his mind said.

"How is the training going?" she asked on a more serious note.

Tan sat up and picked at the grass, ripping it into tiny pieces.

"Good... at least, I *think* it is. Hard to tell with his way of training. I don't know if I'm ahead or behind in training compared to you. I'm pretty sure he wants me finished within the next two moons."

"He *what?*" she was gaping at him again.

"What?" Had he miss spoke? "I said- "

"No! I mean…he thinks you will be done? As in, mastered all of the styles and forms?"

"I already did that…" Tan was confused. "That was the first thing he taught me, then he taught me how to store power into a crystal. I can perform heat vision quite well, and he is just now teaching me how to fuse a weapon. Oh! And I've almost learned Flash Step."

"Tan," she warned, "most of the others in my class, including me, have only learned three of the Forms, and I have only just finished training to regulate my aura, much less store power into a crystal. Our teachers tell us we won't be fully trained until the end of the Seasonal Rotation. It's almost like you're on an entirely different level."

Tan was silent at that. Was he really that far ahead? It hadn't felt like he had been training for long under his master. But at the rate he realized Nicodemus had been pushing him. It sounded plausible. When he had left, he had been a class behind Dancer. To now be this far ahead of her? It brought confidence in himself and made him appreciate his mother's last wish even more. He would have to thank his master when he finished his training.

"He must be some mentor…"

This made Tan smile. "Yeah. He's a really good teacher. I don't think I would be able to do anything that I can now without him."

A slight breeze crossed the small hill, and a cloud slowly crawled across the sky above them. Birds chirped and bugs buzzed as they lay in the cool shade. The sounds of the clansmen working below echoed across the hill. The slow vibrations of Tyrone's sleep echoed was a subtle touch. Tan could feel the calmness, the serenity of the space had him drifting towards sleep.

"How about you?" Tan gasped out in an attempt to keep himself awake. "How has warrior training gone?"

"Father says I am ready, and I would like to agree," she answered from deep within her conscious, then lay back with an arm over her face.

If she wasn't careful, she would be asleep in no time, Tan thought.

"We have been working on a bit of a style between three and five to add more attack with the mobility."

"Sounds like a good strategy for you. You are pretty quick." He always seemed to tie with her whenever they had raced as kids.

After that, she talked about her duties as a Dragoon trainee. She talked to Tan about how a patrol had been attacked along the western border again. The southern border along the Lightning Province had actually died down a little as the normal feuds and occasional skirmishes had slowed. She assumed it had something with the province politics, but was unsure.

Oh! And she was finally assigned a dragon of her own. A scout dragon! His name is Razor. He is a beautiful dragon and Tan should see it. The gushy bubbly way she got about the smaller dragons was a little much for Tan, but he forced himself to endure it. He actually liked that she got excited, but it was always to the extreme with her.

When they had been kids, Dancer would go on and on about wanting to become a Dragoon Huntsmen. She had constantly bugged the older huntsman when they tended to the dragons, and she had always wanted to train or go out with them if they were going on patrol, or just about anything really.

And it appeared to Tan that she has been training hard towards that effort. Her body looked quite tone now for fifteen, so she must have been training hard. Tan supposed the warriors had finally given in and let her train with them. He noticed she had a small falcata strapped to her leg.

The thought of her becoming a Dragoon was a kind of comfort, as he now knew he had someone that he could count on if ever he needed help. And having an ear on the inside of the clans was always a good thing, even if Tan didn't want to deal with any of it.

'It's better to have too much information than none at all,' Nicodemus had said one day when Tan had groaned about how much of his academic studies there were.

After a minute, she slowed, and he could tell her words weren't coming as fast or excited as before.

She finished with, "...been training a lot..."

"Yeah, sounds like it. I hope you pass your trials," he offered when she went quiet.

But all he received was silence as she had drifted off to sleep. It must have been a long flight for her to have fallen asleep so fast. He remembered when they would stay up until midnight talking about random stuff.

Tan smiled to himself and decided it was time to do the last item of his daily routine.

He stood and made his way back down the hill, walking toward the cabin as he watched the Huntsmen tending to their dragons, running from the stream, and filling buckets of water up every time a dragon drained the contents of the barrels. *Dragons sure go through water like a drunkard through beer.*

As he passed the cabin entrance, voices from within, reached his ear.

"...the Owl's messenger was quite clear..." His master was saying. "...they have begun again, but this time it is a more subtle tactic."

"If they are making a rise to power again, then surely we need all the help we can get." Gran stated. "And you and Tan would need to return to the clan—"

"No." Master Nicodemus' voice was firm. "We are quite safe where we are. I highly doubt anyone wants anything to do with a hermit and a street boy student. No, we will remain here."

"And if we take him with us?" Gran's tone challenged.

"You try to take him, and see how hard he fights you on it."

Tan smirked at the way his master said it.

"That boy has enough power to take on even one of your poorly trained Dragon knight squires out there."

This made Tan blink in surprise. Sure, he wanted to test his skill. But against a huntsman in Armor? He wasn't too sure about that. He hoped his master was just bluffing.

Focusing back on the conversation, he only caught the last half of something his Gran was whispering about.

"… you really think he is ready, Nicodemus? Honestly? Is he that close?"

"Yes." Nicodemus's voice came from further in the cabin.

"Not even the King learned it that fast…" Orion's voice came from closer to the door. "He is his father's son. Aideen was always better at Elemancy than me. I guess that is a good thing that the boy is progressing so well."

"No! It's a very dangerous thing!" Gran's voice was tight. "You know what it did to your brother, Orion. The power blinded him. He was such a young king when he joined the Dark Lords and their reformation. Thinking that if he was to put in a bind that he could protect everything and everyone. That was his downfall. One that Dark Lord Obsidian foresaw. Your brother's arrogance and pride caused his downfall, which the Dark Lords used against him. If it weren't for the Owl Legion, we might *all* had been caught in the purged like the Golden City."

"Yes, *Mother*, I know. But it is good for the boy to be trained and taught how to control his impulses and his power…"

Peeking inside to see if that was what they had noticed.

The conversation went quiet. He knew he had already stayed too long. He glanced through his heat vision and then instantly released his heat vision as he saw a form slowly coming towards the door. Releasing the sight, he glanced at the cracked door, only noticing that his shadow from the sun was now casting itself into the cracked door. He cursed inwardly at this amateur mistake.

Tan swiftly bounded around the corner of the cabin and off toward the woods as someone swung the door open. By the time they had though, Tan was already disappearing into the woods.

The crest of the sun was disappearing behind the horizon and the dark purple of night's arms stretched from the east by the time Tan stopped running. He had made it to the stream further down from where the Warriors dipped their buckets.

As he caught his breath, hands on his head, he paced in a circle, dismantling what the adults had been talking about. What had Gran meant by those words? And why did she think it was dangerous for him to be doing so well in his studies and training? What did his father have to do with any of that? His thoughts were racing all over the place as his adrenaline still raged in his ears from the run.

Unable to think straight, he threw his top layers of clothing to the grass bank, and wearing nothing but his britches, he jumped into the chilly stream. The cold rush of water enveloped him as he jumped into the water, thankfully deep enough to swim underwater. Even with the summer days coming to a close, he still found the water refreshing in the night air.

He stroked to the other side of the stream and back, creating a small circle before going against the current as his mind settled. He was attempting to battle the current, not that it was terribly strong, but it was enough to give him a pleasant exercise.

Swimming to a shallower spot that allowed him to sit and relax in the water, he watched the reflection of the white moon glinting at him from the surface. The night sounds echoed all around him as he let the water wash over him. He released a big sigh before standing and exiting the stream.

Those thoughts, and that conversation, would have to wait for a later date. He needed rest if they were going to be waking early to head for the venue of the Trial, the Golden Plateau. And he didn't need anything distracting him from the trials. Especially if he was going to be flying all day tomorrow.

16

FEAST OF HUNTS

The enormous dragons flapped their immense wings, propelling themselves through the air. The wind hit Tan's exposed face; thankfully, it was cloudy, and they didn't have to wear the entire riders' garb. He wore a head wrap that draped over his shoulder and his regular light clothing had been discarded in favor of a more huntsman-like garb Nicodemus had acquired when he had been in the camps last. They fit him well.

The clothing was good for all weather, any type of fighting he would do, or for riding dragons. The leather padded rear side of the trousers were a must.

And if one wanted to protect oneself from the intense sun and chafing from riding dragons for more hours than one should, like what they were doing now, then wearing these leather guarded trousers would be a wise choice. The Clansman of Dragons and Fire had adapted their kit over the course of history to best suit them for their type of nomadic warrior life they lived.

An entire day had passed since they had left the cabin beneath the volcano. The caravan of dragons made suitable time across the mostly desert plains of the ruins. But now they were out of the great Desert ruins and flew over a small line of trees, and in the distance appeared the colossal form of the Golden Plateau. The huge hill stuck up out of the ground like a brown and golden cake sitting on top of a plate.

The large plateau with a lake atop it, was a sacred place for the Clans, and was where many Trials have taken place, as well as other seasonal rituals. Guarded by the Sanguis Bellator, or as everyone called them the Santory. A full wing complement of dragons was ready at a moment's notice. And as the procession approached, a small wing of dragons took flight, three in total, and formed an escorting pattern around them.

The caravan flew between the two escort dragons and up onto the plateau, all landing with ease as the ground came up to meet the dragons. The ground's grassy cushion atop the plateau was like a green blanket across a table, with a lake at the center and a small batch of trees on the waterfall side farther to the group's left side.

Tan marveled at the large body of water, only staying full due to the water spring beneath, from what researchers had found. The clearness of the water was plain enough and with the amount of water, there was no fear of the dragons drinking up the entire pond.

They dismounted, and the hunters led the dragons to the water to drink their fill as Tan followed the elders toward the encampment closer to the stream. They departed the lake to fall off the edge of the plateau. A small bridge allowed one to cross the stream of water to the other side of the encampment. There were rows of tents lined across the grass, in orderly fashion, according to the color of clans and their rank. There were smaller tents for the regular single clansman that grew to a medium-sized tent for Hunters and couples, and then two large tents at the center for the elder and head of each -clan.

When Tan studied the colors, he marked all the ones he knew in his mind. The Ignus Clan's red tents with the Fire Phoenix crest were situated close to the lake and were very noticeable. There were five rows of tan tents with his uncle's large brown tent next to Gran's gray tent nearer the center, in a more defensive posture.

Additional clusters of tents were present. The gray tents of the Draconus, the brown, brown and green tents of the other houses.

Across the stream was Clan Treus, their blue-gray tents, Clan Herkin with their dark green tents, surrounded by House Frinrear and House Vixian with their blue-gray and green-striped tents. The small stream was a visible representation, in Tan's opinion, of the divided clans.

With each row of tents representing a family unit separated between the head of the house, the lady of the house, the children, the servant, and finally the one taking the trial. The rest of the tents, the extra Huntsman that were brought along as guards and soldiers. Roughly there were about eighteen rows of tents, meaning there would be that many taking the trial this cycle.

They approached the main tent. Separated by a path through the clan's tents, the monstrous tent sat off to the side of the lake and was big enough to hold an entire war party procession beneath. Tan was sure that five full grown dragons could easily rest inside the tent with room for about two scout dragons.

The sounds of a large party, with music, laughter, and cries of glee, escaped from beneath the tent.

Guards at the entrance, wearing the tradition clan turban and robes, held the flap open as they all walked into the tent, and the party seemed to encompass everything as a wave assaulting his senses hit Tan. He hadn't been in such a crowded and boisterous place in quite a long time. Tan stopped at the entrance and took in the scene as the others moved along the edge of the large tent around the proceeding festivities.

Men of all creeds drank, ate, bellowed songs, and spoke loud enough to be heard over all others. Woman mingled about with their respective protectors, for if one were caught unaccompanied, they would instantly be surrounded by hungry young warriors looking for a chance to prove to the maiden their strength and prowess in… many skills that required much, yet little.

Tan moved to follow the group toward the back of the large tent, where a flap separated what he assumed was the common folk from the elders, chiefs, and their families. Dodging servants with trays of empty mugs and full plates, Tan caught up to the group just as they disappeared behind the flap.

Within this portion of the tent, it was much more "civilized." Though it did still hold that air of alpha status and ale, Tan felt this was a bit more timid than what was happening on the other side of the divider.

Master Nicodemus suddenly appeared before him, cutting Tan off from going to the buffet table.

"But master..." Tan protested, but Nicodemus was holding his shoulder.

"Nope," the old man held up a finger as he chided Tan. "Before you go gobbling half your face away and ruining yourself, remember why we are here. I will not go having my student making a fool of himself like those ruffians out there." He motioned with his finger toward the loud party on the other side of the flap.

Tan contained the sigh that almost escaped. He knew his master was right. Even if this was one of the greatest feasts ever thrown, there was also the trial tomorrow, and most of the contestants were preparing as they weren't allowed to partake in the Feast of Hunts until after they'd passed the trial and become a Huntsman themselves.

"Yes, Master."

"Good lad, now get something small; you don't want to throw it all up when the trial starts. Trust me, I've seen hunters do that very thing. Your uncle is one of them, even though he passed."

Tan laughed, wondering what the large bear-like man had been like when he had gone through the trials. Especially him emptying his stomach in front of the clans.

Which made Tan wander what it was like for his father to go through the trials, too. What had his trial been like. It was supposed to be his father's duty to prepaire him...but–

"Tan!"

Tan looked to see Dancer motioning him to come to where she stood next to the table of food.

"Off with you. And mind your manners."

"Yes, Master." Tan gave a head bow before walking to Dancer.

"What should we get first?" she asked as Tan picked up a plate.

"I would have said the scarab soup. I haven't had that in a while..."

"Scarab soup?!? Really?" Dancer's scoff was hard not to miss. "Tan, your taste must have been ruined by that old man if you want a street urchin soup."

Tan blinked at this. *Guess a year on the streets and then living with Master Nicodemus changed me. I hadn't realized...*

"Why not the bread and krim on a stick?" She offered. " That is way better."

"Sure..." Tan didn't mind bread and krim. It wasn't his favorite by any means. But it differed from what he had been eating.

Even though they called it the Feast of Hunts, only about a third of the clans' men and woman were true huntsmen. How the trials usually went was that if you wanted to become a huntsman you would do a test that involved a particular task, like farming, herding, or such. While the rest would attend the Huntsman's trial and either go the way of the hunter or pursue a different station. Most who passed and decided not to become true huntsmen were still given a hunter's name and all the privileges that came with it. Like good food.

A good majority of the young clan members went through the basic tests earlier in their training, like Tan with politics and his studies, then called it there. Only those that truly wanted to be a huntsman would go through the Trial of Blood, like those whose family were primarily huntsmen, usually went the hunter's route.

If your family Huntsman class and you went a different path, usually they ended up falling into debt and having to take the hunter's path, anyway. Very few that were in hunter families did well outside. Not that the other jobs and tasks were beneath them, they tended to just not do as well.

Tan pushed the thought to the back of his mind as he began to drool over a piece of well-cooked red chickery, a flightless bird that lived near the edges of the dune wastes, that was steaming on its platter a good six plates down the table. The bread and krim would not be enough for this meal.

But there was also a large roast brown karish, a fish from the river Stix along the eastern border of the Black Mountains, sitting not two dishes away that almost seemed to ask to be eaten. The decision was hurting him as his stomach growled in protest. Which one?

"Why not both?" An elderly bald man leaned over next to Tan.

Tan flinched back and almost threw his plate at the man reflexively, but stopped himself before his muscles acted. He hadn't even noticed the man walking up behind him. Tan chalked it up to being too distracted by the food.

Looking the bald man up and down and seeing the gray robes, it made Tan think that the old man was some warrior monk or hermit.

"Because one is a fish and the other a bird...?"

"Ah, but between the two well-cooked meats, regardless. If you desire both, why not take both?"

"Because if I choose both, the taste of one will sour the other. That and they clearly have two different seasonings which most likely don't mix well together."

Tan spat all this out so fast the old man blinked several times, as if taken aback by this young man's adept perception of food. At least, that's what Tan imagined. The old man smiled warmly and nodded.

"I see. Well, you are quite right, and since that is the case, go with the chickery. There are more items on the table that go better with it than the karish."

Tan turned to regard the table and indeed saw more of the items regularly served with Chickery, like the white rice, red beans, and potato slices. Whereas the karish only had a small dressing dish and some greens.

"Yeah...there are. Thank you," Tan said with a slight head bow, and then proceeded to fix the rest of his plate. The old man filled his plate before turning to move down the table in front of Tan.

Someone nudged him in the back and Tan turned to see Dancer with a raised eyebrow as if to say, *who was that?*

Tan shrugged as they reached the end of the table and grabbed cups of water. The attendant standing guard to prevent any underage drinking watched them with hawk eyes. Though, if Tan had watched and believed the man to have let one of the younger men get a tiny cup of ale.

They turned to look for a seat at one of the bench tables, as the old man did the same.

Tan spotted a seat at the end of the center table and nodded his head in that direction.

"There. Come on."

When Tan placed his plate on the table, Dancer doing the same beside him, Tan watched as the old man placed his plate across from him. Well, now that Tan could better see the man, he looked old and wrinkled but was lean and muscular, like the body of a warrior.

In that moment, Tan felt like the three of them were the only people at the table, as the surrounding sound slowly faded away almost unnaturally.

The old man's warm smile was inviting when he noticed Dancer staring, while Tan just awkwardly watched the man for a moment. Was this some sort of...test?

He glanced at Dancer. She had a look that said, '*I don't know*,' then shrugged and began eating as well.

Tan grabbed a stick of bread and munched on it as he studied the old man. *He's probably Nicodemus' age, maybe younger?* The forehead wrinkles were long across his bald head, and his skin was full of faded black tattoos stretching to the base of his collar, and when Tan saw the man's exposed fingers, he saw more tattoos spread across them with the marks of some ancient mystic symbols or lettering.

The old man's face was clean-shaven with no hint of hair at all on his head, which seemed strange to Tan, but he liked the way it made the older man look sharp. A man with eyes half his years but reaping knowledge one could only imagine.

Not quite hunched like some of the clan Elders were, this man had a gray cane with an owl head as the pommel. It sat resting against the table. The man's gray robes concealed all other defining features, other than the sandals wrapped in cloth. He definitely seemed like some warrior monk to Tan.

After eating most of the plate, the old man looked up and spoke to Tan, as if a sudden thought had crossed his mind.

"And what clan are you young folk from?" The man cocked his head as he looked Tan over. A curious action, almost like a bird looking over a new shiny coin. "Not Trauities, they like water far too much, and you don't seem to be growing any gills..." Dancer snickered at this joke. "You don't look like you are a part of the Herkins, they are far rounder. Not the Treus," he eyed tan with narrowed eyes, "your tongue is quick but not sly like those snakes. More like...a dragon. Hmmmm...perhaps Draconus?"

"We awe of Cwan Igwus," Dancer said with a mouthful of fish in her mouth. Unlike Tan, she had no qualms with mixing food.

"Ah, yes! Clan Ignus. How obvious it is now. Thank you, young miss. And pray tell, what are your names?"

Tan swallowed his bite of chickery before answering. *Why did people always seem to want to talk when you tried to eat something?*

187

"I am Hagitan Ignus, and this is Dancer Ignus," he nodded his head to Dancer. "And who are you, old man?" Leaning back and crossing his arms, Tan watched the old man stroke his chin, seemingly deep in thought. Tan didn't know what to make of this man's interest in them, but this was not some coincidence.

The surrounding room seemed to move without having noticed the little bubble the three were now in. The distant sounds of shouts, laughter, and stringed instruments caught Tan's attention, as he knew he was not impaired.

"A bit defensive, aren't we? Are you always like this, young phoenix?"

"Depends…"

"On what?"

"On whether I like someone. Their name can tell you a lot."

"Ah. And if someone answers wrong?"

"How could your name be wrong?"

"Well… that is a good question, now, isn't it? Can a name be wrong? I would say yes. For a Ravin is a Ravin, not a Robin."

"No, that's what it *is*. Not what its name is," Dancer pointed out. Tan noticed she had finally finished her plate as well. Tan set the last stick onto his empty plate as he watched the old man.

"You have me there, young miss. But I wonder why the Ravin doesn't tell us its name… Maybe because his name holds a tremendous power over it? I have found that a name matters a great deal, and would agree that it is extremely powerful. For what if I were to say that I am the Dark Lord Obsidian? What then?"

Tan froze at that. This man was *not* the Dark Lord. For one, the Dark Lord was dead, and besides, this man didn't seem like a dark Lord. It was the second time Tan had heard the name in the past few days and he didn't like it.

Everyone knew this Dark Lord's name. The leader of the Rau Council, the group of Dark Lords that started the Great War, the ones responsible for the Purge for betraying the Rau Council and joining the Alliance of Nations.

"That's not a joke I would use around here," Dancer quipped. "Some of the elders wouldn't be too happy."

"Indeed, child. But thank goodness they aren't near." The man chuckled.

Tan felt confused by what this crazy old man was talking about. It felt like swimming through fog.

"You still haven't answered me," Tan commented.

"Ah, yes. I speak of the power of names and words having meaning, not using them properly, while you use them as they were intended. Communication and dialogue are a remarkable thought provoker... forgive my rudeness... My name, young Prince, is Master Arien de Traès, of the order of the Owls."

The old man stood slowly and the strange feeling of being under a blanket lifted and the sounds of the feast cleared around them.

Tan mulled over the name; *Arien de Traès*. Tan liked the way it rolled off the tongue. But what made Tan pause was the last bit. The order of the owls? Tan had heard of no such thing. He knew of all the Clans and houses, but he had no clue what the order of the owls was.

Some type of merchant guild? Or a traveling monk sect?

"There you are, boy." Nicodemus emerged out of the sea of people around them. Being outside, it was easier to hear one another in the vast crowd that had amassed.

"Master..."

"Master Traès. Strange to find you attending. What brings you to the Plateau?"

"A special request from the Great Matron Ignus," the old man answered with a smile. "She offered an invitation to the feast and added a seat at the trials as a bonus, for the time I had helped at the last trials. This time I am but a guest."

189

Gran had invited him? Tan thought Gran disliked outsiders, with how she had treated his mother. Much less strange ones like this man.

"I see. Abree did, eh? All the same, it's still good to see you again, old friend."

Nicodemus shook the man's hand with a smile that didn't seem to reach his entire face. Tan saw a bit of tension behind his master's eyes.

"Likewise, old friend. Now! If you fine gentlemen, and miss, would excuse me, I just saw Paltor Draconus and I need to speak with him before the feast truly begins. If I don't catch him before he is lost among the boos I'll never get a chance before tomorrow. Excuse me."

The man stood, bowed, and walked off into the small crowd towards the tall figure that stuck up out of the crowd. Nicodemus stared after the man, making Tan look from one to the other and back.

"What is it?" Tan asked.

"You two just met one of the Masters of the Shadow League, one of the five GrandMasters in fact. A Druid that is considered legendary, even in his own realm. He is one of the best assassins ever known. Fortunately, he is retired now. I hope."

"He's a GrandMaster, of the *Shadow league?!*" Tan couldn't believe it. When he glanced at Dancer's wide eyes, he knew they were thinking the same thing...

"He's known as the Owl Legion. He was the one that killed two of the Dark Lords during the great war. As well as an entire legion of Imperial soldiers with two of their Silver Masks and their wolves. And those are just a few of the more well-known contracts he has committed..."

Tan was unimpressed, both from his own lack of knowledge of Druids and the Shadow League, other than as assassins, as well as not actually seeing these impressive feats. So, Tan held on to the knowledge and his skepticism.

"What are Druids? I've heard of them, but don't know what they are." Dancer squinted after the man known as the Owl Legion. "I heard they were just a bunch of witches doing witchcraft. But he seemed just like some crazy old man..."

Master Nicodemus sat down across from the two leaned over the table, so he didn't have to yell as loud.

"Don't let that old fool trick you with his nice old man act. He has many scars and secrets that young folk like you don't need to know about... Also! Druids..." — he took a sip from his tankard that he held between his hands and Tan had failed to notice earlier — "... they use a different type of skill than we do. They must use symbols and words to activate their powers, at least some do. They can do anything from making themselves light enough to walk on water, or able to change their entire shape into any animal. The GrandMasters? Think of them like the Mages and their great association, but for the Druids."

"Any animal?"

"*Most* any. But Arien says that most can't do that now. Though, I don't believe him."

"Wow." Tan leaned forward. "Can...can anyone become a Druid?" Dancer bounced up and down next to him excitedly.

"Yes, and no. You have to go through what they call the *Melding.*"

"What's the *Melding?*" Dancer asked. "Sounds like something a bug would go through.

"Er...It's...how they gain their powers. The tattoos that you saw on that old owl were a few of them. Each tattoo is a different Druid...Art, I think, is what they call their skills? Apparently, the Shadows are the only ones that still know the craft of making Druid Art. And to gain this power, you must go through a painful process that drives most people mad, kills them, or causes a defect. At times, some have gone mad and destroyed entire cities."

191

"Can we become Druids...?" Dancer asked. "I've always wanted to know what it was like to be a cat."

Tan was glad she asked, because this sounded like something he could use. But he was pretty sure how his master would answer. *'It's worse than the Burning...'* or *'...don't leave the clans,'* or some such.

Something worse than the Burning? There was no way that something was worse than the Burning. Tan had gone through a Burning. It was, by far, the worst thing he had ever experienced. The pain of being burned alive from the inside.

That's what he would describe it as. There was nothing worse than that. Thankfully, Master Nicodemus's ointment had helped a tremendous amount. Tan had learned how to make the cream as soon as he had his first Burning.

"Not if you want to remain in the clans," his master answered.

Tan smirked and shook his head. His master continued as if he hadn't noticed.

"The clans don't necessarily trust Druids, nor their...*Arts*. And when I say that obtaining that power is far worse than even the Burning, I mean it. Unless you want to go through something worse than that, don't do it..."

Tan knew it. It was amazing that he was learning to read his master as well as he was. It had only been a few moons since...

"...I said, *"Do I make myself clear?"* Nicodemus asked, raising his voice, and pointedly staring at Tan.

Tan blinked, dumbfounded. Tan had spaced out and missed the last bit of his master's words.

"Y-yes master."

Nicodemus sighed, and Dancer giggled before Tan elbowed her in the side playfully.

"The Mage Association has forbidden people from joining in the past but haven't been *around* as much as they used to, and so people have been joining the Shadows with a bit more...frequency. Just don't go to the Grey Taverns. They're recruiting stations for the

Shadows and the Druids. They know how to get what they want. Don't let them fool you with their honey words."

"Is that some kind of Druid Art they have?" Tan asked.

"You could say that..." Nicodemus sat back, stroking his white beard. "Enough talk about Druids and assassins. Go, you and your cousin need to rest. You both have a big day tomorrow and don't need to fret over this stuff."

He shooed Dancer and Tan away with a hand. Then pointed a finger at his nose. "And no talk of this to anyone. Your Gran will have my hide if she finds out I've been filling yall's heads with this nonsense!"

"Yes, Master." Tan gave a head bow before turning and disappearing into the crowd with Dancer to go find some place to set up his tent.

Tan had wanted to ask more, but when the veteran put his foot down... Tan did not want to test that foot. Besides, they had far more exciting things to look forward to.

17

NOTHING BUT DARKNESS

With the rising sun came the last day of the trial, and Tan was thankful for it. The first few days had been boring and upsetting. He was ready to get back to his training and do something productive.

It had been two days of watching other people take a trial, one flying on a dragon's back and using flames or arrows to strike at targets on the cliff side. Another trial where they had to hunt in the forests below the plateau in search of a Goliath Boar. A massive beast of a pig the size of a bear. Tan wished he could have seen one of them, if not partake in them. But he, like Dancer, had been assigned trial by duel.

Focusing more on combat than hunting or dragon back riding, though he supposed Dancer could have done since she was on track to becoming a Dragoon. The only thing that the trials did was allow the elders to see the progress of each warrior. And most were only clansman, the farmers, shepherds, and gatherers, not Huntsman or Dragoon level, much less dragon knight.

There apparently weren't any dragon knights at the trials this season.

After asking about it, Dancer had only said, "They are helping with some raiders that had started pouching some of the caravans and bask of their cragon's had been attacked. The elders are getting worried that this might become a normal thing."

After that, Tan officially declared he was bored. Other than the dragon flying trial, spectators couldn't see what was going on. So, he had gone through his drills and did some light sparring with Dancer. Both seeing how far they each had gone since the last time they had done this nearly two full seasons ago.

Dancer had a strange technique that always kept her spinning and windmilling for attacks while Tan remained light on his feet and used his quick jabs and strikes to keep her swings and spins from getting close. It had been some good sessions for both of them.

They now stood next to the other candidates as the elders whispered among themselves. Sage Fuma seemed to be in a heated discussion with Tan's Gran over something and after a while they turned to address the crowd, albeit with heated faces. And on one side of the stage was the Owl Legion, far enough back to be unnoticeable but close enough to hear.

While on the opposite side stood the red-robed mage, the man never attempted to speak with Tan as the Owl had. But Tan would avoid the man. Like now, as the man's eyes always seemed to watch Tan at odd times throughout the speaking.

"Welcome to the Trial of Blood," Orion announced to the gathered attendees and onlookers. "After this Trial, if you have completed your task successfully, you will be acknowledged as a Huntsman and will be given a hunter's name. This test will decide whether you will be able to use all of your skills and knowledge to complete the task given you."

"Each task will be performed to the best of your abilities. There are three tasks you can be assigned, Trial by combat, Trial by the hunt, and Trial by flight. Each of these three tasks will show your abilities that you have learned as well as your knowledge of how to complete the task.

"The trial by combat is a duel to the death against a sentenced criminal. Each of you who have been chosen for this task must bring justice to these criminals. Or they" — he stared intently at Tan at as he said this — "will bring it to you." The pause as the man scanned the crowd made those in attendance shuffle nervously. Clearly not many wanted that task, Tan thought. Which was probably the task he would be given.

"So, be warned." He broke his stare to look over the rest. "These villains have been promised their freedom if they are able to kill you... and they will kill you."

The crowd grew even more sober after last night's feist. They all shifted uncomfortably as Tan looked over the elders. Nicodemus seemed thoughtful, Gran looked angered, and the rest seemed to be a bit more passive as they listened to Sage Fuma.

Except for the GrandMaster, who looked amused at all the frowning and shocked faces. The Druid had probably killed plenty, especially with his title of Deadliest Assassin. The man caught Tan staring and winked. Tan smirked and returned to Gran, who was now speaking.

"If you wish to step out, now is the time. There will be no repercussions for dropping out now. You will have the title of Hunter for reaching this far, but only those who pass this next trial will claim the title of Huntsman."

No one moved for fear of showing weakness. It was an honor to have gotten this far; to hold the title of Huntsman was the greatest honor in the Clans. And no one wanted to be known as the weaker Hunter, though there were a few that held the second-class title.

Tan's mind drifted and he missed the next few bits of the briefing, until he heard a name.

"And finally, Hagitan Ignus, who will be tasked with Trial by Combat. And will be facing Killion Peaks..."

A gasp rose from the gathered crowd, and Tan was already confused since he had never heard that name before and apparently with this kind of reaction, he was glad for it.

"What's that about?" Tan whispered to Dancer who stood with a very pale face. The crowd began clucking like a bunch of hens in a frenzy.

"You've never heard of The Kill?" her jaw dropped as Tan shook his head. With a sigh, she explained, "He's the mass murder of the Hannibal House. That guy who went crazy the season before you left? He's been locked away for all that time."

"Oh! That famous war hero that went crazy?" Tan remembered that but had never heard the name since he had arrived well after the fact, and the name was considered to be taboo at that point. "I remember a little about him."

"They say he kept screaming in his cell for several weeks that your dad had ordered him to do killings because that was what he was good at. Ranted on and on about him doing his duty."

Tan felt his face go numb at these words. A tinge of Fire pulsed within him. That wall of glass humming low as if to tell him that the power was there and ready to exact justice upon anyone who dare use his father's name to justify something like that. His father was many things, but a mass murderer was not one of them.

The surrounding voices whispered and reached them through the crowd.

"I'm surprised they haven't executed him already..."

"Maybe they were saving him for this?"

"Just glad that I don't have him..."

"...doesn't that seem unfair?"

"Bet the exile prince won't last two minutes..."

Tan just filtered the voices out. There was no need for him to worry about something he couldn't change, other than preparing for the inevitable. Let the nay sayers and gossip hens have their say.

His mind was clear. He would pass this test, gain membership, and then continue his training with Master Nicodemus.

"Remember," Elder Fuma called over the whispers, "this is a fight to the death, yours or theirs. Only you can choose to fight. You may back out at any time."

Sage Fuma seemed to stare directly at Tan as he said this. Making the point that the elder hoped that Tan would lose, and allow Lighten to take the throne. Tan scoffed at the man's schemes. If the old man thought Tan would just roll over and walk away from this? He was sadly mistaken.

Tan didn't break eye contact, forcing the elder to blink, looking away to regain his composure.

"Ehm. We will begin in a moment, so prepare yourselves. We will meet back here and then fly to the Grounds."

The cheering crowd was all but background noise to Dancer as she fought. The man before her was a strange one. His left eye was bigger than the right, one nostril larger than the other, and a buck tooth stuck out around his mouth. It had almost made her laugh when she first saw it.

Now, all she could think about were the words the man had half snarled, half spit at her with his clogged nose.

"Don't worry girly," goblin face had said, "I'll make it quick and easy so that daddy won't have to watch me beat you to a pulp."

That had made her angry. She had felt her face heat and had immediately gone for her now chosen weapon. The Rope Dart. A long rope that had a metal ball on one end and a knife-like dart tied to the other. It was used on foot, cavalry, or dragon back. And after using the weapon for the past five seasons in secret training with her Master, her father, the training was paying off. She smiled now as the man, who had scoffed at her weapon when he had first seen it, now cowered behind his shield with his sword useless in his other hand.

"What's the matter?" Dancer called as she snatched the blade back with a spin. Catching it and then quickly igniting the blade before launching it back at her target. "You're awfully quiet now, goblin face!"

The man only grunted as the dart struck his shield in a small explosion that made him stumble back. His useless sword arm that was now burned from the first attack Dancer had used. It had caught the man off guard, but he had scrambled back in hopes that Dancer was worse at longer ranges. Sadly, for him, she was almost just as accurate. Maybe not on her father's level, but still pretty good.

Then, with an animal like growl, he attempted to throw the sword at her. Dancer didn't even move from her spot as she watched the sword tumble end over end, flicking her dagger around her head like a lasso encase the man did something stupid, which he did. She watched the sword hit the sand a good three paces off to her left while she spun her rope in her hand. She shook her head with a sigh as the man, only after the sword hit the ground, roared forward in an attempt to rush her. He was a good twenty paces away from her. Her rope being almost thirty paces long, and the arena only being fifty.

A tad late on the distraction there, goblin face. Dancer spun in a circle before bending low dragging the rope just over the sand to whip around the man's legs and tie them up.

Locking his legs for a split second caused the man to stumble to the ground. Dancer flicked the rope loose and snatched the dart back to her hand.

This is all but over, she thought as she glanced to the Ignus clan box where she saw her father biting his fingernails in that dreadful habit. *Oh! Stop worrying you muscle brain of a father! Didn't mother tell you, you needed to stop that bad habit?!*

Goblin Face grunted a few paces away from her. She turned back to see that he had recovered quickly from the fall. Dancer

199

smiled at the man as he panted, bringing the shield back up to ward her dart off again. He did not charge this time.

At least someone is learning to stop bad habits. She brought the rope short to spin around like a sling before launching it in an underhanded pitch directly at the man's shield.

Sitting on the stage, Nic watched as Dancer fought a nasty-looking goblin of a man in the arena below. The box he sat in sat at the center of the arena, giving Nic a good view of the field and the stands that wrapped around it.

The flight over had been brief, as the prison was at the foot of the plateau. The boy had been silent ever since the end of the briefing. More distant than when Nic usually gives him a chore or lesson to do.

"Oh! Stop that, Orion!" Abree chided her son from the seat behind Nic.

Nic glanced over to see the large man standing at the edge of the box with his entire focus upon his daughter fighting down in the field below. The man was biting his fingernails again, a habit the lad had been fond of since he was a youth. Nic shook his head before standing up, walking over, and smacking the Clan Head on the back hard enough to jar the man from his thoughts.

"If you're that worried, then leave," Nic pointed at the door to indicate which way the man should go. "Otherwise, give your daughter the respect she deserves and stop acting like a nervous father and act like the clan head."

Orion blinked before crossing his arms. Nic met the man's eyes and saw a shine to his eyes now. Nic smirked. These Ignus boys sure do like to sulk sometimes.

"Good. *Now*, stop fussing like an old hen and cheer her on..." Nic turned back to the fight, "Not that she needs it. She's just about won."

As she was. The girl...young woman in a few moments, was keeping her opponent at back with her rope dart. She kicked the blade, snatched it back, and sent it twirling around her like a saw blade weel. The goblin man seemed so confused and frightened that the only thing he could do was to attempt a pitiful throw of the sword, which landed harmlessly to the arena sand beside Dancer, and then cower behind the small shield he was using as cover. The man already had several red lines across his exposed face, his helmet tossed aside to track the dart better.

It was pointless in the end. Dancer yanked the dart back, caught and through the dart straight at the man. The man brought his shield up to block, but there was no impact.

Dancer had snatched the dart back so fast and then launched it over the man's head.

With no impact, the man peered over his shield and then tracked the rope into the sky above him. Nic watched as the man's face when pure white as Dancer twirled and slammed her foot down on the rope to bring the dart smashing down into the goblin man's face.

The man's body twitched before falling to the sand in a heap.

"That settles that then." Nic stood with a grunt. Nic picked up the sack he had brought with him from his trip to the clans and slung it over his shoulder before limping towards the door. "I'm going to go check on the boy and make sure he aint puking his guts out all over the place like you did when you took your trial..."

"That was because the man's hammer took me clean in the stomach, and you know it!" Orion called after Nic. "I wasn't nervous!"

"Tell that to your fingernails!" Nic called back. Not looking back as he gave a wave upon his exit into the hall that would lead him around and down into the staging area.

Nic nodded to Huntsmen, old and young alike, as he made his way past several venders that had taken up shop. *There always seemed to be traders and merchants at these stoking things.*

'That's because they make a lot of money when they happen,' Corax pointed out. 'Which tends to be good for businesses.'

'Not mine!'

Nic was passing one said vender when a dark-skinned man with a broad grin, one that some would find heartening, but Nic found revolting, stepped in front of his stand and waved over the various items on display. A Ravin pendent caught his eye but quickly dismissed it.

"Ah! My friend, would you care to browse my shop? The Great Wran Veer has a vast collection of pieces, or knowledge for one to go through..."

"No." Nic said flatly as he passed.

"But—"

Nic raised an eyebrow at the man.

"Fine. Don't then. Wran Veer will find a better friend anyways."

Nic shook his head before continuing his trek. 'Stoking crazy man, say'n his name as if he would forget it...'

'I don't think—'

'That was rhetorical, bird.'

'Ah.'

Nic made it to the doorway that would lead down into the staging area but stopped a few paces from it. Beside the open door stood the bald tattooed man Nic had hoped to not have had to run into for the second time in three days.

"Beginning to hope you might leave me alone," Nic said to the man.

"You and I both know, Nic, that we need to speak..." Arein de Traes, the Owl, pushed off the wall, holding the dueling cane in one hand. Nic knew the old man didn't need to use it. He was almost twice Nic's fifty-five seasons, Nic guessed, but had the body of a man in his early fifties.

"I already told Talibee, I'm not interested in helping any more than I am. I will give you information if you ask. But right now, I am training the boy."

"And after you finish training him? From what Talibee reports, the boy is nearly complete. He has already had a Burning, and he has summoned a Ferox Fire. How much more do you really need to teach him?"

Nic growled at the bald man with narrowed eyes, "I'm not going to work for you, Traes."

"Oh, I am quite aware of that." The man stepped up to Nic.

Nic eyed the cane for the briefest of moments before realizing that the assassin would have probably used some other trick if he had wanted to kill Nic. "You soldier dogs keep your nose to the ground once you find a scent. Bone headed to the end."

"Then what do you want?"

The man's eyebrows rose at this. "What do I want? My friend, since when has what I wanted ever mattered? Or yours, for that matter? No. I am here, one, to warn you that there is a very dangerous assassin after you..."

"I can handle myself. You know that." But Nic knew what the assassin would bring up in retort.

"Which brings me to the second matter..."

The bald man glanced down the stairs to the staging area. Nic kept his voice low.

"The boy—"

"In your care, he is a liability, my friend. You have a price on your head." The assassin turned back to Nic. "And the young prince needs more guidance. You have done a fantastic job, just like you did with his father and uncle."

Nic felt a sudden stab of regret at being reminded that he had installed some of the savior complex into the late king. He had trained the man to protect. Was he doing the same with the boy?

"*But,*" Arien continued, "if you, *or* he, wants to be prepared for what is to come. You will need more assistance." The Druid raised an eyebrow. "Have you spoken with Magus Ardoris? He has already expressed an interest in the boy."

"Of course he has," Nic scoffed. "Why wouldn't the mages want a piece of him? He has the potential to be one of the most powerful Fire Elementalists in the Realm."

"And the most powerful *weapon*...Don't think the enemy hasn't noticed that you are training the boy, either. They have ears everywhere."

Nic hesitated at this. Was the old owl telling him that there was something worse than assassins after him? Could it be about the whispers of the Rau Council?

"They are growing, Nicodemus...deep within the depths of their castles, within their lairs and laboratories of vile creatures. And within the Mist Mountains. They are coming for you, and eventually, the boy."

"He's stronger than they could even imagine. You can be stoking certain of that," Nic hissed.

"Oh, I don't doubt your word, old friend. I don't. But...what happens if you are no longer there to aid him? Allow him to wander back to the life of a street rat searching for answers he won't find on his own? Alone? He has no true friends other than his cousin, who is doing quite well, perhaps his grandmother and uncle, but you and I both know the boy won't go willingly. If he only stays within this small circle, he will be crushed by the much greater mass the enemy is compiling to defeat him, his family, your country, and the continent."

Nic remained silent at this.

If something were to happen to Nic, he wasn't sure how the boy would react. Would he become more determined? Would he step back from his role as heir? Did he even want to become king? From what Nic had learned about the boy, he seemed to resent yet respect his father, the late king. But seemed to wish to all but dismiss responsibility. If the Rau Council was returning, then the Clans and Realm...the continent itself would be in danger.

"They are already moving to bring the honorable knights to their knees," Arien commented. "They have been planning this attack for quite some time."

"What of it?"

"What of it?" Arien seemed aghast at Nic's question. "My friend, if the provinces fall then all that is truly left between a reasonable society and a world of slavery and darkness is the Empire, the weakened warriors of those blasted Forests. The clans are scattered, with no true leadership, and the Rangers, well...who knows with them?"

Nic remained silent. Unsure where his "old friend" was getting at.

The Druid sighed. "The enemy is beginning to make their move. And I am attempting to stay ahead of it this time. But, I cannot do this alone..."

Nic didn't know what to say to this. If the Provinces fell, Nic knew it would begin the collapse of the Alliance of Nations. After fighting, and spilling all that blood during the Great War, and then for it to have meant nothing? Nic could not stand by that. He sighed in contempt but knew that, if he was going to get the boy to take responsibility, he would have to do the same.

"I have some contacts that I can give you, but I won't be of much help until the boy has been trained." Nic met the assassin's gray eyes. "When he reaches Api Biru...I'll bring the boy back and we can attempt to gain some footing through the Clans. I would like for you to train him in some of your ways if you might..." He hesitated, but added. "...If something does happen...to me, make sure the boy is taken care of...don't leave him out in the dark."

Arien smiled, a sad smile that a man who has lived through three wars could only offer as comfort.

"My old friend, all we are, are Shadows. There is nothing but darkness here..."

Nic watched as the bald, tattooed man bowed and turned away. The strength in the man's steps something that no one missed as he made his way towards the Ignus Head's box.

The words were a bit unsettling, but as Nic hefted the bag on his shoulder and turned to the stairs, he knew one thing he could do.

18

BLOOD TRIAL

"How are you feeling, boy?" Nic asked from where he stood looking out into the gladiator Grounds.

"Good, Master," the boy glanced up to see Nic enter the door. "Just finishing up."

Nic watched as the kid slid his leather armor, given to him by the coordinators of the events, on over his undershirt and began strapping the vest down. The conversation he had just had with the old owl wasn't sitting well with him yet. Like there was something he was missing.

"Are you ready?"

"*Maybe*," Tan gave his master a smirk which the man returned in kind.

"That's my boy." Nic set the bag down at his feet. As he spoke, he moved over to the gate that opened out to the arena. "I can only tell you what you are doing wrong, or right, in my eyes. Soon, it will be up to you to decide whether you are ready, and ashes help anyone on the other side of that decision."

He turned back around to see the boy squinting at him through the light. The boy raised an eyebrow, as if he wanted to question the way Nic had said it. But only nodded.

"I'll never know until I try, then." He began putting the arm guards over the shirt sleeves and tightening them down.

"That's one way of putting it..."

Nic turned from the light from the arena reflected from the boy's face as he worked.

"Remember to take the forms you have learned and apply them with the sword. It is the same concept I have just been training your body to get used to the movements. Now, you will apply them for real."

Nic walked back over and picked up the sack.

"Here...take these."

The sack made a clinking noise as he sat it on the bench next to the boy.

"What is it?"

The boy untied the string holding the sack closed and peered inside.

"It's a...err, an early seasonal gift. Don't tell your grandmother! She'll have my head, again."

Nic watched as the young face gaped into the sack. The boy was so stunned he looked like a statue sitting in eternal shock. After a moment Nic had felt like the boy had done enough gaping.

"Are ya just goanna stare at it like a fish or are you going to put them on?" Nic finally barked.

"Y-yes, master!" The boy reached in and pulled out a black and red armored vest and then a pair of armored boots. A vest that Nic had specially made from the scales of the king's now dead regal. "How did you-?"

"I got your grandmother to make it for you and promised I would give them to you on your season day. We will have to wrap them. Since you don't have a proper under suit, wrapping them will be the best we can do. In the bag."

The boy reached back in and pulled out the fabric that Nic had bought and wrapped the tan fabric around the vest, leaving the arm and neck holes exposed. The boy fastened the straps of the vest chest piece, preventing the armor from shifting. Taking off his boots, the boy cut the second piece of fabric in half and used them to wrap his feet.

"Thank you, master!" the boy said as he slid the boots on. They were a tight fit as Nic had them size the armor's thickness down.

Then he saw it faded to a boy, same face and nose, wearing similar armor, clean cut hair, and his crimson sparkled red eyes beaming back at Nic. Then the image faded and he was met with those other messy hair, and crystal blue eyes that nudged him forward.

"Thank me later." Then he noticed the boy struggling. "Or you could put your armor on properly... let me see that!"

The boy smiled as Nic fussed over the "lousy craftsmanship" and, "Who stoking taught you how to put on armor, the cook?"

When Nic was satisfied, he stood back and looked Tan over.

"Not what I would wear but you work with what you've got... Let's wrap the boots up. Don't want that maniac to know you got these on. You know what to use these for right?"

"Yes, master. Oh! I forgot to tell you that I was able to do it! I got the leaf all the way across the field right before you got back."

"Good lad. And don't forget what it will take to use that."

A horn sounded beyond the gate leading to the arena. The two looked in its direction before Nicodemus turned back to him.

"Now listen..." — he pointed a finger at Tan's nose as the other hand grasped his shoulder — "when it comes down to it, this stoking man is a beast... treat him as such, because *he will kill you*, especially since your uncle is the one who jailed him. Understand? And do not let him get in your head. He will always try and get in your head. Remember that."

"Yes, Master."

"Good lad. Now get out there before they send one of them stoking blokes in here and start whining."

Tan stepped out into the sunlight, pulling the strap that held his blade in place across his back as the heat wrapped around him while he strode out onto the sandy dueling ground. From the staging area Tan could only see a section of stands but stepping out into the arena the expanse of the coliseum felt like he was in a large bowl. The blue sky over head and bright sun casting his shadow upon his feet. The crowd was loud as they screamed and cheered as the announcer, a medium aged man with a greying beard called into the horn that projected his voice across the sands.

"Ladies and gentlemen, you know his name, you know his title, please welcome our challenger of this final trial. I present to you, Royal Heir apparent, his highness, Prince Hagitan Ignus!"

There were a few boos mixed into the screams of excitement. But Tan wasn't paying attention. His attention was much, much more concentrated. Feeling the Dragon armor hugging his chest perfectly, the slight pulses of element into the armor giving him a warm sense of comfort and strength. The slight breeze that swept in from the north brushed his curled hair, which he needed to trim soon as it was almost in his eyes now.

The only sounds he could hear were the sand crunching beneath his new Dragon armor boots, and the echoing heartbeats as he took a deep breath, he forced the air around him to dissipate as he looked across the patches of red and white sand of the pit to where others had either met their fate or received a blow. He noticed the spot where Dancer had taken down her opponent off to the right. She had opted to use a rope dart, and a Fire technique he hadn't seen before. It was quite impressive. And he thought to ask her about it later. He might be able to use it in junction with his own style.

As Tan reached the marked spot on the field where he was to wait, the sound of the crowd quieted. The main event was about to start, and everyone was anxious to know the outcome. Would the exiled prince defeat the murderous fallen hero? Or would the Hero turned villain claim his freedom? The fight between a mad warrior and a talented prodigy. Who would prevail?

Tan half noted that the crowd looked a bit larger than first thought, word of the upcoming trial must have spread. Who would pass up seeing a sanctioned fight from the mass murderer, Kill, and the once lost Prince?

Tan stopped before coming to the center of the arena. The crowd grew louder again before the second horn silenced them, and the opposite gate entrance opened. The silence was only barely contained as the crowd held their breath.

"Ladies and gentlemen," the announcer had the same enthusiasm, but he spoke with a reserved temper as the gate came to a stop, "you remember his name, you remember his crimes, without further ado, Killian Peaks."

The sounds of sand crunching before the boots were seen was loud to Tan that it felt like there was no one else there in that moment.

The shadows gave way as first a pair of dirty boots, then ripped trousers of an old uniform Tan recognized design being from the Army of the Realm, which had been disbanded nearly five years ago now due to lack of funds. The man slowly emerged from the holding cell, like a lion from its den.

Tan narrowed his eyes as he watched more of the man appear. A white stained shirt, worn leather breast plate, and forearm guards. In one leather gloved hand the man held a long sword by the blade. The other empty as he moved forward with the grace of a wild cat. Shoulders back, but head lowered, the look of one prepared to spring into action at a moment's notice.

The long sword was a sword that had seen its fair share of combat already, with a huge notch near the hilt guard. Tan's own sword didn't look much worse when he had inspected it. There had been a notch at the point, but he didn't expect it to impede the blades use.

Kill's eyes never leaving Tan as he smoothly glided toward the designated waiting spot. When the man drew close enough Tan took in the man's features. Tan assumed the man was in his forties, with long black hair pulled back out of his face by a cloth tie. The tips of the man's black beard were turning a shade grey-white hair that draped around his scarred face. The man's eyes glinted in the light, a shade of gold like that of the fresh morning light reaching across the sky, not white but not quite sun yellow. The man had a small scar that ran over his lips, making a sideways cross made crooked by the sneering smile on the man's face.

"Well, well, well. Look what we have here. So… the little Fire Prince finally coming into his rightful place, eh? Finally picking up where Daddy left off are we?"

Tan remained silent as the man waited for a response.

"What's the matter, girly? Cat got your tongue?"

Tan remained silent.

"Ah, I see. Someone warned you of me, did they? How thoughtful of them. To cowardly to face me himself, was he?"

"My master does not need to prove himself to you, murderer."

"Ah, so do you have a teacher? I thought there was a rumor spreading around about some old dog giving you some new tricks… clan gossip is all the rage down in the box."

The man thumbed back toward the holding cell that led back to the prison that sat behind the coliseum.

"Tell me, how many Ignus' will Nicodemus let die because of his stoking stubborn head? Is he here?" the man made a weak show of looking into the crowds behind Tan. "Guess he's still a coward letting all the Ignus die for his ignorance."

Tan gritted his teeth. *The man's tactic is to rule you up. Remember what Master Nicodemus said.*

"I wonder what the late *king*," the man rolled his eyes at this, "if anyone actually thinks that man was a king, would say about you training under a man such as that one."

"Wouldn't know. He was always off being *king*."

Which was true. His father, when the man was alive, had been away at war for a good majority of Tan's life. Visiting to see Tan, his mother and sister only for a few cycles before heading back out to fight. *Leaving us and mother alone like that night.*

"Yeeees, I guess that would be the case, wouldn't it? You were quite young when he died, and we were at war with half the world for a bit. Well, maybe that is a good thing. Because there were a lot of things the late king did and ordered us soldiers to do.

Things that you probably shouldn't know about...like how he ordered us *heroes* to murder an entire village that wouldn't surrender to him. The frail people up there," the man glanced to the stands, "can't even fathom, much less stomach, the things he had us do. Yet, they blame us for what we had been ordered to do. And when asked about it the king always seemed shocked that anyone would do such a thing, like he hadn't ordered his men to kill a whole innocent clan house just because one man overheard something he shouldn't have.

"But does he get blamed? Was *he* imprisoned? Nope! Not the good ol' King. He's too honorable and good for that." The man cocked his head as he squinted at Tan. "Are you like that, boy? Are you too good for the rest of us?"

Tan remained silent.

What this man referred to was entirely nonsense. Tan's father had been dead for over three seasons when this crazed man went on his killing spree. These lies were only to confuse Tan.

The announcer was saying something to the crowd, or was that to them? Tan wasn't listening. He watched this mad man, coiled up in his carefree attitude, ready to explode into action at any moment. They were a mere five paces from each other, still standing at their starting points. *If the man made to strike...*

213

Tan slowly brought his sword hand with his sapphire ring to grasp the hilt of his sword, but not drawing the blade yet.

"Oh, that's right! I almost forgot that we are dueling. That old hen up there sure likes to squawk. The clans are so content to wallow in their exile and nomadic life that is slowly ruining this nation. But you wouldn't know too much about that, would you? Always running away to hide."

Tan squeezed the hilt of his blade and gritted his teeth. *If this man was implying...*

"Yes. You ran off with dear old mommy before any of that took place, didn't you? Ran off to hide away from good ol' Daddy's sins and the big evil world. But where is Mommy now? Is she in the crowd?" another mock turn of the crowd, before he stopped, as if realizing something, "Wait... Oh! That's right. She died on the streets, like the little whore she wa —"

The loud *"Clannnnnng"* of the swords crashing into each other reverberated across the arena. Tan's face grew hot as he drove his sword down on the man. Feeling the pulse deep within him roaring to burn this vile man. The man's voice was cut off as Tan had exploded forward, bringing his sword up to catch the blow and directed away from him.

Tan had used a more subtle technique for this sudden attack. By increasing the elemancy he was exporting slowly to fuel the Dragon Armor boots, the power was stored like a dam on the verge of bursting and he allowed the power stored up to launch himself forward as he poked a whole into the dam allowing it to burst forth, propelling him far faster than the average person to his opponent.

"And make sure you don't put too much into it, or you'll stoking crush your foot if you don't watch it. The better you get, the more you can put into them," Nicodemus had said in his rushed crash course of the properties of the armor techniques.

The crowd erupted in exclamations of various degrees, some shouting that the elders hadn't started them yet, and others on the edge of their seats in anticipation.

Tan kept his footing as Kill brought his blade around. The man's longer blade arched around, and Tan could bring his blade up and block the downward strike. Their blades clashed and the bigger man pressed his blade down, locking the blades as Tan used one gloved hand to press against his own blade from beneath for leverage.

"A-and there it is, folks!" The announcer began once he found his voice. "The young Prince makes the opening strike with an impressive forward lunge!'

"Oh-ho ho?" The man smiled down at Tan as a cat might would while playing with its food. "So that's your little itch, huh? Sweet, dear, old Mommy..."

Tan pressed into his sword, face to face with the maniac that was smiling like the King's jester.

Aligning his back leg, Tan was able to gain some leverage on the blades, grunting as Tan bullied the man back to a more evenly matched position. Apparently, the man had not kept up with his strengthening training while in incarceration. With a shove, Tan threw the man back.

"Now, now," the man chided, as he caught his stumble. "Didn't your mother ever tell you to be kind to your elde —"

With a sudden small explosion, Tan launched forward, not like with the enhanced armor boots. This was more like being shot from a bow. While running at a speed that was inhuman and which few Tan suspected could barely keep up with. Like his opponent.

 The man cried out as he swung his sword wildly, a burst of red flames arching across his sword's path. Tan slid underneath and brought his sword up, crashing into the man's lightly armored chest.

The man grunted and Tan kicked the man in the side, causing him to stumble away.

Again Tan moved with the same ferocity, a speed that only allowed him to see the man's eyes growing wide in fright, the white of his eyes almost all you could see before a terrific "*Boom!*" sent him flying off his feet.

Tan had caused a minor explosion to manifest at the edge of his blade as he thrust it at the man's chest. The man's body was tossed backwards into the dirt a good many paces back. Kill coughed a few times as he came to his knees.

Spitting blood to the side, he coughed out, "Nice... one, kid. Wasn't expecting you to use the Flaaa—"

The sound of metal cutting through flesh an instant later had the man grunting in pain, for Tan was not taught to wait when performing his training, instead to follow up, or follow through, to be relentless in battle is the key.

"This is a fight to the death," Tan whispered only so the man could hear, "not some court dialogue for you to tell me your lifelong grudge with a man I hardly know."

The man stared in shock at the blade in his stomach.

"And there's another thing you should know..." — the man's eyes met Tan's, and Tan could see the glowing blue light reflecting in them from his own — "...you will *not* insult my mother."

Then Tan stepped back, kicking the man off his sword. With a snap of his fingers, Kill ignited into a blaze of scorching crimson Fire that was so hot the criminal had no time to scream before he was no more than ashes as the burned husk collapsed to the ground.

And with that, Tan turned from the burning corpse as the crowd cheered.

At first, he felt nothing. Empty, like the vast nothingness of a deep ocean. Then he felt drained, like finishing a long race that took several miles, but with blood on his hands. It was a feeling he didn't like too much. And the words from his mother rang in the back of his head, "*Be a good person.*"

When he met his master's gaze across the pit, Tan felt his chest well up with pride at the glint in the old man's eyes and the hint of a smile, the slight curve of a grin. Tan returned the smile as he made for his next step to his destination.

19

DECEIT

The saddle groaned beneath Tom as he adjusted himself in his saddle. He tugged on his safe line to make sure he was still strapped in. The wings of his gray pegasus a calm rhythm as they soared in the sky. The beast stretched its long powerful wings out to catch the wind as they descended from the cloud cover towards the small caravan moving along the road below.

A gust of wind pushed the pegasus up and back before the horse tucked its wings and dove a good way before leveling out. Tom held onto the reins lightly, allowing the beast to make its way through the sky to their destination.

That the winds were picking up was already a bad sign in Tom's book. It meant that the Autumn Winds were fast approaching. A time when the pegasi were grounded or sent to areas within the provinces that didn't have large gusts of wind that periodically struck the sky. The winds of autumn were not a pleasant thing to be a part of. And for some strange reason, the winds never reached the ground.

The winds would skim the top of trees and buildings but would not affect those upon the ground. A phenomenon that seemed to be naturally accepted by the citizens of the provinces. Even though they had only become this way since the Great War.

It made Tom wonder what really happened to make the winds so angry to where they could snap a pegasi's wings off.

Approaching the caravan, Tom's mount glided in before fluttering it's wings as it lightly dropped into a canter alongside the carriage that held Tom's charge for this trip. The pegasus folded his wings into a neat shell that wrapped around Tom's legs to better maneuver whilst grounded.

"Good boy, Nero," Tom said, patting the horse's neck with a gauntleted hand in praise. "Remind me to get you a fresh bag of oats later."

The horse nodded its head up and down with a snort at this, showing its delight at the potential snack. Tom smiled as he pulled off his helmet to hold in one hand, directing Nero closer to the carriage so that he might speak with the man inside without having to yell what he said. Though he trusted the knights around him, the servants, aids, and other entourage of the man, he did not.

"Mister Tiften?" Tom called into the carriage.

It was a modest craft with fine decorations of silver and maroon curtains for privacy. Knobbed fingers pulled the curtain of the window back as a man in his late fifties stuck his head out.

"Yes, Sir Fulmen?"

"I am do to inform you that there is a forest ahead and that we will be moving the caravan around the woods so that-"

"Around some woods? Again? How long might this one take?" the man seemed annoyed and worried at the same time.

"Well sir, it will add in a half day's ride. But we-" Tom was cut short again.

"Absolutely not! I gave into your little stunts last time we came upon that last group of trees. That had added an entire day to the trip, and you had said that it would have only taken a third of that. *Now* you say half a day?!"

It was only a day's worth because you had us stop so that your cooks might prepare you a feast that lasted for the afternoon. Tom almost said this aloud, but bit his tongue.

"No. We will go through the woods. I am already late as it is. The king requested that I get this done as fast as possible and I will do just that! So, move us faster, *Knight!*" then he slammed the curtains back.

He keeps using the word fast, Tom mused, *and I don't think he knows what it means.*

With a sigh, Tom did as the Mister instructed. Tom was the security head, but the Mister was the party's leader for this mission they were tasked with. The simple task of collecting the tax statements from the southern province.

Glancing at the sky to see five other pegasi and knights flying around the caravan in a scouting pattern. They had seen several woods and avoided a majority of them. With the potential ambushes by bandits being a dire threat, Tom and his knights had aired on the side of caution rather than haste.

But the Mister had finally had enough of being safe. He must think that six Tempus Knights can hold off an entire arm of bandits.

Not if there are other Elementalists we can't. Tom moved Noro forward and away from the road to a full gallop as the pegasi spread its wings slowly and then pushed back into the sky. Tom was always amazed the beast made it into the air with him in full plate upon its back. But the beast did it. Tom glanced out to see electricity running across the bird like gray feathers as the horse flapped its wings.

"What did he say?" called another knight riding a white pegasus, as Tom and his mount came level with him. The Tempus Knight Sir Remington, the knight of Titin with a large fist indented upon his chest plate.

"We are to head through the woods."

"To the Seven Hells with this fool! Is he trying to get himself killed? He does know we are not but a few leagues away from the Bandit War, right?"

"I know. Just keep your heads about you. Tell Drent, Berrdy and Hastings to stay above the caravan. You, me, and Landel will land and travel by foot."

"Aye, Fulmen."

Remington spurred his mount around to send the message along to the other knights. And as Tom watched the disgruntled knight inform the other knights, he couldn't help but agree with his friend.

It wasn't as bad as Tom had first thought it would be. The woods had very little undergrowth with a thick canopy, and the trees were spaced far enough apart that he could see for a long way. The sounds of the woods echoed around them as horses and men trudged along the beaten path.

"I don't like this," Remington stated. "It feels…odd. Like we can only hear what's inside the woods."

Tom raised an eyebrow at the man. "That may be the strangest thing you've said to me."

The knight shrugged in reply.

"Don't know what to tell you. But that's what it sounds like."

Tom shook his head as Noro plodded along. They rode near the front of the caravan of three wagons, one carriage, ten-foot soldiers, and four horsed knights. Regular horses, not pegasi as pegasi weren't as plentiful or easy to train.

Landel was at the back of the long train to bring up the rear. They had been traveling along the road for about half a league when Tom thought he heard the sounds of a loud thud off to his left.

"Do you hear that?" Remington asked. They searched the woods, but nothing moved. The woods were suddenly quiet as the creatures within felt the tension as well. There were some falling leaves and Tom almost wrote it off as a tree limb falling.

"You see that?" one soldier asked further back in the line. "Over there, next to that tree? Something shiny."

Tom pulled Noro around and Remington followed.

"Where?" Tom ordered.

"There sir," the soldier pointed to one of the larger trees where something large seemed to be hidden within its shadow. "Can't tell what it is though..."

Tom turned Noro, and they shot toward the object. Tom felt his heart beating inside his plate so loud he thought his ears were ringing.

The form grew to that of a body, two bodies. One smaller one in armor crushed by the larger form of a horse with wings.

The sound that Remington had hinted at earlier seemed to disappear as Tom suddenly heard the clashes of metal, the screams of men and beast fighting high above.

"Ambush!" Tom cried out. He slammed on his helmet and turned to the caravan. The men there were positioning themselves in a defensive posture around the wagons and carriage with swords drawn. Officers were screaming orders to hold their lines and prepare for attack when a shout pulled Tom away.

"Fulman!" Remington cried out.

Tom whirled around and only saw the form of a man in shadows as he was tackled from his steed. Noro neighed in fright, rearing back as a lightning bolt struck the large tree behind him.

With a grunt, Tom hit the ground and rolled, tossing the body that had seized him away. He came to his feet gripping his sword hilt, watching as the nimble form of a man in dark black robes and hood flipped to his feet, pulling out two wicked curved blades.

Tom drew his blade out of its scabbard slowly, the sunlight gleaming from the polished metal blade as he raised it with both hands to assume a forward neutral stance. The assassin cocked it's head as if judging what to do next before reaching behind and pulling a small pouch and throwing it at Tom.

Tom instinctively stepped back, slashing his blade at the sack before it hit him. The bag burst into sand that the assassin leapt through, blades raised.

Tom grunted as he dropped his now leading armored shoulder into the assassin's gut, passing the dangerous attack with brute force.

The assassin lost his blades with a huff of air and landed on the ground with a thud. Gasping for air as Tom recovered instantly.

Without hesitation, Tom acted, instincts of an entire season of war with bandits, thieves and cutthroats had taught him to act in the face of victory. A respite now would mean death.

He rotated his grip to reverse, driving the sharp tip down into the assassin's exposed stomach, pinning the body to the ground with a sickening *"shlunk"*. Tom felt the assassin's body spasm, then relax under him, the telltale sign of the soul leaving the body.

Using his boot to pull the blade free, Tom turned to see what more needed doing. He had heard fighting and as he scanned the woods nearest him, he found the end of a fight.

Remington was now slumped awkwardly in his saddle of his confused mount that could now smell the blood of the dying around it. Another black robes assassin, smaller than the one Tom had faced, stood with a strange weapon that was looped around the knight's neck.

"No!" Tom roared as he moved on the assassin.

But this time, he did not use the simple forms of the sword. Drawing upon the power stored within the blade's gem, Tom let a bolt of lightning arc across the space between him and the assassin, directing the flow of the power into the subject.

The assassin lunged behind a tree that took the attack with an ear shattering *crack!* The tree groaned and Tom was forced to jump out of the way of the falling tree. Coming up, he brought the blade, high gripping it like a pole ax to block an attack of a shadow nearest him. The action was too slow, and thankfully his helm protected him from the glancing blow to his head as what looked like a vine lashed out at him.

A Nature Elementalist? Tom brought his sword up and cut the vine before it was able to snare him, as the assassin came whirling at him with a spinning thrust of a thin fencing blade.

Why would a Nature Elementalist be here? He was familiar with their fighting style a bit, the Tempus Knights were taught a great many forms of fighting, but it was still odd to find one this deep within the Provinces.

If Tom was right, he would need to stay on his guard. The group that was usually known for this sort of ambush was not to be taken lightly.

Tom paired the weak attack of the small blade aside and countered by pushing his blade point back down the length into his opponent's flesh. This assassin was skilled but far weaker and inexperienced compared to Tom, who wore his Silver Armor that enhanced him far more than the normal person and battle reflexes honed by several years of training and an entire season at war.

Tom drove the blade directly into the assassin's heart. The assassin cried out as the blade pierced flesh and Tom sunk the blade into his enemy. He met the eyes of the assassin with a grimace.

"That...was for Remington..." Tom growled.

Then he pulled the blade free, spinning it around to lop the assassin's head from its shoulders just for good measure. He didn't wait for the body to hit the ground as he spun to meet a third Shadow. Which confirmed his suspicions.

A three-man hit team, all wearing hoods, and dark robes, and with a potential fourth member. These were Shadow League assassins. But who would hire the Shadows to take out some low-ranking bureaucrat?

This assassin was far bigger than the previous two, as big as Tom *in* his armor. The massive assassin brought his broadsword down and Tom caught the blade with his own, their cross guards locking as the assassin pushed into Tom with all his weight.

Tom strained to keep the man from forcing him to his knees. The effort was a strain on him, so he seeped some power into the armor.

"I'll kill you!" the berserker yelled at Tom.

"You can try," Tom grunted from behind his helmet. With a grunt, the man pushed Tom even further back. "What are you? A bull?"

They were in a shoving match now. They were so close that Tom almost thought of just head butting the man. But felt it would over expose him if it didn't have the desired effect on such a large opponent. As they tussled, Tom could see the man's exposed neck, unlike the mask covering his mouth and nose, and he got a glimpse of a tattoo. It looked like some winged rat...a bat? The man roared again, bring Tom to focus on the man's sudden denied strength.

Tom grabbed his own blade with his metal encased fingers further to the end to push like a pole into the man's downward momentum. Then, Tom had the stupidest idea. With a war cry, he gathered all the energy stored within the sword's gem and released it in directly into the man's sword.

With a guttural roar, the man locked up, dropping his sword as electricity fried his nervous system. Tom watched the man's eyes roll backwards before the body crumbled to the ground.

Panting, Tom took in the situation.

Turning to the road, he saw several soldiers on the ground, and the carriage the Mister had been in looked intact, except for the torn curtains and the gnarled finger hand draped limply out the window with blood stains.

Then he caught the faintest sound of a whistle.

Tom rolled and came up with his sword raised for another attack. The sound of two thuds in the tree he had been near indicated whatever projectiles had been thrown at him.

"Well done," a voice commented from a shadow to Tom's left.

"Stix!" Tom spun, angling his blade towards the sound to prepare for the attack...that never came.

"*Very* good reflexes. You are quite a warrior, young knight."

Tom kept his blade leveled at the Shadow, peering down the length of the polished metal reflecting sunlight. He noticed the bit of blood still on the end and along one edge.

Focusing on the tree, he attempted to discern where the Shadow stood. The tree sat at an angle towards the shadows, allowing the assassin to remain hidden.

Until slowly, a form stepped just to the edge of the darkness. The hood still hid most of the face, along with the cloth mask, but now Tom could face the demon before him. And this truly was the demon of the four.

This would be the master, the other three just trainees. Most true Shadow League assassins were usually solo, or a mentor for a new batch of potential assassins.

"Who sent you!?" Tom ordered. He adjusted his grip for a maximum thrust if he needed to attack or defend. Holding his arms up and close to his chest as he slowly maneuvered around the assassin.

"How do you know someone sent me?" The assassin asked.

"Why else would you be here?"

"Maybe to settle a debt? Or perhaps I am a bandit come to liberate this caravan of all its goods?"

"I am no fool, assassin. Why were you hired to kill the Mister? Who was the one ordering you to fight against the king?"

"Fight *against* the king?" the assassin chuckled. "Now that is rich, since we were hired by one of his aids."

Tom froze at this statement. His sword blade dropped before he realized what he was doing.

"You're lying!" he leveled the blade back at the Shadow. "You came to rob, kill, and sow deceit. But what I want to know is why?" Tom would not allow this man to dissuade him from his duty.

"They did say you were smarter than you look. Well, in any case, *I* have completed what we came to set out, regardless of these..."

The assassin glanced at the three bodies Tom dispatched, "...disappointments. I hold no resentment to you and your duty, and bid you farewell, sir knight. May we never meet again..."

The Shadow slithered deeper into the tree's shadow,

"Coward!" Tom roared as he lunged for the Shadow.

Tom's sword only struck wood as the assassin disappeared without a trace.

Tom finally felt the fatigue of battle wash over him as Linden rushed to his side. But he had no energy to engage the man as he knelt before the tree as if in prayer.

"Fulmen? Fulman! Sir Thomas!"

Tom could hear his name being called, but the effects of releasing so much elemancy was distorting his thoughts. Then a hand gripped his shoulder and lightly shook him. Turning, he met the face of a young red bearded knight.

"Landel?" Tom shook his head, remembering himself. He reached up and removed his helmet, taking the surrounding scene more fully now. Landel looked battered but unharmed, other than a bruise upon his forehead. Three bodies in black lie around him, one in armor a ways off, six soldiers near the caravan, and the Mister in the carriage.

"Where is..."

"Dead. The other four are...dead, sir. It's just us."

Tom blinked at the man's blunt words.

"All of them?"

The knight nodded. "There was some sort of flying bat that attacked them. I only saw it after it killed the last one...Drent, I think? How did we not notice that?"

Tom did not answer, for he did not want to sow anymore fear in the men of Druids and Wraiths. If the men got spooked at every shadow, Tom would have a hard time getting them to safety. They still had a league to go to reach the capital.

"We will find out later, have the men gather the dead in the carriage and stow the wounded in among the wagons. We are too vulnerable here."

"Y-yes sir!"

"And gather those bodies," Tom pointed to the three bodies in black robes. "They may hold answers..."

Tom trailed off as he realized the bodies were now smoking, as if a Fire had been started. And then a Green Fire engulfed the bodies with such intense heat that Tom could feel it through his armor. Tom watched dumbfounded as the bodies burnt away to ash within ten heartbeats.

All of that evidence, it might as well be scattered into the winds now. He cursed the gods turning from the bodies as he reached into the small sack tied to his waist of various items and grabbed the cleaning cloth to clean his sword before sheathing it within its scabbard.

The men thankfully hadn't seen this event as they attended to their tasks. It had happened so fast that Tom had been helpless to do anything. The cowardice and then the desecration of the bodies were so dishonorable that Tom wished he could chase after that last assassin and kill him as well.

The sounds of a horse plodding up behind him and the huff of breath as Noro brushed the back of Tom's head with his snout gave Tom a small comfort.

He turned to meet the beast's face. Giving the horse's head a good scratch on his forehead. The pegasus nudged its head into his hand to get Tom to feed him.

"I am glad you were not harmed, my friend. Let's get out of here so I can get you those oats."

The assassin had tried to fool him, he was certain. They had been here to assassinate the Mister. But he could not think of a reason why. The man had been a snob. This much was true, but not warranting a Shadow contract. There was something more at play here. Tom just couldn't see it.

Tom set his jaw as he turned to stare at where the bodies had been moments ago. His eyes drifted to where his friend, his brother, now lay motionless in his brilliant armor, now stained red. Tom would do better next time. He would not let his drive to be overcome because of a stupid decision of an ignorant fool.

Tom went over and bent to the body, stripping the silver armor and wrapping the body in cloth for travel. He would be laid to rest with the fallen in the great tomb of valor. Tom would ensure that he performs the proper rights. When he finished stowing the valuable armor on his friend's mount, and placing the body across it. He moved to Noro, who was standing alert next to him.

A pegasus trotted up next to Tom, the last remaining knight in his troop holding the reins of two pegasus carrying the bodies of the other fallen knights. Tom looked away, feeling as though he had failed these men in so many ways. What would he tell their families?

"We are ready to move, sir," Landel reported.

Tom nodded and was just about to swing up and into his own saddle when a lightning flash and a loud boom of thunder cracked overhead.

"What is that?" Landel asked.

Tom swung into the saddle, passing off the reins of the last fallen knight to Landel, sliding his helm on, and letting Noro race to the more open canopy of the road and launch into the sky.

Breaking the through the trees, Tom scanned the now clear skies.

The flapping wings caught his eye almost immediately. The silver armor of the knight upon the approaching winged horse shone in the light of the falling sun.

Flapping in the wind, the sight of the Lord Commander's banner upon the knight's spear made Tom worried something far worse things than an ambush from assassins was on the horizon.

20

TO BE KING

"Congratulations!" Gran stood in front of those who passed with two other warriors holding bowls of liquid. "You have each passed the Trial. Step forward to receive your Huntsman name and receive the mark of the Hunt."

Being last, Tan stood behind Dancer in line as they waited for each to step up. The deer-skinned tent was lit by an ominous red Flame that sat in the hearth behind the small, carpeted platform that Gran stood upon.

All in attendance wore the ritual furs and cloth, as the huntsman of old would have. The decorations around the room were fashioned as such. Tan felt the softness of the fur carpet against his bare feet, as he had been stripped of everything except his trousers and undershirt after being newly blooded.

Tan watched Dancer, so excited that she was bouncing on her toes, with a huge smile on her face. A content smile on his own as he felt the looming decision coming closer and closer with each Blood born moving forward to take their place, along with the many thousands of Huntsmen before them.

"Tan, can you believe it?! We did it! After all that time and training, it paid off. We passed!"

Tan hoped his smile in turn was as excited as she looked for within. Tan felt...hollow.

"Hard to believe," He replied. Though he said these words, he felt no joy within himself over his accomplishments. It felt more like there was still more to do. But here he stood on the verge of accomplishing his first task of becoming a Huntsman. And after this, he would finish his training with his master and continue to become even stronger. *"There is always someone out there stronger than you. You train for them, not the ones you can beat,"* a bit of wisdom Master Nicodemus had imparted on him.

This test had been so far beneath the training that his master was teaching him that it had felt more of a distraction than anything. He was only here because his master had told him to be, not for the clan or the broken kingdom that his name held claim over. In truth, it wasn't even *his* name that held power, it was Ignus. That this wasn't the first time that Tan had killed...was that why he felt this way?

The beating rhythm he felt within had what felt like a rhythm of irritation, as it wasn't allowed forth to consume the enemy as it had wished. As if it knew there was something, or someone, that was still out there, but Tan didn't know exactly what that meant. Who else was out there? And why did he feel anxious about it?

Pushing these thoughts aside, he did as instructed, waiting while he watched Dancer step up with almost a girlish glee to her step. Gran smiled as Dancer took a knee before her, the girl attempting to control her excitement as she bowed her head.

"My child, rise and accept the sign, for you are now known as FireDancer."

Dancer rose with an even brighter smile now as Gran dipped her thumb into the ink bowl one of the warriors carried and drew a small flame on Dancer's forehead. The ink ran down her nose a bit before drying quickly.

"Thank you, Gran," Dancer whispered, then bowed and stepped away to another warrior who gave her a Huntsman's robe, a new rope dart that had black ink staining the rope with a bejeweled anchor point for her to store her power within.

Next, she was given a new breast plate armor with the phoenix of clan Ignus emblazoned upon it, and led her toward the tent flap.

That was all Tan caught as he stepped forward, kneeling before his grandmother, eyes upon the carpeted ground at his feet. He felt... strange kneeling in such a way that left him vulnerable to attack from those around him, even if they were fellow clansman and huntsman.

Tan did not feel comforted by it. It was to display that he was loyal to the clan and those within it. That he would offer his life for the clan.

"Rise, my child, and accept the sign, for you are known as Dragonborn, for your Fire comes from their breath." She smiled with pride in her eyes, as he looked up; most likely she was the one to choose the name for him.

All new Bloods were allowed to keep their original names, and most did, but many warriors used their new names as a brand of honor. Tan would most likely just add it as a second name between his true name and clan house.

Putting on a smile, he stood, closed his eyes, and felt his Gran's finger as she painted the symbol across his forehead. After she finished, Tan opened his eyes and was about to step off before he stopped at the sound of a rustling tent flap behind him. Tan turned to see that two clan elders, then Nicodemus, his uncle, and an older man in red robes, entered the tent.

Tan also noticed that the Owl Legion, with his bold tattooed head and gray assassin robes, as he now knew them to be, had suddenly appeared in the tent's corner as if he had been there all along. Tan blinked at the old man before turning back to Gran.

"What's this?" Tan asked. All he wanted was to know why he wasn't being treated equally. He assumed he would receive a sword since he had been partially trained in using one. He received his Huntsman attire, but no new weapon. He wasn't angry, just slightly disappointed. And then, after receiving his new armor, he would be led away like the others to the feast...or, at least, he should have.

"Good day, your highness, I am Magus Ardoris of the Mage Association. I am here to formally request that you attend the Mage Academy to become a Mage Champion. This is to help the stability of the country as king, and head huntsman. From your performance here today, you have exceeded all expectations and have so much more potential that we of the Mage Association would most graciously wish to help guide you in."

Tan crossed his arms; he felt like this man, as old as he looked, was strange, but that was beside the point at the moment.

They want me to be a Mage Champion? Why? Were the Mages expecting another war to break out? In past records they were known to do so to prepare for a looming disaster or some terrible war...

"Thanks." Tan nodded to Nicodemus. "But I already have a master. And no offence, old man, but I prefer to remain with him."

"Is that so?" Sage Fuma stepped forward with a sly grin. "Well then, do you wish to take your place as king? You are now a man of legal age, and have completed the trials. And, from my understanding, you have actually *completed* your training with the Captain, especially after the performance you have displayed during the trial..."

"Completed?" Tan looked to Nicodemus.

"Now, listen here Sage, I said he was *near* completion with me, not that he had finished training." Nicodemus glared at the silver tongued elder next to him. "Don't you *dare* go twisting my words like some Province politician."

"Wouldn't dream of it, Captain." The man turned back to Tan. "So, I take that as a no, then?"

"No! I'm not."

The room grew a bit too quiet for Tan's liking at his proclamation. He turned to Gran.

"Did I say something wrong?"

"By saying no," Sage Fuma stepped in, "you forfeit your birthright to the throne. You still have a right to it, but now, so does every other member of the clans."

"So, anyone can take it, is what you're saying?"

"Yes…" The old man drew out the word as if contemplating if he should answer before Tan interrupted.

"Good, then my answer remains the same."

"*What?!*" several people said at once. Tan looked from Orion, to Gran, and then back.

"If you want to remain in control, put Dancer or someone else from the clan up for the throne," Tan answered. "I don't want it."

This made Sage Fuma's face light up with a grin that Tan almost thought fox like. Orion stepped forward to convince Tan to rethink his answer. His gran and Nicodemus were both attempting to do the same, and the voices all just meshed into one loud shouting fit.

GrandMaster Traès stood in the back with raised eyebrows and an amused smile playing across his face as he watched madness unfold.

The mage attempted to placate, Orion recited creeds of responsibility, Gran pleaded for Tan to see reason, and Master Nicodemus just seemed to wish for an answer as to why.

Having enough, Tan shouted and tossed flames that dissipated over everyone's heads.

"Enough!"

The sudden bright red of the hearth grew, causing a few to flinch.

The room grew silent, and when Tan looked over the faces, he received a bunch of mixed expressions. Some were of fear, anger, confusion, but only one seemed amused by the entire thing.

"I said no! I will not be taking the throne. Not as some stoking impulse, but because even if I did, I have nothing but empty promises and blood on my hands thanks to the actions my father took during the great war."

He turned at Gran. "You said so yourself, Gran. I'm not ready."

Sage Fuma's eyes glittered even more then, as Tan glanced around. He met Orion's confused face and decided a compromise was in order if he were to be given a reprieve for his decision.

"If the throne isn't taken by the time I am finished, and there is no suitable candidate by the time of the Trial of Kings, then I will take the trial. But for now, you will not find a candidate in me. Not until I work through some of my own...faults. And to you, *Mage*." Tan turned to the old man in red robes. "I have a Master. I don't need you."

Tan glanced over at the Owl, then to the mage.

"Also, I thought that you Mages didn't like Druids or some such?"

The bald assassin smiled from his corner.

"Indeed, your highness," the Mage turned and gave the GrandMaster a respectable head bow, "However, the Owl and his creed are a...how should I say? Special case."

"I see."

The room remained silent after this, taking in all that had just happened. Tan took the room in, meeting the confused faces of those he cared deeply for but could not truly explain his reasonings. About his promises to his mother. He wouldn't let that dying promise end here. He refused to let anyone stop him.

"I'm going to return to my training tomorrow," Tan announced. "That is my priority right now. If anyone needs me, you know where to find me. But know that if it has anything to do with that *stoking* throne, I won't have any part of it!"

With that Tan turned on his heel, slapping the tent flap out of the way, and leaving the path others had tried to set up for him behind. He had a different path to follow.

21

PROMISES

The shock of what the boy had said didn't quite register with Nic until the others began speaking in worried tones, or smug pride in Fuma's case.

Abree was attempting to send Orion after the boy to talk sense into him. The young clan had attempted to calm his warmongering mother. Nic thought he might have seen smoke coming from her ears at the amount of worry the woman was putting off. The other elders of the Ignus clan and Houses whispered in hushed tones of what they should start planning on doing next.

Nic shook his head. *The stoking fools didn't even give a second thought to getting the boy back. Shows how much they really cared.* Though the boy had just given up the throne...so Nic guessed he could permit some haste in figuring out what to do next. If this was what the boy truly wanted.

Nic knew it was, though, and knew the elders were making the right decision in moving forward. When that boy made up his mind there was little to no stopping him.

Nic glanced and saw Arien standing with an amused smile on his face as he watched the events unfold around him. *The man wants this to happen,* Nic realized. *The stoking assassin wants the boy*

238

for himself, after all. What better way than to separate him from his responsibilities and clan?

Then Magus Ardoris clapped his hands. But not in the normal way. When he clapped in succession, he seemed to create a small concussion of Fire that erupted, creating a small crack that captured everyone's attention. Smoke rose from his hands, but the man seemed unaffected as he crossed them into his robe sleeves.

"Thank you," the mage bowed his head. "I believe that there are things to be discussed later, especially since there will now need to be a King's Trial to be held. I will now be returning to the Association, unless my assistance is still needed?"

When no one said otherwise, he nodded.

"Thank you for allowing me to attend this cycle's Trials and I hope to be back for the next one." The man bowed to Abree and Orion, "Matron Abree, a pleasure as always. Prince Orion, thank you for your hospitality."

"Our pleasure, GrandMaster," Orion said, stepping forward and giving the mage a respectable head bow.

Then the mage turned to Nicodemus. Eyeing him as if he were debating whether it was a good idea to say anything. They had not parted on friendly terms last time. Throwing that aside, the man bowed to Nic.

"Captain, I apologize for springing that upon you earlier and the young prince. I had not the opportunity to speak to either of you before now and fear it worked against me. Still, *it is* good to see you in good health."

Nic blinked before giving a head nod, his attempt at being respectable even though he didn't want to.

"Have a safe trip back, Magus."

The man gave a small warm smile and Nic saw the appreciation in his eyes as the man exited the tent.

Others followed soot, retiring for the evening or too more private tents. Until it was just Abree, Orion, Nic, and...the Owl. Nic gave the assassin a flat stare.

"What?" the old man still had that stupid smile upon his face. "If you recall, I promised to not influence the boy while he was in your care. I have done nothing to him, mystically, or psychologically. If anything, I dare say there is something more behind the boy's motives than he lets on."

Nic remained silent as he watched Abree's expression darken towards the druid.

"Now listen here, you—"

"He's right, Bree..." Nic cut her short. Closing his eyes in preparation for her verbal and physical attacks.

When none came, he cracked an eye to see her standing with her head low. Her eyes searching the carpeted floor as if it held the answer as to what happened.

"I think we do as the boy said, and leave it be for now," Nic finally said. "We won't get any answers tonight..."

"He's right, mother." Orion, bless the lad, wrapped a comforting arm around his mother, who stood an awkward head shorter than the giant. So, it was more of a strange side hug. "Let us rest. In the morning, we will decide what to do."

The woman seemed to be in a daze as she let Orion lead her from the tent. Nic watched as a woman who had not only lost a son, but her daughter-in-law, granddaughter, and now grandson in just a few short years.

The Owl was beside Nic now. Nic did not need to turn to feel the man's presence. The assassin was very adapt at hiding it when he wanted to.

"The actions the young prince has taken up to this point, leaving the clans, taking a teacher who has self-exiled himself, completing the Trials with ease, and now pushing the responsibility of kingship aside, they have all been *his* decisions. The sooner you realize that. And what he is attempting to do, the faster you can help him accomplish his goals."

"And what might those be?" Nic asked, not turning to the man as he spoke.

"Whether or not those foolish elders care to admit it, they abandoned the boy long ago. When the boy's mother died, it only solidified it. He is attempting to fill that space. And I fear he has made you a part of it. And I am not so sure that is a good thing, my friend."

Nic didn't have the same zeal he would normally as he spoke "What do you suggest I do?"

The day's events had drained him. He was not as young as he had once been. *Curse this druid for being able to stay lively for so long.*

"Help him, in the best way you can. Let him go."

And with that, Nic felt the assassin's presence vanish. When Nic glanced about, he stood in a deserted ritual tent.

Tan grabbed the small sack he had brought and began stuffing his belongings into it. As he reached for his spare clothes, the flap of his small tent kicked open and Dancer came storming in. Tan let his head hang, an inward groan wanting to escape, before sighing and turning to meet her glare. She stood hands on hips, foot tapping away, with creased eyebrows and a red face.

"Just like that!?" she tossed her hands about animatedly. "You're leaving, again?!"

He sat up to better talk to her. "Dancer..."

"No!" she shook her head as she stepped into the tent. "No. Not again. *You* said you would be done after you finished your training with Nicodemus, remember? Or was that a *lie?* From what I heard, Nicodemus says you've basically finished. So why not come back home? What about what we had talked about?"

Even as she said the words, he knew then that he wouldn't come back. Home? He didn't have a home, not since his mother had died. Yes, the clans are home, but not in the way it used to be. After his mother died, he had nothing, not a penny to his name. In fact, his name was all he truly had, in a way.

Though, he guessed Dancer could fit into it. The hyperactive, aloof cousin? Gran was trying to make him be the king, despite her conflicting emotions. And Uncle Orion was, for lack of a better term, a mamma's boy.

And now he had Nicodemus, and at least with the old veteran Tan had someone…someone he didn't know where to place yet. He hadn't put much thought into it.

Tan knew one thing, he wouldn't be able to come back to the clans after today for quite some time. With the way he had left things within the ritual tent…

"Dancer, I… I can't. Not right now. I'm sorry…" was all he could say.

She stood above him for a minute, glaring at him as he met her gaze. Tears began to well up in her eyes.

Then the sound of the warning horn sounded, sharp and clear from the watchtower. There was a bandit party nearby, nothing Tan needed to worry about, but clearly Dancer was going. Though he could see the conflicting emotions in her as tears welled up in her eyes as she glared from him to the direction of the horns.

"You-" she coughed to clear her throat before continuing. "When you finish, you're coming back, r-right?"

Tan felt his heart plummet at this question, to which he had no answer to. Would he? His goals seemed to not align with him returning to the clans. If the mages offered more training, he guessed he might have to take them up on their offer eventually if the Magus said there was still far more for him to learn, and Nicodemus had finished teaching him all the veteran knew…

Dancer seemed to read his answer in his eyes and a tear fell down her cheek. With a solemn nod and a cough to hide what he suspected was a sob, she turned and smashed the tent flap out of her way as she exited with a fury.

With a sigh, Tan resumed packing his small bag of the one extra pair of clothing he had brought and the armor Master Nicodemus had gifted him.

Tan stared at the armor wrapped in cloth, rubbing a thumb over the fabric as he decided. He would return and finish training under his master, then he would search to find another teacher, or take the Magus up on his offer, and that would be that. Maybe afterwards he might return to the clans. He would only finish after completing his training under his master. He would keep his promise.

22

NIGHTMARE AWAKE

Tan lay back in a grassy field, letting the warm summer airbrush his skin. He twirled a long piece of grass between his fingers, studying the way it moved in the air.

Relaxed in the sun, he couldn't help but smile. He had completed the trials and was now back at the cabin, about to learn the secret of the Fire Guard and what it took to be a Master Elementalist.

A noise distracted him. He heard a weird croaking sound from behind him. He stretched his neck back until he could see what it was.

Strange... why is the Master's Ravin here? Tan mused as he twisted over.

The bird cocked its head before hopping about a bit, getting ever closer to him.

Tan pushed up until he was sitting back on his knees, the bird quickly hopping up and then pecking his knee and then hopping back. It was cocking its head in a way Tan could only interpret as an expression of confusion. Tan didn't know what to make of it. The bird did this several times. But after every peck, he would start to hop further and further away.

Tan stood and took a step after the bird. The bird squeaked happily. It hopped ahead of him in the grass before taking flight and flapping over the next hill. Tan chased after it, smiling all the while.

This was such an odd thing to happen to him. Usually, the bird just hovered around his master or laughed at Tan whenever he failed or when Nicodemus reprimanded him. And the thing *never* interacted with anyone, unless Nicodemus nodded his head or yelled at it to fly away.

The bird flew ahead of Tan, close to touching the hill as it glided up and over. Tan padded up the mound after it. But his run slowed to a trot and then a cautious walk as he watched the black bird land upon a branch of an immense tree.

Tan slowly looked up as the large trees towered over him. The forest floor was a sea of mist with the occasional bush popping out. Not only that, but the trail he had been running along plowed straight into the ominous woods.

The wind picked up and threw itself into him. He steadied himself and turned to see three large tornadoes slowly following the path he had just taken.

The Ravin croaked at him from the tree line.

"Wake up..."

The echoes of the words rippled all around him. The wind tossed it away from him and into the forest. He took a step back.

"Why?" he asked.

A sudden change of wind pushed Tan from the woods.

The Ravin twitched its head.

"They aaare near!" the bird cawed at him, hopping from its perch to a lower limb.

"Who? Who is near?" Tan was confused. What was this bird talking about? *How* was it talking?

"If your highness does not hurry, it will be a sahd morning. A sahd one indeed," it croaked, before shouting out another series of Ravin calls.

Then it spread its wings and flapped away. Many feathers twirled about like the tornadoes behind, engulfing him. He batted the black feathers away, watching them fall to the ground and degrade to a black sandy substance.

When he looked up, dead black trees scattered the dunes about him. He had heard of a place such as this, the Black Sand Desert.

"There will be dark times ahead..."

Tan whirled around to see a red-tattered robed figure standing in the black sand. The hood covered the face and clutching to a staff with a red ruby set at the top.

"If you do not make a decision, they will take advantage of us, young prince. You need to decide. What will you do?"

At that Tan knew he was speaking with the Fire Mage from the tests. The mage had seemed nice at first. But the way he and the elders had talked about Tan like some prized pig, something to use, something to obtain like an artist's collection, it had sent a Fire chill in the back of Tan's mind.

"*Why*!? *Why* should I?! I don't want to lead them. And they clearly don't want me! They didn't even know I was still alive! The only ones who really want me to rule are people who wish to use me. All of you are nothing but power hungry liars looking to gain respect for where you have lost it."

The man stood in the sand like a lone tower against the storm.

"And all *you* want to do is use me like some tool. No thanks. I'm not someone's lap dog that does parlor tricks for them on the occasional whim..."

"It's not too late." The mage said it as if he hadn't heard Tan. "You will need to decide. The Rau are close at hand. I will see you again, young prince." The dust around the man kicked up.

"No, stop asking! *Hey!* I'm not finished with you yet!" Tan launched himself at the man, but before he could grab the man's robes, the figure crumbled back to black sand.

With that, the black, lifeless trees and black grainy sands swirled about until they morphed into that of a dark alley that twisted and turned deep into a city.

Trash blew about so much that one could barely see.

The street looked like the one from his childhood.

One of dirt, grime that never truly left, and dark loneliness that is never truly forgotten.

For how can one forget when they lived it most of their life?

Then it all halted, and the scene fell away to blackness.

Still, like the world stopped spinning and came to a point frozen in time. Tan felt the weight. That crushing heaviness within his chest as he heard that sound... that sound that haunted his dreams.

"Hagitan?" called a voice as familiar as the smell of the sea.

Out of the darkness, Tan could make out a disfigured, stumbling woman. But this thing was not who he remembered. As the thing with the voice of his mother stumbled slowly toward him, he knew this was not her. His mother had a warming smile that made him feel safe, her large crystal blue eyes inviting and understanding.

With tattered clothes and hair that was a mockery of its former beauty, the corpse slowly met his eyes. Beady, white, empty eyes stared back at Tan. A bone-thin, deformed claw reached out to him in an act that made him step away.

"Tan... My little Fire...why did you leave me...?"

Tan jolted awake! Sitting up with a scream caught in his throat, he forced it back down.

Gasping for air, he sat in his bed rubbing sweat from his face. He leaned back with his arm over his sweating forehead, panting. The dream had been a bit much this time and was by far the strangest one he had ever had.

Then he frowned. Sweating? Why was he sweating? He was sweating as much as the first day he had arrived at the cabin. Had the dream disturbed him that much?

Calming his breathing, he focused on his heat and stored it away within his ring. But it was not quite enough, as he felt his mouth was dry from what he assumed had been yelling in his sleep. He rotated off the bed to his feet and walked to his small cabinet in his room. The cup of water he had pre-poured before bed went down fast. But it was not enough to quench his thirst.

Brushing a bit of water from his lips, he grabbed his undershirt from the back of his chair, punching his arm through the shirt as he tiptoed down the hallway to the lavatory. The wooden floor creaked ever so quietly. He cringed, hoping that it didn't wake the old man sleeping downstairs.

He listened... but could hear nothing. Though it was strange to not hear any snoring from Tyrone outside, Tan assumed the enormous beast must be off near the volcano, warming up. It was beginning to get chilly outside and the light snow would soon be upon them. Even with the volcano so close, the temperature did do weird turns every now and again. When they had been flying back from the trials a few days ago, he had felt a cooler breeze.

Smoothly shuffling his feet so as not to make any more boards squeak, he pushed into the lavatory. Coming to the metal tank of water, he put the cup underneath the tap, uncorked the top, and twisted the knob.

As water slowly trickled into the cup, he listened for any rustling from downstairs for any indications that he had woken his master. When he heard nothing, he tightened the tap back and put the cork back on top. He took a mouthful of the water and sighed in satisfaction at the cool fresh water of the previous day's chores coming in handy again. Content, he turned and stepped out the door.

As he shut the door, the click was very loud. Like someone had put him in a closed-off room that made everything clearer. The surrounding sound he could hear well, but that was the thing; he could hear nothing else. There were no crickets chirping from the woods, nor frogs from the stream croaking into the night. There was nothing...

Tan focused his sight on the dark hallway, searching for anything out of the ordinary. Was this another test? No, his Master hated doing tests in the middle of his beauty sleep, much less when they already had a full day's worth of training and work.

Tan crouched at the edge of the hall and peeked around the corner. Looking down the stairs, he could barely make them out there in the darkness. He thought of making a small firelight but knew that would be foolish if he was trying to sneak around. The light would just be a beacon for all to see.

Then he noticed that nothing seemed to move. The dust he could see in the light cast by the moon from outside sat frozen in place, neither rising nor falling, like he was looking at a perfect portrait. The best artist in the world couldn't rival this tranquil moment.

As Tan grew closer to the first step, muffled crunching and crackling rose from the direction of downstairs. Carefully, he stepped onto the first step, and as he did, it felt like a spell had been broken, bringing the world into focus around him.

And all he knew... was Fire.

The red-hot Fire was what first caught his attention. Bright flames sprang across the room. He saw what looked like two bodies burning in the center of the cabin, their forms slowly churning to ash.

Was it the Mages? Did they seek retribution for him rejecting them? But why? There was no need for them to do that. They wanted him on his side, not as an enemy.

Then the next thing that caught his eye was the ice shards stuck into the walls, like someone had played darts on a much larger scale. The ice, however, was beginning to melt from the heat, water falling like sweat and sizzling as it evaporated from the Fire's heat. Tan could feel the amount of heat that still gripped the flames.

How was this possible? How did he sleep through all of *this*? Was his master dead? Was he that inept at sensing danger?

Taking stock of what happened, another thought occurred to him. He had heard *nothing*. Was this Druid magic? Master Nicodemus had said that the Shadows could do unnatural things that an Elementalist couldn't do.

Could he even fight someone that uses this type of magic? Elementalists were one thing, but a Druid assassins were an entirely different beast.

By this point, he was at the bottom of what was left of the stairs. He stepped off and turned toward the back of the cabin. The back of the cabin that led to the kitchen and his master's room was empty, but already the blazing flames were reaching those points.

However, he saw a trail of blood that smeared across the ground from the direction of the room all the way out the front door.

Tan withheld a shout as he ran to the busted open front door. He flung himself through the black smoke and instantly stopped in his tracks. The firelight set the entire scene before him alight. But he didn't want to see this...

The large black scales rippled as the firelight danced across them. Tyrone lay in front of the cabin, lifeless as the rabbits Tan would skin for dinner. Tan didn't walk any closer. He already knew. There was no heat coming from Tyrone's body.

The large gash in the beast's side had dried blood crusting around it. The great dragon's neck was at a disturbing angle that looked as if it was thrown back in a pain. A way that didn't seem natural at all.

One of the warmest, friendliest creatures he'd ever known was now empty, and disfigured with what looked like ice shards boring out of the right side of his face where his eye had been. The feeling of pain he had to force down for now, no matter how much it hurt him to see the majestic beast brought low.

Tan focused on the heat. He needed to breathe. Taking several breaths before expanding his senses, he felt the large burning flames from behind him, then he felt a small flame near one of the trees. He dashed to the tree where he found Nicodemus's ravin stuck to the tree with more ice shards.

Tan reached the bird and quickly produced a flame that began to crack the ice apart. Tan made sure to not harm the creature, but the bird definitely got a little warm. He needed to find his master and hopefully the bird could lead him to the old man.

The bird began to squawk and peck at the ice near its wing. Tan moved some of the flames over the wing and the bird began wiggling as the ice slowly broke from the frozen wings.

Then the ice shattered, and the bird fell to the ground. It squawked in annoyance, and flapped its wings, sending ice everywhere. Tan raised a hand to block the ice and cursed the bird for it.

"Where is my Master?!" Tan had no clue why he was asking a bird this.

Dreams were nothing like the real world. And he hoped what the bird had said in his dream would not come any truer than it already had right then.

The bird croaked at him before flapping its wings and taking flight into the night. The dark plumage of the bird made the creature disappear into the shadows of the trees, toward the darkening woods.

Tan quickly expanded his heat vision, allowing himself to intake the heat around him and transform the picture in his mind's eye, catching the bird's core dwindling as it flew away from Tan.

Tan quickly tore after the creature. The tree's faint glow of heat allowed him to navigate around the large evergreens, stumbling over a rock here and there from the lack of heat. The bird flew over a deer path from which Tan could pick up the slight heat residue of footprints and drag marks. People had been this way.

The bird then slowed and landed on a low branch as a bright heat source bloomed in front of Tan. Just beyond the next row of trees and large shrubbery, he slowed to take a more light-footed approach.

Voices were coming from just the other side as Tan crouched behind one of the bushes at the edge of the small clearing. There was a bit of hooting, hollering, and grunting of pain mixed in, but Tan was unable to distinguish any of the voices before a loud shout quieted the clearing.

His heat cast over the scene in short order, until Tan's vision froze on Master Nicodemus. Tan's lungs wanted to hop out of his chest and his stomach seemed to want to join. His head was racing.

There, in the center of the small clearing next to the pile of sticks that were set ablaze, the old man sat on his heels. Hands were tied behind him. Blood dripped from his chin. The crooked nose showed where the blood came from.

Scratches, bruises, and black eyes were evidence of beatings the men surrounding him must have given him. Five men stood about the clearing. Two stood next to Nicodemus while the other three were slowly walking around the center to form a perimeter within the clearing.

Those were a few of the thugs from the tavern. The night Tan had attacked those bandits along the road.

All the men seemed to sweat profusely. The men were not well adapted to the humidity that still clung to the air, even with winter slowly approaching.

Tan's eyes locked onto the man in the center, and he knew, leaning down to hiss something into his master's face, the blue robes and disgustingly clean-cut face were hard to forget. Especially when there were very few Imperialists in the area.

The Imperials didn't travel far from their northern homes, but when they did, they made sure that everyone knew they were always wearing their blue coats. But they weren't as uncommon near merchant lanes. Out here, it was strange.

So when Tan had seen the man at the tavern before his out-of-control incident, Tan knew it was odd.

The Water Empire had a colony in the northern portion of the Fire Realm, which they had gained during and a bit after the war through invasion and treaties. But they tended to only like to stay amongst themselves. It was strange to see him with these other men.

The other man standing next to the Imperialist Tan did not recognize. The man wore a hood and a face mask that covered all but his eyes. A sleeveless leather vest protected his torso, with many knives strapped to his chest and a short sword to his back. The man was fit in his leather vest, arms exposed. He looked like he did more than just a few push-ups. The way he stood was like a panther, relaxed but ready to pounce.

But what really caught Tan's eye were the tattoos etched across the man's arms. He most definitely was a Druid. And most likely the one who had put up that barrier in the cabin. Tan could only naturally assume that he was an assassin hired by the Imperialist.

That was probably the reason his master was in the state he was in. The thugs and their leader would have had a much more difficult time with Nicodemus on their own. But the assassin most likely evened the playing field.

The Imperialist muttered words that Tan could not hear at this distance. He seemed to make a remark that had his master laugh. Nicodemus said something, and that's when it escalated a bit.

The Imperialist backhanded Tan's master. Blood sprinkled on the ground as Nicodemus spit. The old man glared at the attacker before a boot kicked him in the chest. Tan went to move towards his master, but when he moved to defend him, black shadows seemed to enclose around him and trap him in place.

Tan froze, thinking that a hidden assassin, whom he had failed to identify and who was waiting in the bushes, had just found him out. But when Tan turned to see where the shadows led to, they traced to none other than the Ravin. Looking down, he could now tell that it was shadowy feathers with a faint glow of red like pulsing, wrapping around him.

Feathers were holding him back? He had no clue that the bird could do this. Tan wanted to shout at the bird to release him. But the bird almost seemed to pay Tan no mind as he stared at the field, to its master, bloodied and beaten on the ground. Tan turned back and found himself locked in place. His master's gaze grasped him with a power he could not overcome.

Nicodemus, from his position on the ground, seemed to pin Tan within the Ravin's grasp. The light of the small fire seemed to flicker reluctantly, as though the world appeared in slow motion, while Tan watched his master slowly shake his head. As if saying, 'don't you dare do something stupid.'

His master's face was rock solid, the way he looked whenever he didn't want Tan to do something he specifically told him not to do.

But this time, this time Tan wanted to disobey that order so badly that his veins felt like they would burst, yet he couldn't. The look his master gave him revealed his determination to ensure the protection of his ward.

"Not so talkative now, are we?" the Imperialist spat as he kicked again. Tan could hear the man a little now. "I have waited for this. Waited-mhm-for so long." He punched the old man.

Tan tried to shake the Ravin off again, desperate to get to his master. Staying hidden, unable to help, was tearing him up inside. But his master locked eyes with him.

'*You stay right where you are! You hear me?*' Tan looked on as the imperialist walked around Nicodemus.

Nicodemus grunted as the younger man lifted him up back onto his knees.

"Let me ask you, old man. Do you remember the North Wall? Do you remember the commander of that base?"

Nicodemus grunted as the man grabbed his head and yanked it back, so he stared up at the blue-eyed man.

"Commander Dwin Gelida... was my brother, and you killed him. You stormed the keep and killed all his men. But even though you had won and killed them, you had each one beheaded and mounted their heads on pikes to be displayed on the wall you had taken. And then you left without a second thought. Do you remember?"

Nicodemus said nothing and stared up at the raving man.

"Nothing?"

The man seemed to be in a frenzy at this point, almost hyperventilating. Eyes wide, like some mad animal. Tan sat in horror as this crazed man ranted, trapped within the confines of his fears. And then a horror stuck him...the connection of why this man looked so familiar.

And Tan was back there, back in the alley, watching as the man in a blue coat stabbed his mother with an ice blade. The same design as the one this man held now.

That ice blade, the way it seemed like a translucent short sword, but Tan knew! This was the man- this was the murderer that had taken his mother away from him. And now he was going to take Nicodemus from him as well.

Tan screamed into the black material that held him back pulling, punching, and kicking. But it was no use. He was standing, watching as his mother locked eyes with him. The vision faded to Master Nicodemus staring right into his eyes.

"Well, Drake of the North, tell my brother hello for me when you see him in hell..."

There was the sound of cracking and the breaking of meat with what sounded like a butcher's knife. Tan looked down at his master's chest in disbelief. The Firelight flickered off the ice shard where it sprouted from his chest.

No, no, no! Tan couldn't breathe. Blood built around the stained white shirt where the ice blade protruded from Nicodemus's chest. Tan was gasping for air now. As if something was in his mouth, he couldn't spit it out.

The Imperialist stepped back, leaving the blade in place. Nicodemus slowly brought his gaze down to stare straight at Tan. Blood was building around his lips as he smiled at Tan with a pained face. Tan couldn't look away, caught within the moment.

This infinite moment. His master coughed and spat blood before his body pitched forward like a tree being chopped down.

In that instant, as Nicodemus's body keeled forward, the shadows faded, and Tan broke... as the world burned...

23

THE MASTER'S LAST HOUR

Nicodemus sneezed as his sleep was interrupted by a chilly breeze wafting in from his open door, the door which he always kept open, even in the wintertime because even on the coldest day, the volcano kept the cold air at bay. And that's when he knew the intruders were already inside.

The draft hit his back, which faced the door, but he remained unmoving as if he were still asleep, while he projected his heat across the room just enough to be able to see what was around him. The heat came into contact with several heat sources. There were eight that he could see within the house, as the cold engulfed the outside of the cabin, keeping him blind from any activity.

The bodies inside the building slowly made their way toward his room in the back. None seemed to notice the stairs that led to the second floor where the kid still slept. At least, he hoped so, but when Nicodemus tried to project his heat into the upper rooms, it was like he'd hit an invisible wall.

Druid magic was at play and that was what probably kept Nicodemus from being able to detect any enemies, and why his companion's voice was nowhere to be heard. Curse that bird; the one time that he needed Corax to speak, it didn't make a sound.

Three bodies were now just outside his door, slowly walking within, while the remaining two stood back at the front door. The three inside seemed to hesitate once they entered, like they weren't sure what to do. Until one of them stepped forward, arms outstretched, with something in his hands.

Nicodemus knew what needed to be done and hoped that the kid was safe within his room. He took a slow, deep breath to calm his nerves and center his core, and then opened hell. With the power of a storm, he erupted the room in blazing orange Flames.

As he rolled off the bed and to his feet, the shocked faces of the men were instantly engulfed in screaming fire, unable to protect themselves from the hungry Flames. Nicodemus moved past the bodies of the three dead men into the next room.

The two men at the door were ready, unlike the previous three that were being dwindled to ashes, and with swords out, they stood posed to intercept the aged guardsman.

Nicodemus used the heat from the room behind him as one man produced a vine whip and the other formed ice shards from the little basin in the kitchen area. But Nicodemus was not planning on getting in a drawn-out fight.

Releasing a torrent of fire at the man with the ice, Nicodemus summoned more flames as a shield just before the vine whip struck him.

The man with the ice tried dodging the blast of fire and sending one of the ice shards at Nicodemus, which harmlessly hit the wall, but he received a scorching burn to his shoulder and arm. He cried out before Nicodemus doused his screams with even more flames.

The last thug attempted to counter Nicodemus with the planks of wood from the floor. The flames slammed into the wood, but it only delayed them for half a second before the flames ate through the wood like a beaver.

Nicodemus had planned for something like this and had purposefully chosen to make his cabin out of Fire Elementalist's favorite and most Flammable wood, Elder wood. The wood would burn long and when Nature Elementalists tried to use it against him, it would only help Nicodemus.

The Fire burst through the wood and struck the injured man and, spraying the man with the whip, the men screamed and Nicodemus waited until the smoke was too much for even him to handle. He brought the flames to a low burn, knowing the fight was still not over as a man dressed in the standard Druid assassin garb stepped into the room. The buff-hooded man looked about his feet at the burning bodies and shook his head.

"You just can't find good thugs these days." The man's muffled voice was gruff and weathered as he moved deeper within the room, displaying his tattooed arms for Nicodemus to see.

"Maybe it just wasn't their day?" Nicodemus stood in his pants and undershirt like an old man who had just woken up from a nap he very much wished to get back to.

"Or maybe they underestimated their opponent? You are an imposing man when riled up. I told them."

"Oh, you're going to make an old man like me blush with those compliments."

"Only because it is deserving of a man of your pedigree and skill, *Drake of the North*."

"Yeah? What of you? You seem to know who I am, who are you?"

"That was rude of me. I apologize," the man said, bowing at the waist. "I am known as the Barrier. I have been hired to capture you by an individual who wishes to keep his identity a secret."

"I see. So... you're *not* here to kill me?"

"All I am here to do is bring you to someone, though I don't know his name. But that is the extent of what I am to do. However, they do not care how I get you there, so we can do this one of two ways. Either you surrender to me and I take you to him. Or we fight it out and a certain ward accidentally gets nicked by one of my poison blades."

The man cocked his head toward the stairs behind him. With this sort of threat, Nicodemus was in no position to protect Tan with the Druid between him and the stairs, and with his tattoo designs of the crest of shields, he would easily be able to keep Nicodemus at bay long enough to deal with Tan.

It confused Nicodemus, however, since this man could have done that from the very beginning, so why didn't he? Maybe he was trying to use a more subtle approach, or he just didn't want to get his hands dirty. With this all-in mind, Nicodemus didn't want to involve the kid any more than he had to.

It also set Nic at ease that they hadn't technically taken the young Prince as a hostage, which means they thought Tan was just a student and less valuable than Nicodemus.

"So? What will it be?"

"If I leave with you, then swear that you will not harm the boy."

The assassin crossed his arms for a moment before slowly approaching Nicodemus and offering a hand.

"I swear on the Shadow's Curse that I shall not harm the boy until my deed is done. And if you are to die, I will leave in peace."

The man's tattoos glowed for a moment before fading again. Nicodemus had heard of this curse before; if any Druid swears by it and breaks this creed, the curse of the shadow engraved would kill him. Nicodemus nodded in approval and shook the man's hand, finalizing the pact.

"This is acceptable." He held out his wrists and the Druid bound them and escorted Nicodemus out of the house and into a scene he thought he would never come across.

Tyrone lay on the ground with blood beginning to lose its bright red color and darken to a dead black. The beast probably didn't even wake up from his dream of eating cows or whatever that gentle beast dreamed of.

Corax croaked from the left. Nicodemus turned as they walked to see the blackbird frozen to a tree, its torso and wings stuck in place as the bird pecked at the ice.

'Nicodemus?' That stupid voice was in his head again. *'There you are! I was so worried-uh... What's going on? Where are you going?'*

'Does it look like I know, Corax?'

'From my perspective, it looks like you have been captured.'

'Really? What gave it away?'

'Well, there's no need to get offensive. At least you were able to somewhat defend yourself. I was leapt upon from out of nowhere and-'

'I don't have time Corax!' The old man cut the bird's rambling short. *'The kid's inside, not sure if he is okay or what. Get yourself free and get to the kid.'*

'What about you?'

'Don't worry about me, the kid is the priority.'

'Okay, okay. I'll make sure the prince is okay.'

Nicodemus and the Druid were now a good ways from the cabin that was beginning to burn a lot more. The dark woods began to block the light, and the moonlight was all that shone them along their way. With this distance, it was hard to make out what the bird was saying with their limit being only a certain amount, but it varied from person to person.

'Make sure he's okay, and then go straight to town. Do you hear me?'

'Nic... I...yo...'

Nicodemus could barely hear what the bird was saying at this point, with the distance so great and what Nicodemus would assume was a barrier disrupting their communication.

"Where are you taking me?" Nicodemus asked as an orange light began to bloom ahead of them in the woods. He remembered there being a small clearing where he would take Tan to train at times.

"Just up ahead. He has been impatiently waiting to see you."

Upon getting to the small clearing, Nicodemus saw four men standing next to a fire lit by what looked like torches they had just tossed on the ground. They turned when the Druid called out, Nicodemus recognizing only one. The man that stood in the center with that blue coat and stupid grin was an Imperialist.

Most likely the one the boy had told Nic about. The one asking after Nic and his treasure trove or something of that ilk. They will be sad to know that Nic had no trove and instead had an allowance that Abree gave him for the boy.

The Druid marched Nicodemus to the men, who all seemed to be smiling until they started looking behind them, as if something were missing.

"Where are the others?"

"Dead," the Druid responded, not missing a beat.

"Dead?"

"What?!"

"How?"

"Not possible..."

"This old man?"

"Can't have been..."

"It must have been that dragon!"

"Boss, you hear this?!"

The thugs all began talking at once like hens in the coup, clucking with their heads cut off. Nicodemus was getting a headache just listening to the stupid things they were spouting.

"Oh, you think it's funny to kill our friends, old man?"

"I bet he enjoyed it, too!"

"Why don't we teach him a lesson in why it's not a good idea to kill our friends!"

The men stepped forward, one punching Nicodemus in the gut, another smacking his head. Then someone kicked him in the chest, knocking him to the ground. They all just started kicking him in the dirt, pain from every inch they touched as he couldn't fight back with his hands tied in the rope that the Druid had used.

There must be something about this rope that prevents Elementalists from using their power, because Nicodemus had been trying to burn the ropes away since they had stepped into the woods.

The men began to pant more and shout less, but they're laughing, kicks, slaps, and insults kept coming. The pain they caused wasn't as bad as what he had done to their friends. Nicodemus had to admit this was still painful. But not the most pain he had ever felt.

"Enough!" came a crisp voice, familiar and with the accent of an Imperialist. "So, it was that brat, huh?" A pause. "Get back to patrolling the area. This is still Realm territory, and I don't want any surprises."

The men ceased their assault on Nicodemus's body and did as the blue coat man ordered They walked in different directions with dirty glances toward Nicodemus while they did so.

Nicodemus sat up on his knees with a painful sigh. The cracks on his ribs made him gimp to the side, and the bruise on his face was already beginning to swell around his eye.

The Imperialist slowly walked to where Nicodemus drooped his head.

"I promise that is not the worst to come..." the man hissed into his ear.

Nicodemus grunted a chuckle.

"Sure, kid..."

The young man's face went red with rage, gritting his teeth as he backhanded Nicodemus to the face. Nicodemus felt his cheek sting as he spat blood from a cracked gum, slowly glared up at the boy standing before him, and who then proceeded to kick Nic in the chest.

Nicodemus did not know where he was for a split second as air returned to his lungs in such a way that it felt like being revived from the dead. He gasped for air, which tore into his already stressed lungs.

'Nick, the kid is trying to get to you!' Corax shouted in his head.

Nicodemus's mind was in a spin now. Why were Corax and the kid here? He thought he'd told that bird to take the boy away.

'You, in fact, did not tell me to take the Prince away. You told me to make sure the boy was safe. But the reverse happened, and we came here to assist you.'

'You will do no such thing! You will take the boy and leave here at once!'

Nicodemus was finally regaining his senses, other than his annoying thoughts. He slowly looked toward the woods where he felt Corax's presence and locked eyes with the young man being restrained from jumping into the fray by the bird. Not looking away, Nicodemus slowly shook his head in an effort that he hoped conveyed his will to leave.

'You keep him right there, you hear me, Corax!?'

'Trying,' the bird responded. *'His highness is pretty strong for his age, remember?'*

"Not so talkative now, are we?" the Imperialist spat as he kicked again.

Nicodemus grunted and groaned in pain from the impact on his cracked ribs, curling into a ball to try to protect his ribcage.

"I have waited for this. Waited-" the man punched him again with a grunt, "-for so long."

Nicodemus looked to Tan again, wishing, praying the boy to remain calm and stay where he was or leave. This was not a fight he should take alone, especially with the Druid here, even if he swore on a curse.

'Don't you dare let him do something stupid!'

'I got him, Nick, don't worry. Focus on yourself right now.'

"Let me ask you, old man. Do you remember the North Wall? Do you remember the commander of the Hackrim Castle?"

Nicodemus grunted as the man grabbed his head and yanked it back so he stared up into crystal blue eyes. Nicodemus's eye was so swollen he could barely see out of it.

Why was this blabbering idiot asking about a war that was nearly thirteen years ago? Didn't he know it was over and done, and the Allies and the Fire Realm were pardoned for their efforts in betraying the Dark Lords?

"Commander Dwin Gelida…" the crazed man growled, "he was my brother, and you killed him."

Nicodemus remembered the Commander very well once the man said his name. The man had slaughtered innocent women and children, raping and pillaging as he conquered the North in the effort of "bringing back order." All the while shouting that stupid name. That man and his men had got what they deserved.

"You stormed the keep and killed all his men," the young man continued his rant, "but even though you had won and killed them, you didn't stop there. No! You had each one beheaded, and mounted their heads on pikes to be displayed on the wall you had taken. And then you left without a second thought. Do you remember?"

Nic didn't feel like answering such a stupid question. If this idiot was trying to get him to beg for forgiveness, then he came to the wrong person. So, he said nothing and just tried not focusing on his bruised ribs.

It was evident that one of them was definitely cracked. The pain whenever he tried to breathe and not being able to take in a full breath was clear enough, but the burning pain in his side that kept wanting him to keel over was hard to ignore. But he needed to fight through the pain and focus on the task at hand.

The real danger was right behind him; he could not let this man get to the kid. That was Nicodemus's one true goal, to protect the Prince. This man didn't scare him one bit… The fear of losing the boy was…

"Nothing?" The idiot seemed to be losing it and he kept panting like some expectant mother whose waters just broke. His eyes were wide, like some mad man craving his daily fix.

"Well, Drake of the North," — the sound of ice and the freezing cold air hit Nicodemus's skin along his neck like a wave of cool air — "tell my brother hello for me when you see him, in hell...and tell the queen that our chat in that ally way was too short..."

What!? Nic tried to comprehend what the man had just said. This brat was the one to kill her majesty!? Nic thought he could hear the smug smile on the bastard's face.

In that split second Nicodemus tried to think of a way out of this. His elemancy was all but out at this point. His dagger was in the wraith's hands. He attempted to rip his hands free of the bindings, but to no avail.

There was nothing he could do as he felt the pressure of whatever blade cut into his back. All thoughts seemed to only go to one thing... the boy, hidden within the bushes not several paces away.

The sound drifted away, remembering when that scrawny twig had stood outside his shaggy old home in the middle of nowhere. When he first brought the youngster to this place to train, it felt like so many years ago. And now that youngster had almost mastered Fire, one less than four moons! And not only that, but was on the verge of getting his Blue Flame. If only he could have seen it.

The sharp pain from his back to his chest broke through him, and Nicodemus was unable to breathe as the cold ice that protruded from his chest hurt more than he ever thought it could.

Blood built on his stained white shirt. He was unable to breathe at this point, and his vision was fading in and out as his head pounded. The Imperialist stepped back, leaving the blade in place. Nicodemus slowly brought his gaze down as the taste of iron was building in his mouth.

The blood was already flowing so much that he felt lighter. There was no holding on, not this time, Nic knew that. He met Tan's eyes one last time and smiled through the pain.

The sudden impulse to share what he knew with the boy, about the Owl and the Dark Lord Obsidian... but...

A sudden pain in his lower back caused him to keel forward. The world was blurring, and as it faded, the bright flash of blue erupted all around him, as the world blurred around him into a mesmerizing color of light...

"They were after me. If you make it through this, they'... be after you too," Nic found himself speaking to the bright colors around him, unsure if anyone heard. "They are coming...They want to take the world... the owls ... go to them... they will help you... I don't have much time left..."

He coughed again...

"My... ring, bird help... you..." He struggled with every word as he spoke.

"N-no. Don't talk..." a distant voice said. *Was that Hagitan?* "... it'll just make it worse."

"It... is too late, boy..." then he realized something, this kid wasn't a boy anymore. Not after the Trial, and certainly not for many years. Not since the passing of the queen. But Nic sputtered in an attempt to say this, coughing up more blood.

Feeling the emotions of regret and pain fill his eyes and fall down his cheek. The sky was dark with a world of color around him. His vision focused one last time, and he saw the face of Nic's misunderstood king, and the eyes of his loving queen.

Suddenly there was more that he wished to say, to give, about that night in the Purge. About what happened to the king. He hadn't failed, he had in fact won. That the king didn't abandon his family. Nic so desperately wished he could, but all he could say was.

"...I'm... proud of you...my king..."

24

LOSS OF PAIN

The ravin released Tan in a panic as Blue Flames erupted from within the broken soul, flapping its wings to get away from the destructive flames, but there was no escape from the heat that seemed to be everywhere. Tan roared as the fire exploded across the small clearing.

Fire engulfed the closest man, who screamed in horror before turning to ash. The Fire covered the distance across the field within the span of two breaths. All living things, the grass, bugs, rodents, trees—everything, was burnt to a crisp.

When the screams and cries of death went silent, Tan took a deep breath and let the Fire grow its own way, losing its unnatural blue color and turning to the natural red and orange of true flames. The smoke from the fire was thick, but Tan could see just the hint of something near the center of that small clearing.

There, within the Flames, stood the man in strange garb next to the Imperialist. An invisible barrier was blocking the flames from reaching them, as they stood unharmed. The druid's tattoos glowed green upon his skin as he stood between Tan and the Imperialist.

Tan locked onto the man in the blue coat as the heat within him raged. Tan's anger re-lit to full strength as he summoned the surrounding Fire to create a large fireball, gathering all the strength he had into this attack. The ball of burning hot blue-white flames hovered in the air as Tan amassed enough power to break through the barrier.

But before Tan could react, the Shadow turned and grabbed the Imperialist's arm. And in that instant, a black substance appeared from the druid's shadows, now a swirling black void. That was when Tan knew the assassin was also a Shadow Wraith.

Tan roared his frustration and threw the ball of Fire at them, even though he knew it would not reach them in time. The Druid stepped into the portal, dragging the stunned Imperialist in with him.

In the storm of rage Tan watched as the portal disappeared and the Fire passed harmlessly over and crashed into a tree in the distance. The concussion blew apart the tree, incinerating it to a pile of ashes. The explosion ruptured a small crater in the ground leaving a gaping hole.

After the shock wave of the blast dissipated, Tan raced to where his master's body lay. Tan split the flames into a pathway to the small patch of grass.

The Flames were becoming more of a nuisance at this point. Tan silenced the flames to a whisper. Ash and smoke covering the sky with the smell of burned wood and flesh protruding on those nearby.

The sight of his master lying face down with a large hole in his back made Tan's stomach roll over. The pool of crimson blood Tan knelt in did not make him run or flinch as he kneeled next to the old man's body, holding back tears as he moved to his side and rolled him over as gently as possible.

A wheezing noise escaped Nicodemus's mouth as Tan delicately held his master's bald head off the bloody ground. The old man's face had dirt and drying blood stuck on it and Tan attempted to brush it off but only smeared it. He abandoned cleaning his forehead and face and looked over his body... he was at a loss at what to do.

"Master... I don't know... W-what should I do?" There was so much blood.

Tan's hand hovered over his master as the man gasped for air. The Flames Tan had created were so hot that the ice shard that had plugged the wound had melted away.

Nicodemus's eyes seemed to look past Tan as he slowly whispered, "My... ring, bird help... you..." He struggled with every word as he spoke.

"N-no, don't talk, it'll just make it worse."

"It... is too late, boy..." he sputtered, coughing up more blood as Tan tried to hold him steady.

Tears fell onto the old man's cheeks as Tan watched the man's gaze grow distant, like he was looking at him from very far away.

"... I'm... proud of you... my king..."

Then, Tan felt his master go limp, just like his mother's had those many season's ago. Dead at the hands of the same man.

Tan's head drooped as the weight of it all hit him. *Why?! Why are you proud of me? I didn't even save you.* He couldn't even do that much. *What good were Blue Flames if they couldn't help me protect even one person I care about?*

The air seemed to leave the old man as his body became limp in Tan's arms. The lack of life within him was deafening as Tan gripped his master's shoulders. Tan felt the buildup of more tears before he could stop it from happening, streaming down his face as he cried out in anger at the stars.

That pain... That loss he had felt before, hitting him with the force of a tide, hammering him as he let the waves of emotion wash over him, gripping the lifeless body of his beloved mentor. If Tan would have chosen a role for Nicodemus, it would have been grandfather, but it was too late now. He was alone, alone again, as he poured his sorrows out into the cruel world of destruction around him.

From the depths within him he felt that wall that mirror of Flames within him. And as he allowed himself to focused on the reflection the Flames within morphed into a blue Fire dragon. The rumbling grew louder and the dragon's deep voice growled. *You know what needs to be done...*

Then, Tan was back. His sobbing calmed, the body shaking, waves receding, he became lightheaded.

As the world grew dark around him, there was one thought that went through Tan's mind...

I'll burn him!

EPILOGUES

I

VALENTINE

"There! After her!"

The panicked panting, eyes searching, scrambling down the alley as fast as she could. Looking over her shoulder at the shadows of approaching torches.

Where? Where? Where—? There!

Turning down an intersection, she sprinted to a fence with a board loose. She slowed and turned sideways, thanking, for once, for her slight frame. She squeezed through and continued to the end of the alley. Gripping her palm where she had scraped it. Hissing through her teeth at a piece of the gravel still in the wound.

The street on this side was less active, the street lights all lit to show the way down the cobblestone path. Looking back, she caught sight of the orange light and the grumbling of her pursuers.

Continuing across the street, she ran down until she came across another alley.

"There she is!"

She saw one of the men stumbling out of the alley behind her and her eyes went wide. Ducking into the shadows of the new alley as the voices called after her.

The alley was shorter than the last and she came out on the other end and cut back up the street. The streets were a bit more active further this way. Men talking and walking with woman. Pubs, and other nightly activities where music and laughter came from as she passed.

The road curved down after a few buildings and brought her up to an intersection with a large building in front of her. Lit with red, orange, and pink lights.

To the left, the road only opened towards the city wall with only one row of buildings left. To the right, a street that would bring her almost back in a circle.

Where? Where should she go? They were almost here-

"Hey, you. Miss, you okay?" A deep but soft voice asked.

She looked at the large beast of a man who stood in front of the enormous building, his face showing scars but also an expression of kindness and concern that she hadn't seen in a long while.

"I-I'm being..." she glanced back to the sea the men coming out of the alley. With a gasp, she stepped away from them. And then the man was stepping past her and pointing back to the extensive building.

"Inside! We'll handle this, miss. Isn't that right, boys?"

And with that, four other men, all just as big or menacing, stepped up with him to make a sort of wall. She stood in shock for a moment before seeing her pursuers finally seeing her at the end of the street. With a gasp, she backed away before turning to the building. And only just read the name of the sign above the door before she swung the door open, pushed in, and slammed it shut.

Welcome, to Lady Thedral's.

II

SCARLET

The inner sanctums of the Black Fortress always made Scarlett feel uneasy. The black, gray, and ash colored fortress gave it a gloom that matched the surrounding landscape. She recalled her father's stories about how the land didn't always used to be so dark and gloomy. It had been before the first Dark Civil war, before the people of the Mist Mountains, the Black Dunes and the Gray Forest were enslaved.

And the Dark Lords of these lands of darkness were dead set on making sure those that were responsible for that first civil war paid the price.

Scarlet stepped through the broken doors to the decimated throne room, her black cloak billowing behind her as she stepped over debris. Concrete blocks crumbled from that broken statue set in the center of the room.

But she avoided looking at the broken statue of the two distinguished men that brought the Land of Mists from the Dark Lands it had been. Instead, she looked to the man lounging on the broken topped throne. The flesh and blood of one of the statues behind her now. The throne beside him was still a pile of rubble from the battle fought long ago.

Coming to a stop at the steps leading to the throne, Scarlet bowed her head as she took a knee.

"You summoned me, father…" Keeping her head lowered until she was addressed.

"My Lord has a task for you, daughter of red." A voice, the weasel of a man, spoke from the shadows next to her father. When Scarlet looked to her father, she could see that his pains were great this day, and he was probably forcing himself to be present here even though he should be resting still.

"It pains me and my Lord that he must send you and your sisters into the hands of the enemy. But we must move, daughter of red. There will not be much time left before there is nothing we can do."

She slowly lifted her head.

"What is asked of me?"

"There is a special task that requires someone that my Lord can trust. Something that only you can do. Your sisters will help you if need be. They will be near Titan City and Seaside. We need an insider within the Shadows. Our sources there have become unable to communicate with us safely without exposing themselves."

"I understand."

"We also believe there will be an important…person that will be thrust into the mix. That fool, the man calling himself Iceman, has made a mistake. He has killed the Drake of the North and brought attention to himself that the Rue Council was not ready for. The Clans are stirred up and have been made aware of our presence."

The form upon the throne shifted as the weasel continued.

"That fool has brought attention that the other Lords have not wanted. We need to do what we can before the west collapses to save our interests. Hopefully, by putting you into place before the plan is enacted, we can prevent more from falling. Go. Become a Shadow and do what you can. There is a carriage with further instructions for you that the daughter of brown will inform you of."

"I need you, my daughter," a scratchy and bruised voice she hadn't heard in years said. "Our enemies…they wish to finish what was started…we can't let them…"

Scarlett met her father's gaze with wide eyes. He hadn't spoken in quite some time. She was honored and relieved that his recovery was that far along.

Scarlett felt her hands shaking, but it surprised her to find her voice steady as she answered.

"As you command, father."

Scarlet stood, her eyes searching the dark face of her father as she bowed one last time, before turning and marching out of the room.

She would do what needed to be done. And she would make sure her father's plan came about. To see the color of the world brought back to these dark lands.

End of Arc 1

ARC 2

RAVIN THIEF

1

HE'S NOT DEAD

It has been four days since the trials, and Dancer was still unsure if she should bring up what Tan had told her before he left. Gran should know...probably. But she wasn't sure that her father, the elders, and other clan heads should know.

Dancer wiped down her small light blue scout dragon, Razor. A four-legged, blue Sky Dragon, was the size of a horse with a wingspan double its length. She used a hard brush to get some dirt the dragon had acquired the day before when she let him take a mud bath, something she very much regretted doing. The dragon, however, was purring in its sleep as she toiled away.

"Curse you and your cuteness!" she hissed at him. But she couldn't stay mad at him. He was an adorable and exquisite dragon. Sleek and lean, he was also one of the fastest in clan Ignus, if not the entire Realm. Tan would probably say he is a spoiled brat, with the way she treated the dragon. But he hadn't gotten the chance to meet her dragon as she hadn't been able to take her with them to the Trials.

The thoughts of that last night attempted to raise their head, but Dancer punched them down by humming a tune of Willow Whisps.

Drifting back to present events, she knew the elders were planning on moving the entire camp this time, for another trial.

This one is much more important. The Hunters Trials. One that Dancer herself would take part in. They still hadn't decided on the King's Trial. She hoped it wouldn't be for a long time.

After nearly three years of training, she was sure she would pass. Her father wasn't so sure, but other Hunters, and clan members would always come to watch her spar or train with the others. Her Master, an older dragoon named Freil, was considered the next best Master, with Captain Nicodemus being the best. She wasn't worried, much.

Scrunching up her face in an annoyance at a spot that would not clean, she tossed the brush in a bucket and went to pick up a wired brush.

The call of, "Flyer approaching," went up and Dancer turned from her dozing dragon.

Up in the rafters of one of the dragon barns, some of the only permanent buildings the clans used, she had a good view across the clearing where dragons came to land in, the space was big enough for four Regals to land in, about eight scout dragons. Beyond the clearing was a small fence with rows and rows of large tents exploding from the dragon area like an explosion.

Dancer watched as a scout dragon came in so fast, the call had almost been too late. A Red Salamander dragon, it looked like Reid's. The tight wrapped clothing worn by the rider is for better aerodynamics. With a thud, the dragon landed as the rider's face remained hidden behind goggles and a peculiar leather helmet. The rider unlatched themselves from the harness and rigging and jumped off the dragon and raced towards the Ignus Clan tent, Dancer's father's meeting tent.

What was that about? Wasn't Reid's supposed to be patrolling near the volcano? She put the brush she was holding back in the bucket and walked to the ladder.

Dancer arrived at the tent entrance just in time to hear her father's voice.

"...and you're sure?"

Another man spoke shakily as Dancer passed the guards and pulled back the tent flap.

"Yes, Sire. There is nothing left..."

"Nothing left of what?" Dancer asked the group. Heads turned to regard her as she stepped up beside the table. "Why does everyone look so..." she trailed off as her eyes went from her father's now set jaw to Reid's ghostly complexion.

Glancing around the room she saw the group of four men, her father, Reid in his scout garb still, another Clan head, and Elder Paxi, stood next to the table. All with clenched fists or wide eyes as they stared at the table where a map of the area sat.

Gran, Elder Mincie, and Weis of house Draken, we're near a group of chairs at the back of the tent. Gran had a hand to her mouth and looked horrified at something. The other two women supporting her back into her chair.

"What is it?" She demanded, all playfulness gone as she stared the scout down.

The room seemed to shuffle uncomfortably as if the very order was something uncomfortable.

"I-I don't thin-"

"*Reid!*" she warned. "What is it?"

"It's Captain Heliken and the young Prince, FireDancer..." began Elder Paxi. "There has been an incident..."

Her father urged them to send out groups to scout the area. The large man whirled on a guard standing at the edge of the tent. "Send out a raiding party. Search that entire forest!"

"But..." Reid began, "they can't, Sire..."

"Why stoking not!?" Her father growled at the scout who flinched but attempted not to shy away.

"I regret to inform you, sire, that there is no longer any forest. It was all *burned* to the ground."

The room went silent as the realization struck them all. Dancer couldn't believe what she was hearing. Was Tan dead? Was the old man dead? Were they attacked?

The room slowly moved as men seemed to gain their wits.

"There has to be something- "

"-if we search that town-"

The voices mixed as Dancer tuned them out. She stared at the map where the cabin would be. It was a day's flight, and Razor can beat that time. She would need to grab a pack of supplies but...she knew what she needed to do.

Spinning around, she strode back to the tent entrance.

"Dancer!" Her father's voice made her stop at the flap. In a gentler yet commanding voice, he said, "Where do you think you are going?"

She turned to meet her father's eyes. He seemed to try to search her eyes for any hint of what she was thinking.

"I'm going to find my cousin." She could hear it in her own voice, the anger and worry.

Then she turned and brushed out the tent back towards the dragon barns. The sun was high in the sky as she passed people moving throughout the camp in their normal day rituals, unaware of what had transpired in mere moments.

This would upset the clans even more than Tan just stepping down. The forgotten Prince murdered? That would send the clans into a frenzy. Especially after he had survived the Purge. But to die by what she assumed had to be assassination? She would bring a full gear set. Glancing up to the sky, she saw few clouds. With a groan, she realized she would need to get a full riding suit as well. It might end up taking longer than she had initially thought.

That wouldn't stop her. She decided. And Ignus never let up on something they set their minds to.

She reached the edge of the dragon barn and whistled long and low. A blue streak shot out of the open barn rafters. Razor hopped right to her with a happy little chirp as Dancer walked to the saddle rack under the little shed at the edge of the dragon landing ring. And one thought kept to staring in her mind. Like a chant. *'I will find him.'*

Razor landed, and Dancer jumped from her dragon's back. Racing up the hill, Dancer felt the soot crunch under her boots. The broken remains of the cabin sat at the top of the burned ground. Smoke drifting on the breeze as she came to a stop. She looked down at the two tombstones.

Reading the names, she felt her knees hit the ground and relief and guilt washed over her. She rubbed a finger over the two names engraved on the stones, whipping away soot and ash.

"Here lies Nicodemus De Halkin...Here lies Tyrone..."

Her tears were that of sorrow for losing them, but also for the one who's name was not on either of the tombstones. She stood and marched back to Razor and swung herself into the saddle. As she did, the sounds of thunder wing beats reached her ears.

The Regal landed off to her left and two Dragoons landed to her right.

Dancer did not turn, staring at her hands as she gripped the reins.

The sounds of the passengers sliding off their mounts and hurrying up the hill reached Dancer. There was a pause, the sounds of the dead forest empty around them, and a moment later Dancer could hear her grandmother crying and could imagine her father holding his mother as she wept for a lost friend. Dancer gripped the reins until her fingers hurt.

The sounds of heavy footfalls came, and she saw the large shadow approach out of the corner of her eye. Stopping beside her dragon, her father was silent as he reached up and gave Razor a scratch behind his cheek frills.

"Dancer..."

"He's not dead." She hissed.

"We don't know that," her father began again. "All we know is..."

"He's not dead," she repeated. She met his eyes with her puffy eyes. "I know it."

They stared at each other for a long moment before he nodded.

"Okay," was all he said, and stepped back.

Taking that as an indication that she could leave, she spurred Razor into the skies. And didn't fail to notice the one dragoon that followed her, albeit at a distance. She didn't care. All she wanted was to find Tan.

After several hours of flying, she had gained a sense of where the Fire had started, near a small open field that didn't seem to have any trees a little away from the burned down cabin. She landed Razor, the dragoon following her landed a long distance away. Dancer paid the warrior no mind as she walked around the space.

Until she reached the center of this small field where a tiny patch of grass sat. There was blood staining the ground in one spot. She tried not to imagine what had happened there and instead focused on the one other item sitting in the grass.

A small burned piece of wood. She kneeled and could see words scratched into the blackened wood. Squinting, she read it aloud.

"I will burn him."

Confused, she reached down to pick the piece of wood up. Doing so, the wood seemed to fall apart.

"No, no, no!" Dancer cried out, but it was too late. It was nothing but broken ash now. The words lost to the winds as a breeze.

She heard the heavy footsteps of the dragoon running up.

"FireDancer? Is everything alright?"

Dancer shook her head. Then cleared her throat.

"I'm fine," she snapped. Standing to her feet, she marched back to Razor. "I still haven't checked the town yet."

It took two days to search the entire area. After visiting the mining town and getting vague statements of a Blue Fire that had engulfed the entire forest up to the town, she had thought she might have something.

When the townsfolk only said that the Flames had gone out even faster than they had begun, Dancer became confused. She couldn't think of anyone besides Captain Nicodemus, her father, and a few other clan heads, and elders who could summon Blue Flames. But after the people retold what Dancer had found at the burned down cabin. She knew these people didn't have any other useful information. No strangers entering town. No people coming or going, in fact, other than her and the scout that had reported the incident.

Dancer was back at the Clan's tent city sitting in the lounge area of the Ignus house tent. The trip back had been even more uneventful than the last time. But when her father and Gran had let her search for nearly two days with no other evidence, they had first told, then ordered her back to the encampment. One that the clans would most likely be leaving in two days.

She pulled the blanket from the tangled mess to wrap around herself, not sure what else to do. She was already beginning her Dragoon training, her Dragoon Trial was in about seven moons. If she gave up on that now... No. She couldn't stop training.

Knowing that she would not give up on that goal, she needed another way to still search for Tan. He wasn't dead. She knew that for a fact after seeing that last inscription, and that the tombstones didn't have his name. But she had no way of being able to, not right now, at least.

Whether Tan had given up the throne at the Blood Trials, the clans now knew, or thought Dancer had to remind herself, that her cousin was dead. And he had no heir. Meaning there was no one else to take the throne.

So, they make plans to meet up to discuss what should be done. There were three options. One, have One of the still living blood relatives take the throne. They faced a problem because there were only a few individuals who could be considered for the position of a new clan head.

And Clan heads can't take the throne. And Dancer didn't want the throne for almost the same reason Tan hadn't.

Two, they would have an election. Which would get nowhere because each clan would vote for their representative. And the clans that were the largest would end up winning, which was Clan Ignus, as they had the largest houses in their clan.

Or three, have a Trial of Kings.

Dancer knew they needed a ruler, as the country's people were slowly deteriorating. The crops from the caravans were doing well but they couldn't make any trade agreements with anyone because the traders either didn't trust the clans or because the traders feared being attacked by the raiding parties that had been attacking the caravans lately.

If things continued how they were, the clans would look at starvation soon. Being in a land of sand was hard enough, and forests were hard enough. They weren't as able to grow enough crops and relied on trade for a lot of their food. Though their hunting parties were good, they were having to hunt more and more, dwindling the hunting grounds as the trade slowed.

Gran seemed to have the same conversation with her father again, as they entered the tent.

"…if we don't do something soon, the clans will collapse."

"Which is why I propose we move the clans back to their caravans." Her father sounded tired. Dancer turned from where she sat lying in the cushions to watch the two walk towards the cabinet that held the wine bottles and cups. It was their nightly ritual to have a final glass of the day before retiring for the evening.

"If we can get the people back on their barges," her father continued as he poured a cup and handed it to Gran, "we will grow more stocks of our own food. I have also proposed that we increase our caravans and possibly use the calves as a supplement."

"You know that they are too valuable for that. We need every calf to help with the amount of people that will go back to the caravans."

Her father sighed. Finishing his own cup, he turned and walked to the edge of the cushions and blankets.

"You're right. I'm just trying to come up with ideas."

"What if we turn to a different tactic, then?" Dancer asked.

"Like what?" her father took a seat against a stack of cushions.

"Well," she turned on her stomach to better see him. "What if we start a guard escort service with the huntsman? Or use our dragons as a delivery service?"

"That might work," he said thoughtfully. "I'm just wondering if the other clans would be willing to do it. Their pride lies in tradition. They are Huntsman, not Guardsman. They *may* think it beneath them."

"At some point, they will need to get over their pride and do what needs to be done," Gran said as she lowered herself into her chair at the edge of the cushions and blankets. "I, for one, am tired of it. They throw every idea aside. At least I am open to change."

Dancer saw the look he tossed to her as Gran took a swig of wine. A face that said, "*Sure you have.*" Though Gran had put aside her prideful traditions in letting her first son, take an outsider to be his queen.

Even if Gran still seemed prickly about the topic whenever Dancer asked her about the late queen. She didn't really remember her aunt very well, much less her uncle, the king.

Dancer had been born and raised away from the courts of the Realm, out with its first people, the Fire Clans. They were all clansman, but some had moved away from clans and become a bit more...modern, was a way that Tan had put it. Taking on more of a courtly system. But then the Purge took place and eliminated the courts, at least for now.

"I think you're on the right of it, Jellybean," her father's nickname for her, coming out as he relaxed. "We need to expand, not just within the clans, but out as well." He took a sip of wine and smacked his lips. "This is such good taste. You sure you don't want any Jellybean?"

He held the glass out to her. To which Dancer shook her head.

"I'm good. It always gives a bad aftertaste."

"More for me then," he said with a smile.

The signs were there, avoidance of the trip. No questions of what she had found. They were avoiding it with this simple ritual to distract themselves.

The silence that followed made Dancer shift uncomfortably as she wrapped herself in the blanket tighter. The looming conversation between them sat in the air like a dense fog. Dancer opened her mouth to speak but paused. They could hear the sounds of shouting.

Dancer sat up, her father rising as the tent flap to the entrance pulled back and the huntsman guards stepped inside. The bearded man's face was solemn as he spoke.

"Sire, you have a visitor."

www.ingramcontent.com/pod-product-compliance
Lightning Source LLC
Chambersburg PA
CBHW020437130626
46549CB00001B/179